Northern Ireland and the politics of boredom

MANCHESTER
1824

Manchester University Press

Northern Ireland and the politics of boredom

Conflict, capital and culture

GEORGE LEGG

Manchester University Press

Published by Manchester University Press
Altrincham Street, Manchester M1 7JA, UK

www.manchesteruniversitypress.co.uk

British Library Cataloguing-in-Publication Data is available

ISBN 978 1 5261 2886 7 hardback
ISBN 978 1 5261 4589 5 paperback

First published by Manchester University Press in hardback 2018
This edition published 2020

The publisher has no responsibility for the persistence or accuracy of URLs for any external or third-party internet websites referred to in this book, and does not guarantee that any content on such websites is, or will remain, accurate or appropriate.

Typeset by
Servis Filmsetting Ltd, Stockport, Cheshire
Printed in Great Britain by
CPI Group (UK) Ltd, Croydon, CR0 4YY

For Joanna Elizabeth Campbell, with love

Contents

Plates

Acknowledgements

This book is based on research I undertook in the Department of English at King's College London, where I was warmly supported by colleagues. I owe an incalculable debt to Richard Kirkland for his support, advice and insight throughout the writing process. His belief in imaginative research and high scholarly standards has encouraged me to push the boundaries of our discipline. Colin Graham and Alan Read both read an earlier draft of this book and their comments have been invaluable in reconceptualising and rethinking much of this project. John Duncan, Jane Elliott, Paul Gilroy, Pat Palmer and Patrick Wright all read individual chapters and I would like to thank them for their astute observations and assistance.

I am indebted to the following for their help and enthusiasm: Tony Canavan, Garret Carr, Clara Jones, Dominic Johnson, Declan Long, Brian Murray, Caroline Magennis, Mark Turner, Maggie Scull and Victor Sloan. I am also grateful to the staff of the Liberal Arts Department at King's who have encouraged me in the completion of this project. Victoria Baines provided invaluable assistance and intellectual insight when bringing the book to publication. For his friendship, motivation and good humour throughout the writing of this book, I am extremely grateful to Carl Kears.

My family has continually supported my research and I am thankful to my mother for her engagement with this project across all its various stages. My father has offered an excellent sounding board for my thinking and my sisters have provided welcome relief from the writing. Over the years I have also been sustained by my future family-in-law. I would like to thank Ian and Shiennah for their hospitality, and for creating a home away from home.

Finally, and most especially, I am grateful for the companionship and commitment of Joanna Elizabeth Campbell. Her positive outlook has inspired me in my thinking, while her dedication and love have sustained me in my work. Thank you Jo, for listening to me and for travelling with me. This book is dedicated to you.

I am grateful to the following for their kind permission to reproduce copyrighted material:

Ciaran Carson (c/o The Gallery Press), Seamus Deane (c/o Irish Academic Press), Willie Doherty (c/o Matt's Gallery), John Duncan, Derek Mahon (c/o The Gallery Press), Martin Parr (c/o Magnum Photos), Paul Seawright, Victor Sloan and the Craigavon Museum.

Introduction: the price of peace

Boredom is not simple.

(Roland Barthes, The Pleasure of the Text)[1]

To approach Titanic Belfast – one of Northern Ireland's largest visitor attractions – is to behold something of a spectacle. An angulated structure, situated in the slipways where the *Titanic* was born, this building is at once 'a beacon' for Northern Ireland's post-conflict regeneration and an architecture in search of 'global-landmark status'.[2] Emerging from concrete, the building's four corners push out to replicate, from above, the White Star logo of *Titanic*'s owners and, from below, a series of rising hulls. Sized at 14,000 square metres and reaching a height of 126 feet, Titanic Belfast dominates the skyline; it is twice the size of Belfast City Hall. Inside, a series of glass escalators, each in excess of twenty metres, rise up through a jagged central void to reach a set of interconnected galleries that tell 'the Titanic story'.[3] Here visitors encounter 'not a museum, but an experience', a narrative of Belfast as a seamless site for industry: 'one of the greatest workshops the world has ever known'.[4] The British Empire, the Unionist Government, and Loyalist protectionism were all integral to this industrial image – Catholics, of course, were expelled from the shipyards in 1886, 1893 and 1912 – and yet Titanic Belfast chooses not to remember such a divisive past.[5] Rather than acknowledging this site's sectarian history, Titanic Belfast offers the glamour of an ever-changing veneer. Cased in three thousand silver anodised sheets, the structure shimmers with a variety of visual effects, creating impressions that veer, we are told, from 'breaking waves and eroded pack ice to cut diamond and crystal shards'.[6] Enticing its visitors with the promise of spectacular delight and charging a substantial entrance fee, Titanic Belfast might also be viewed as a monument to what Nigel Thrift has termed capitalism's 'technology of allure': the process by which aesthetics have become 'a key means of generating economic value'.[7] Certainly, as Brian Kelly has suggested, the building displays a deep-held 'faith in the market's ability to transcend the city's sectarian past'.[8]

It is at this intersection between capitalism and sectarianism that an affective condition begins to emerge, which I term a politics of boredom. This is not exactly the boredom of Marc Augé's famous 'non-places' (*non-lieux*) – there is, after all, a distinct appeal to the architecture of Titanic Belfast – but rather a boredom created by the cultural and historical amnesia this architecture produces.[9] The process is by no means simple, but for all its complexity such boredom can be metaphorically described, in Lars Svendsen's words, as a 'meaning withdrawal'.[10] In the case of Titanic Belfast, such 'meaning withdrawal' is particularly profound. Here, not only are Northern Ireland's sectarian realities disguised by capitalism's technologies of allure but, in its attractive veneer, Titanic Belfast also ensures those forgotten historical divisions will struggle to return. The politics of boredom stems from this double movement: the withdrawal of meaning on the one hand, and the apparent inability to restore it on the other. The combined effect is to create an almost irrecoverable absence and, beholden to this process, visitors to the site are left increasingly ignorant of the divisive meanings it once signified. In this uncomfortable sense, the politics of boredom is an experience of disempowerment to which we are all vulnerable.

Boredom has not always been viewed in such broad terms. In nineteenth-century Europe, for example, boredom was held to be a privileged condition. In this period it was, as Elizabeth Goodstein has argued, a 'characteristic that functioned both to distinguish the rising classes from the masses and to establish the propriety of their social and material successes'.[11] With the onset of modernity, however, boredom mutated. No longer an 'elitist discourse of subjective disaffection', it gradually became what Goodstein has termed a 'truly universal', even 'democratic' condition.[12] To politicise boredom, however, is to shift her argument. As Geoff Waite explains, 'because politics is always about economics (yes, sure, it is about other things too) … the politics of boredom is also about political economy'.[13] Waite is surely correct in this judgement but, as I will demonstrate in this book, the politicisation of boredom necessarily entails a more complex rendering of the political itself. Nevertheless Waite's insistence that we should focus on political economy when politicising boredom does suggest a productive point of departure. That is, if we are to understand the politics of boredom, we must also understand its relationship to ideas of governance, economics and, most importantly, conceptions of capital. Where Goodstein saw boredom transformed by modernity, I will argue that boredom is politicised by capitalism – a shift that is given added potency if we take seriously Fredric Jameson's wry assertion that capitalism is modernity's 'only satisfactory semantic meaning'.[14]

However, to examine boredom's politicisation against the backdrop of the social and political violence endemic in Northern Ireland is also to witness the more protracted reverberations of this transformation. Set against the atavisms of ethnic–national division, boredom's relationship with political economy comes to hinge crucially upon the containment of disorder and the management of disruption. Empowered by the language of capitalist modernisation, boredom works upon Northern Ireland's divided landscape and reconfigures its ongoing social schisms. This is by no means a new phenomenon: the politics of boredom are as present in the years that predated the Troubles as they are in those that have marked the putative cessation of that conflict. Yet, by exposing the persistence of this process, I seek not only to recalibrate our understanding of Northern Irish history but also to remove boredom further from its recurrent diagnosis as what Saikat Majumdar has called the 'mark of a singular consciousness'.[15] Where philosophical discourse (from Pascal to Kant, Heidegger to Kierkegaard) has constructed boredom as a personal affliction to be internally digested, I argue that boredom is a collective condition externally imposed.[16] Boredom is, then, to use Majumdar's terms, 'an affective consequence of exclusion and disempowerment'.[17] In Northern Ireland this did not begin with an entity like Titanic Belfast or, indeed, with the Peace Process of which that building is a putative symbol. None the less, as I will demonstrate, Northern Ireland's post-conflictual condition has put into sharp focus boredom's politicisation, in ways that reverberate far beyond this context. It is a period that demands an urgent investigation.

Today, it is difficult to miss Belfast's new commercial skin; the city is 'quartered' around this architecture, its signs and maps orientated towards their new designs. Certainly, this entrepreneurial flair caught the eye of Barack Obama during the 2013 G8 summit, held for the first time in Northern Ireland. Stopping to address a youthful audience at the city's Waterfront Hall, the American president celebrated what he perceived to be the construction of 'a thoroughly modern Northern Ireland'.[18] The North's 'courageous' path towards 'a permanent peace' had generated, he argued, tangible 'social and economic benefits' and this was a blessing, not just for Northern Ireland but for the entirety of 'today's hyper-connected world'.[19] In many ways Obama was recycling the official message which had greeted the 1994 ceasefires, what Britain's then Prime Minister, John Major, had called the 'virtuous circle' in which peace would give 'rise to prosperity', while prosperity would, in turn, 'consolidate and entrench that peace'.[20] Nineteen years later, Obama heralded the tangible signs of this circular logic. 'Belfast is a different city', he asserted. 'Visitors come from all over to see an exhibit at the MAC, a play at the Lyric, a concert here at Waterfront Hall.'[21]

Belfast has indeed changed, but an underlying set of disjunctions still subtends these observations. While the city's new landmarks are familiar from a host of glossy commercials, they nevertheless exist, as Colin Coulter has noted, 'beyond the financial resources and cultural compasses of many less affluent residents of the city'.[22] Central Belfast may have been reimagined as a 'place ready to party',[23] yet what, we might ask, of the oft-cited fact that, since the signing of the 1998 Good Friday Agreement, the number of peace walls separating predominantly Catholic and Protestant neighbourhoods has risen by a third?[24] What, to invoke Richard Kirkland's insightful analysis, of the 'traumatised but insistent voices, memories, and spaces around the margins of the process, which refuse to be forgotten and which continue to demand reparation'?[25] What, moreover, of Northern Ireland's dependency upon new modes of capitalist domination, in which its obdurate political schisms are occluded so as to remain perpetually unaddressed? Economic development can doubtless be a source for optimism, but, as Mari Fitzduff observed in the wake of the initial ceasefires, 'if it's not done carefully it can, in fact, create conflict in itself'.[26]

Several issues are knotted here. For one thing, a problem of periodisation is introduced into the genealogies of the Troubles and the Peace Process if the politics of boredom is taken as a theme. As this book will illustrate, the Peace Process is – in many ways – the realisation of a far longer search for a capitalist solution to the unhappinesses of the North. Daniel Jewesbury describes how, 'since 1998, the new Northern Ireland has been undergoing something like the "shock" capitalism foisted on the former communist states'.[27] But, despite its current reverberations, this sudden influx of capital is a process that cannot be confined to the post-conflict moment. Partly due to the persistence of ethnic-national division, and partly due to a prolonged dependency upon the British state, there have been numerous attempts to standardise and rationalise the Northern Irish economy. Indeed, since the postwar period the North has become a site of such 'unproductive labour' that its subvention by the British state has made it, arguably, 'the most socialist region in the United Kingdom'.[28] However, the offering of this subsistence is a policy that must be carefully understood. Though it may have allowed the North's economic inefficiencies to persist, this was by no means its intention. In such contexts we must, as Louis Althusser has instructed, take heed not of capitalism's desire for production but rather of its need for reproduction.[29] The incursion of capital may have proved unproductive, but its ambition – first and foremost – was (and still is) to create the conditions for capitalism's continuance, to perpetuate its ideological inevitability.

Understood in these terms, it becomes necessary to rethink the narrative of the Troubles. While most historical assessments tend to delineate a neat timeline for the conflict (the birth of civil rights to the long war, the Peace Process to the post-Troubles period), my focus on the political economy demands an attention to the continuities within this schema. Rather than perpetuate a self-enclosed historiography, I propose to identify and examine convergences within the putatively discrete phases of Northern Ireland's postwar history. An immediate and obvious starting point is to view the post-conflict insistence on a consociational model of governance not as a new narrative of peace making but as the latest evolution in a longer capitalist response to the conflict. The consociational model was developed by Arend Lijphart in 1968, but it was held to be inimical to Northern Ireland until championed by political scientists during the Peace Process, and then implemented in the Good Friday Agreement itself. Crucial to this change was the work of John McGarry and Brendan O'Leary, who modified Lijphart's ideas as a means of foreclosing the 'overwhelmingly unfavourable' conditions for power-sharing in the North.[30] Foundational to Lijphart's work is, of course, a desire to 'avoid violence' but, as McGarry and O'Leary note, there is also an economic incentive behind this mode of government.[31] Specifically, as Lijphart expounds it, consociationalism forges an explicit link between 'macro-economic management (such as economic growth and the control of inflation and unemployment) and the control of violence'.[32]

Understood in these terms, the distinct shift to peace is actually a continuation of earlier economic strategies, which range from Roy Mason's insistence that job creation would deal 'a hammer blow to the IRA'[33] to Terence O'Neill's infamous pronouncement that 'if you give Roman Catholics a good job and a good house, they will live like Protestants'.[34] The sectarian assumptions that underpin these policies are, as this book will demonstrate, not without their own complexities. Despite this, Northern Ireland's conflation of consociationalism and capitalism continues apace. Just as Lijphart argues that the Dutch origins of power-sharing are rooted in 'Holland's long tradition as a merchant nation', so the visitor to Northern Ireland's post-Troubles shipyards can follow a Maritime Trail that locates the 'beginnings of modern Belfast' in the seventeenth-century: a period when 'Scotsmen dominated the city's shipbuilding industry' even if the colonial conditions that made it possible are muted in the signage itself.[35]

To apprehend this longer narrative of modernisation is not to document the failed construction of a productive economy. Instead it is to focus upon certain 'moments of capitalism' in Northern Ireland's postwar cultural history. These moments may be staged, as in the vision for a new modern city, Craigavon, discussed in Chapter 1. Or they may be a spontaneous reaction to the entrenched conditions of the Troubles, as with sectarianism's spatial replication of the capitalist spectacle examined in Chapter 3. Yet, despite the variety of their manifestations, all these moments involve a forced intersection between capitalism and sectarianism. As such the argument of this book is, on one side, that capitalism's need for reproduction serves to standardise Northern Irish society and, on the other, that Northern Ireland's residual ethnic–national divisions have subverted and complicated these ambitions. Mediated by a language of rationalisation and hostility, the charged interface that characterises this politics of boredom has produced a series of enervating architectures often inhabited by precarious people who have little to gain from such a speculative combat. Capital might claim to have won this contest – a fact that the contours of the Peace Process have made all too apparent – but the concept of capital has not emerged unscathed. Across Northern Ireland's postwar modernity, the conflictual disharmony of ethnic–national division has proved inimical to what Guy Debord has poetically called capitalism's 'motionless monotony', and it is through this incompatibility that capitalism has been both animated and disrupted.[36]

In the field of Irish studies, critics such as Joe Cleary, Mary Daly and David Lloyd have all helped to delineate this contradictory condition by viewing modernity through the prism of Irish culture.[37] Much of this work has been invigorated by what Lloyd perceives to be Ireland's ability to provide a 'postcolonial critique of modernity'. That is to say, Ireland's capacity to offer a 'form of unevenness that calls into question the historicist narrative that understands modernity as the progress from the backward to the advanced, from the pre-modern to the modern'.[38] Additional work by Birte Heidemann, Colin Graham, Aaron Kelly and Richard Kirkland has tried to emphasise the convergences between the often isolated fields of cultural production, the political economy and everyday life in the context of Northern Ireland.[39] The significance of these interventions stems from the way in which they probe the assumed ameliórations of the Peace Process's modernising imperatives, exposing its inner instabilities and the disenfranchisement this can breed.

These points are important because they highlight capitalism's less tangible manifestations and the hidden channels by which they percolate society. Yet these accounts have also remained consciously contemporary, sticking to the post-conflict moment without taking their findings back in time. My aim is to expand their arguments by foregrounding not only the unwritten violence that shadows capitalism's intersection with ethnic–national division but, in doing so, also to investigate the persistence of that intersection across the Troubles timeline. For this reason, I also depart from Conor McCabe's insistence on Northern Ireland's 'double transition': its movement from conflict to peace and its shift from a 'social economy' to one built around 'the financialisation of everyday life'.[40] While I would agree with McCabe's discussion of 'the social fissures that such a transition brings to bear', I contest his sense of the 'transition' itself. Rather than a complete change, I see the Peace Process as harbouring moments of continuity: less a movement 'towards peace and neoliberalism' and more a continuation of conflict and capitalism by another means.[41]

I interrogate the ways in which capitalism is parasitic upon the existence of ethnic–national hostilities throughout this book. In so doing, I examine how this continual violence is manifested at the level of the individual: creating a citizenship constantly coerced into manageable, depersonalised territories from which little can emerge but an exhausting sense of deletion and ennui. Traditionally, Marxist writing has argued that capitalism's exacerbation of ethnic–national hostilities is its final destination: the point at which 'the Irish people might be kept asunder and robbed whilst so sundered and divided', as James Connolly has memorably written.[42] Running against this, however, I argue that, in heightening sectarianism's divisive rhetoric, capitalism also incubates a highly localised sense of 'communalism' that is antithetical to its aims. In the ruins this creates, I ultimately suggest, it is possible to trace the rhythms of a different way of being – an alternative mode of living that helps render the 'progress' of capitalist development both contingent and conditional.

A lot happened to Northern Ireland in 1994. Republican and Loyalist paramilitaries called permanent ceasefires, ending decades of armed conflict. Cross-party negotiations commenced, initiating the North's ongoing narrative of consociationalism. John Major addressed Belfast's Institute of Directors, declaring that 'peace of itself will give a massive boost to the Northern Irish economy'.[43] All these events congealed to position Northern Ireland as a stable political entity, ready to do business with the world. Alongside these shifts, the geopolitical landscape underwent its own, distinct convulsions. The 1990s saw an end to the Cold War and the dawning of a new world economy – one in which fresh, frenetic waves of capital were channelled towards 'hitherto untapped markets'.[44] Indeed, 1994 was the Northern Ireland Industrial Development Board's 'best year for inward investment'. In this year alone a total of thirteen projects were expected to provide 2,300 jobs, while the promise of future international development was strengthened following the New York City Comptroller's pledge to spend $100 million in the North during the next twelve months.[45] Buoyed by the momentum of free-flowing capital and confident of the economic correlatives of peace, Major ushered in an era of 'new money' which was, he claimed, 'specifically designed to underpin reconciliation'.[46]

From Major to Clinton, Blair to Obama, there has been a diehard – even messianic – belief that peace and prosperity are mutually reinforcing. 'There is a well of economic goodwill and potential inward investment out there just waiting for the right opportunity', proclaimed Blair when visiting Belfast in 1998. 'Let us turn that prospect into a reality.'[47] In response to these external prerogatives, the devolved Northern Irish Assembly has constructed a policy framework that seeks to reiterate and realise these ambitions, with the construction of Titanic Belfast as perhaps the clearest manifestation of this imperative. In its final form, however, it is also a lucid example of the inequalities peace dividends can breed. Costed at over £100 million, Titanic Belfast is 'the most expensive tourist attraction in Europe' and yet, despite the commitment of substantial public funds, it has failed to generate the already lowly 'social responsibility goals' tasked by Stormont. For Brian Kelly, this misuse of public money crystallises an inevitable consequence of the desire to remake Northern Ireland in a neoliberal mould: namely, that 'the stark social inequalities that fuelled the "Troubles" remain deeply entrenched'.[48] Such setbacks notwithstanding, the mantra of peace and prosperity remains firmly in place. 'What the world saw this summer', declared David Cameron in the aftermath of the 2013 G8, was 'a new Northern Ireland strengthening the foundations for peace, stability and prosperity'.[49]

The link between capitalist modernity and ideas of progress is so often evoked that it is almost axiomatic. But such rhetoric is also buoyed by the now seemingly intractable commitment to what political scientists call the 'liberal peace'. As Roger Mac Ginty defines it, this now dominant form of peace making 'reflects the ideological and practical interests of leading states in the global north, leading international organisations, and the international financial institutions'.[50] Through the last category we can glean an understanding as to why such peace making is justified by a neoliberal agenda which, in Roland Paris's phrase, views 'market-orientated economics as a remedy for civil conflict'.[51] While the insistence on marketisation as a prerequisite for peace has been duly criticised, it is still a foundational element of recent, spirited defences for liberal interventionism in divided societies. 'Most of those who have criticised the economic dimensions of liberal peacebuilding', argues Paris, 'have not rejected the idea of economic liberalisation itself'.[52]

The inability to jettison the problematic notion of a liberal peace warrants further scrutiny. For David Chandler it highlights the propensity for critics to be 'drawn into a framework in which their critical intentions may be blunted'.[53] This is because these critiques are articulated *within* a framework established by the liberal peace. Consequently any attempt to overturn that model is, in Chandler's phrase, likely to be 'assimilated into the policy discourse of how policy might be reformed and legitimated'.[54] In other words, unless the challenge to liberal peace making is situated outside the parameters of that project, it is likely to reform (rather than resist) the liberalising agenda. Alongside this, the concept of 'liberalism' is also adept at assimilating its antagonists because it has become, through overuse and analytical abuse, a term 'increasingly emptied of theoretical or empirical content'. As Chandler puts it, liberalism 'appears to be used promiscuously to explain a broad range of often contradictory policy perspective and practices'.[55] It is partly for this reason that *Northern Ireland and the politics of boredom* insists upon an analytical framework formed around capitalism itself. As the chapters proceed, I identify peculiarly capitalist modes of conflict resolution to bypass the contradictory agendas an engagement with liberalism could bring.

An attention to the specifically capitalist dynamics of peace building has the added advantage of being more historically flexible than an engagement with liberalism would otherwise allow. As demonstrated by Mark Duffield's landmark intervention in this field, the concept of the liberal peace is cognisant with shifts in global governance that erupted in the so-called 'post-nuclear age'.[56] While this has provided an important springboard for an understanding of how neoliberalism has come to undergird Northern Ireland since the ceasefires, it has also left the longer legacy of capitalism's intersection with conflict relatively unexplored.[57] Consequently, rather than being enamoured by the latest evolutions in economic theory, I advance a methodology that looks back to more canonical and more marginal theories of the political economy, in order to determine how a critique of capitalism's engagement with ethnic–national division might already lie dormant within these texts. Thus I strive to displace the deeper logic of what we might term a 'capitalist peace' without getting waylaid by the latest policies and practices of the neoliberal age.

The idea that capitalism breeds peace is, then, hardly a new phenomenon. In 1848, John Stuart Mill's *Principles of Political Economy* extolled the virtues of capitalism, casting it as a salutary force 'which is rapidly rendering war obsolete'.[58] Writing in a period beset with the 'rapid increase of international trade', Mill saw commerce as 'the principal guarantee of peace in the world'. Commerce, he argued, had 'taught nations to see with goodwill the wealth and prosperity of another'.[59] Where imperialism had created conflict, globalism would instil harmony: creating a set of mutually sustaining relationships where once there had been bitterness and rivalry. In many ways, this is a familiar argument whose outlines can be found in the work of Norman Angell and Thomas Paine and, more recently, Thomas Friedman, Erik Gartzke and Patrick J. McDonald.[60] But Mill suggested that these new commercial alliances could also be a source for 'intellectual and moral' development. Dwelling on 'the present low state of human improvement', Mill claimed that it was 'hardly possible to overrate the value' of using capitalism to place 'human beings in contact with persons dissimilar to themselves'.[61]

With the advantage of hindsight, theories of peace are invariably scuppered by the recrudescence of war. Yet from our present vantage, Mill's belief in the diversity of global capital is equally problematic. In attending to the propitious effects of capitalism, Mill, like many economists of his kind, overlooks the destructive consequences of this economic system. He writes that 'international trade' offers 'great permanent security for ... the character of the human race'.[62]

But, despite the singularity of his terminology ('character'), he ignores the possibility that an increase in trade might also efface those 'dissimilar' sensibilities it is supposed to have secured. The automatic association of capital with a mutually beneficial exchange does not hold true, though the architects of the Northern Irish Peace Process have made a similar set of assumptions. Instead, as Debord makes clear, to unite diverse spaces under the auspices of capitalist production is to witness 'an extensive and intensive process of *banalisation*'.[63]

Debord is all too aware of the violence that lies beneath this banal exterior. In *The Society of the Spectacle* (1967), he explains how capitalism's 'homogenizing power is the heavy artillery that has battered down all the walls of China'.[64] Rather than enabling a mutual accommodation of difference, as Mill suggests, capitalism is a blunt instrument that seeks standardisation. Its 'contact' is neither welcoming nor warranted, while its consequences are decisive and destructive. In emphasising capitalism's 'heavy artillery' Debord is raising the spectre of *The Communist Manifesto*, and through this intertextual reasoning he encourages us to contemplate the full extent of capitalism's homogenising influence – to apprehend the true nature of what financial commentators still describe as capitalism's 'shock and awe'.[65] As Marx and Engels write:

> The cheap prices of its commodities are the heavy artillery with which it batters down all Chinese walls, with which it forces the barbarians' intensely obstinate hatred of foreigners to capitulate. It compels all nations, on pain of extinction, to adopt the bourgeois mode of production; it compels them to introduce what it calls civilization into their midst, *i.e.*, to become bourgeois themselves. In one word, it creates a world after its own image.[66]

Capitalism, in this sense, is what is left when differences have collapsed under the weight of threatened or actual violence. All that remains is a narcissistic image, devoid of its own brutality and enamoured with its apparent civility.

In divided, postcolonial societies such as Northern Ireland, imposing this singular capitalist image is a particularly painful process. Discussing the North's troubled search for a 'peace dividend', Denis O'Hearn describes how 'local political institutions and practices' – 'developed under settler colonialism and decolonization' – are often resistant to the changes that new forms of capitalism represent. As he states, 'entrenched state structures resist changes that could deliver a peace dividend to the communities that require it most, while their narrower concentration on old political relations (from a previous globalisation) impede their abilities to engage in new relations of globalisation'.[67] In Chapter 1 I discuss how the rigidities of capitalist planning are exposed by the legacies of settler colonialism, something I unearth in relation to the development of Northern Ireland's first new city, Craigavon. Faced with the persistence of these residual oppositions – that is, the hostilities between Nationalist/Catholic (natives) and Unionist/Protestant (settlers) – the imposition of dominant modes of capitalism become more pugnacious and restrictive. As Seamus Deane observes, in order that economic development might 'proceed', 'the two communities in the north' are told they must 'surrender' their 'archaic language of difference'.[68] Of course, the irony of this proposition is that capitalism was, in its colonial form, entirely responsible for the very division it now presumes to efface.[69] Capitalism's insatiable march towards an ever increasing universality means that it is – in this postcolonial context – forced to face its own internal contradictions, or, as Marx has termed it, to encounter 'barriers in its own nature'.[70]

The narrative of capitalist modernity claims that the residues of ethnic–national difference are, in fact, 'a symptom of underdevelopment'.[71] Consequently, the 'coercive violence' that facilitates their removal becomes largely deflected; its aggressions are displaced by the discourse of development. Here we witness the erosive logic of the Debordian 'spectacle' in which the violence of banalisation is masked by the construction of new desires – an ever-changing veneer much like Titanic Belfast's glittering skin.[72] Faced with that which impedes improvement, attention is drawn away from the destructive nature of economic growth and placed, instead, upon the enervating symptoms that these new waves of capital claim to redress. Thus, when Deane comes to describe Northern Ireland's 'surrender' to new laws of accumulation, he frames it not in terms of an assault but rather as the logical solution to the North's own internal failings. As he writes, Northern Ireland is told 'it must surrender the archaic language of difference … because it is irrational, improvident, insusceptible to civilization'.[73] The language of capitalist 'improvement' can, in other words, refract its own aggressions on to that antagonistic division it presumes to replace. However, as the chapters in this book will demonstrate, the unwritten outcome of this parasitical relationship is that the persistence of sectarian difference is never entirely foreclosed. Indeed, to do so would be to lose sight of those potential blockage points that give capitalism's monotonous logic such unrestrained momentum. As Marx reminds us, 'the fact that capital posits every such limit as a barrier and hence gets *ideally* beyond it, it does not by any means follow that it has *really* overcome it'.[74]

For those marketing Titanic Belfast, the condition of the city's shipyards was a source of much excitement. 'That area of the city has obviously declined since its industrial use', noted Belfast City Councillor Gerry Copeland. 'But now we have almost a blank canvas and an opportunity to create a new future.'[75] Capital often seeks a smooth surface by which to perpetuate its self-image,

yet in Copeland's use of 'almost' he discloses the obstacles that can also ener-
gise such a venture. Rubbing against the economically deprived and religiously
divided enclaves of East Belfast, the Titanic Quarter seeks 'to diversify the city's
employment' while still serving 'the city as a whole'.[76] What is striking about
the literature promoting this development is its ability to manipulate the rhetoric of urban inclusivity, transplanting it (in a matter of sentences) from being a
'place where the city's residents and guests could freely mingle' to a domain
for a new financial elite: a 'town square for the local neighbourhood of offices,
hotels and apartment blocks'.[77] Denying the actual history of the shipyards, its
communities and their often divisive traditions, Titanic Belfast has helped to
create something of a 'twin speed city': an urban landscape in which the 'image
of a normalised, "post-conflict city"' fails to extend to areas 'increasingly strati-
fied in terms of ethnonational segregation'.[78]

In many ways this schism between centre and periphery is replicated in the
consociational framework of the Good Friday Agreement itself. As a mode of
government, consociationalism presupposes that a lack of political consensus can
be resolved only through an exclusory system of power-sharing. In Northern
Ireland this consists of sundering the political landscape in 'two' (the watchword
of the Agreement) and then institutionalising and harmonising that division via
the Northern Irish Assembly itself. As the Agreement states, Assembly members
must designate themselves as either 'nationalist', 'unionist' or 'other' and, when
voting on 'key decisions', there must be 'parallel consent' or 'weighted majority' from Nationalist and Unionist members.[79] Constructed on these terms, the
Agreement reproduces a system where sectarian division is an overdetermined
problem. As Adrian Little has written, 'it over-simplifies the wide range of
conflicts that politicians need to deal with by suggesting that *the* division is the
only major schism that needs to be addressed'.[80] In this sense, the Agreement has
instituted a depleted form of politics which has proved increasingly difficult to
redress. Chapter 2 explores the apathy that supports this politics, taking account
of the ways in which – to use Chris Gilligan's phrase – a politics that seeks 'to
circumvent confrontation, actually ends up rendering people impotent'.[81]

For Aaron Kelly this structure of feeling can be taken a stage further and
located in the rhetoric of global capital. Building upon Jameson's belief that
capitalism has invented 'remarkable new languages' to camouflage its deeper
exploitative mechanics, Kelly sees the Peace Process as deploying 'a new multi-
cultural discourse of equality and reconciliation' to obscure the fact that it represents, instead, 'the more novel realignment of that society with the economic
and political realities of globalisation'.[82] Where the Agreement promotes a form
of 'regionalised micropolitical enfranchisement', Kelly perceives 'an increased
interdependence of economic micro-units'.[83] Where the Peace Process offers 'a

new ethical dispensation', Kelly identifies 'an ideology whose only compass is the flow of capital around the globe'.[84] The remorseless nature of this positioning reveals the breadth and fluency of capitalism's expanding vocabulary, but it also reveals its own inherent lack of substance: its status as a false wall or virtual window display. As Kelly writes passionately,

> the state-sponsored aspects of the Peace Process – extending British 'Third Way' capitalism westwards and the Celtic Tiger northwards through the promotion of private finance and the exclusion of the poor from public life – aim at establishing a wishy-washy and market-driven postmodern pluralism that actually serves to mask the real socioeconomic divides in our city that threaten ultimately to remove power from the people completely.[85]

Pursuing a similar point, Slavoj Žižek suggests that one consequence of pluralist discourse is not 'the hybrid coexistence of diverse cultural life-worlds', but 'the massive presence of capitalism as *universal* world system'.[86] Rather than an accommodation of difference, Žižek suggests that it would be more accurate to think of the language of collectivism as a 'phantasmatic screen' behind which 'unprecedented homogenization' manages to persist.[87]

In a likeminded fashion, to step inside Titanic Belfast is to embark upon a journey split between a set of unique and uniform experiences. Entering via a revolving door, visitors are greeted first by a central auditorium that plays on 'the geometric confusion of a working shipyard'.[88] 'From the outset', states James Alexander, the exhibition's chief designer, 'the intention was to use the authenticity of place and strength of personal stories to underpin the interactive approach'.[89] Starting with two galleries that take us from industrial Belfast to the shipyards themselves, black and white snapshots from the Welch, Hogg and W.A. Green collections communicate the atmospherics of an expanding economy. These photographs produce a nuanced portrait of the city, but the potential for personal engagement is muted by silhouetted caricatures projected across their surface. 'Titanic Belfast tries to make its own pastiche of Edwardiana the centre of attention', writes Pauline Hadaway.[90] As we move towards the *Titanic* itself, an aerial 'shipyard ride' takes us round a partial reconstruction of the ship's bow. We twist amidst 'the steam, smoke and smells' of industry while 'strategically embedded' holograms counterfeit a generic image of a workforce united in their task.[91] There are queues to see this stand-out feature, yet once on-board there is a pressing sense that we are witnessing commodity fetishisation in reverse. Secured within a six-seater cart, we feel the heat of *Titanic's* labour, but we learn very little about those who actually made the ship float.

Belfast's shipyards are the premise for this exhibition, yet beyond the third gallery they all but disappear. In their place, an ever-more digitised version of the ship comes into view. We watch 'candy-coated vignettes' describing life in each cabin class; we see computer graphics of the mid-Atlantic; in one heightened moment a 3-D cave displays the reality of the ship's interiors: a seamless movement from the Captain's bridge to the conspicuously clean steam of the ship's engine room.[92] We actively imbibe these simulations, but we are constantly reminded not to film or photograph what is on display. Anxious about its own repeatability in spaces beyond its purview, the world's largest *Titanic* attraction begins to offer its own version of Kierkegaard's philosophy of repetition. Where Kierkegaard's experience of the same performance at Berlin's Königstädter provided the variegation of theatre and not the uniformity he craved, conversely visitors to Titanic Belfast encounter the reproducibility of a computer-generated fantasy far more than the authenticity they are sold.[93] 'Some of it was ok', recounts one internet review, 'but it became a bit samey samey after about half an hour'.[94] The contradictions that underlie these affective energies are all the more significant because, in their double movement, they gesture towards the politics of boredom that has come to dominate the North. Titanic Belfast markets itself around its 'emotional connections' with the birthplace of that ship, but once inside the exhibition a set of diminished and depersonalised experiences begin to persist.[95]

Encountering this delimited view of history, we should wonder why the emptiness of a fetishised object is allowed to displace a more dissident engagement with the past. Or, looked at another way, we should ask how this historical amnesia can be so consistently maintained. The consociational nature of the Peace Process has certainly helped to institute such an apathetic condition, divorcing – as it has – the signatories of the Agreement from the people they claim to represent. Yet there are also broader socio-economic forces at work. As Gilles Deleuze and Félix Guattari argue in *Anti-Oedipus* (1972), 'the capitalist use of language is different in nature', it 'does not go by way of voice or writing; data processing does without them both'.[96] Similarly, when Titanic Belfast does grant us access to the lives of those on board, it does so in the form of such raw data – what the exhibition guide calls 'the statistics associated with the tragedy'.[97] Hidden in the wings of the penultimate gallery, a series of interactive monitors contain *Titanic*'s passenger list: a spreadsheet of over two thousand names. When one is confronted with this overwhelming dataset, it is difficult to know how to proceed. We are told that our ability to organise the 'list by survivors, gender, class, age, nationality etc.' will enable us to 'better understand the tragedy'.[98] Yet faced with an avalanche of information, it is easy to scroll listlessly. Searching for connections, we reluctantly partake in this networking of society – computing the *Titanic*'s lost lives like the algorithms that augment investments for companies such as BlackRock. 'It is the modern world of power', writes Adam Curtis in response to this atomised approach, 'and it's incredibly boring'.[99]

Despite its mundane appearance, this statistical rendering of entire populations has a profound effect upon social variegation. For Deleuze, this 'numerical language of control' means that 'we no longer find ourselves dealing with a mass/individual pair'. Instead, these terms become equated and interchangeable, producing something close to that sense of anonymous individuality capitalism creates. In what Deleuze terms 'societies of control', discipline no longer operates exclusively through forms of enclosure (such as a school or prison).[100] Instead it functions via a widespread and unimpeded circuit of regulation – a mode of control 'achieved in part by collecting statistical information on the population'.[101] Developing his argument, Deleuze notes how this insistence on digitisation leads to the construction of '*dividuals*': an impersonal identity compiled from 'masses, samples, data, markets, or "banks"'.[102] Reconceived in this manner, we lose all sense of that 'I' which constitutes our individuality. Instead we become a 'digital "partial representation"', a mechanical entity which can be, in Daniel Martinez's phrase, 'aggregated in seemingly endless ways'.[103] In Chapter 4 I argue that Northern Ireland experienced such a shift following the introduction of internment in August 1971. Here new military technologies and homogeneous temporalities sought to automate entire segments of the North's Catholic population – initiating 'a new apparatus of biopolitical power', the reverberations of which can still be felt today.[104]

The delimited experience generated by these digital matrices tells us something important about the experience of ennui. As Svendsen writes in *A Philosophy of Boredom* (2008), 'information is ideally communicated as a binary code, while meaning is communicated more symbolically'.[105] Understood in these terms, our digital experience of the *Titanic* tragedy is always likely to create something of a meaning deficit: a final 'etc.' that communicates the gulf between computer-generated fantasy on the one hand and the desire to derive a personal meaning on the other. It is through this deficit that the experience of boredom is at its most pronounced. The allure of the Titanic Experience means that this shortfall is often displaced, yet beneath the overwhelmingly positive reviews a handful of visitors are all too happy to communicate the meaninglessness they faced. 'Very boring. Too many videos instead of real innovation', writes one contributor to the TripAdvisor website.[106] Another is harsher still, their grammar and syntax blunted by the vacuity of their experience: 'i am not prepared to waste anymore of my time on this as i have already wasted 3 hours of my time which i will not get back, very poor very expensive very dissapointed [*sic*]'.[107] As the frustrated terms of this account suggest, the experience of boredom is often a far from painless operation. Indeed, as Svendsen has argued, at its most pronounced, boredom is the 'discomfort which communicates that the need for meaning is not being satisfied'.[108]

The tortuous experience that underpins the construction of boredom forms the background to all the chapters in this book. Despite the diversity of its manifestations, boredom's degradation is as evident in Craigavon's uneven urban development (discussed in Chapter 1) as it is in the sensory deprivations that typified internment (considered in Chapter 4). While adopting different forms, its excruciating corollaries are as apparent in the bourgeois apathy depicted in the poetry of Derek Mahon (analysed in Chapter 2), as they are in the oral testimony of the prisoners who resisted the H-Blocks' disciplinary regime (examined in Chapter 5). As I discuss in Chapter 3, these constrictive logics are perhaps most powerful when spatially received. Here, boredom constrains whole environs, policing the experiences of all those who inhabit such hollow domains. In this way, I suggest, boredom becomes an entity that aims to manage disruption and contain disorder; it creates immovable barriers where once there were blurred boundaries; it builds robust structures to combat fluid forms.

It is a small step from the preclusion of instability to the construction of a (false) coherence necessary for capital accumulation. Not only does the Peace Process insist on structuring the complex contingencies of Northern society in terms of two narrowly defined communities but, in so doing, it also neglects the 'shifting political priorities and dynamics' these communities might contain.[109] As Hadaway notes, by bestowing equal legitimacy upon 'two diametrically opposed' communities, the consociational framework has drained them both of meaning, 'leaving only their outer shells intact'.[110] Graham likens this process to a barrier. He argues that, by delimiting Northern Ireland along these lines, the Agreement 'cordons off the people who constitute those communities, trapping them in arenas where they are no better understood, though they may exist more quietly and more peacefully'.[111] The pacification that energises this process tells us something about the underlying logic of the Agreement – what Kelly describes as its 'prior, economic subtext ... scripted by Adam Smith's famous "invisible hand"'.[112] A more important point, however, is that this social segmentation operates at its most invisible, and most powerful, when imparting personal distress and individual discomfort. In a similar vein to Graham's cordon, Charles Taylor writes of the 'real damage' that 'a person or group of people can suffer' when the society 'around them mirror[s] back a confining or demeaning or contemptible picture of themselves'. This politics of 'misrecognition', Taylor argues, 'can be a form of oppression, imprisoning someone in a false, distorted, and reduced mode of being'.[113]

In Northern Ireland the perils of this process are particularly relentless. Indeed, with the North's economic future dependent upon such distortive reflections, there will be seemingly little respite from this 'constrictive', 'demeaning' and 'contemptible' image. The notion of any community has, of course, always depended upon an element of fiction, and this fiction can have its uses. It can, for example, create a sense of personal stability, particularly during a time of extreme social unrest. In the years preceding the Agreement, for instance, the North's Cultural Traditions Group aspired to promote what its then director, Maurice Hayes, called 'the importance of group identity as a means of self-fulfilment and ... security to the individual'.[114] Moreover, in the sphere of social science, Joseph Ruane and Jennifer Todd have insisted that a structural framework of 'two communities' is, in fact, 'necessary to any analysis of the conflict'.[115] Yet, for all these apparent benefits, this should not mean that group identities are hastily defined or broadly instituted as a fait accompli. Indeed, to do so is to create something close to what Stuart Hall has termed a 'corporate multiculturalism' – that is, a disciplinary mechanism which 'seeks to "manage" minority cultural differences in the interests of the centre'.[116] As this book will indicate, the imposition of capitalism has been perceived, at various stages, as marginalising both the Unionist and Nationalist communities. Consequently, by focusing on capitalism's intersection with ethnic–national difference my aim is not to dismantle the idea of cultural or communal identities, but rather to demonstrate the ways in which those identities are more restless, in process, and, crucially, less amenable to the dictates of a capitalist state.

As Chapter 3 will demonstrate, the work of Ariella Azoulay is particularly enabling when it comes to contesting such perceived cultural rigidities. Her insistence that we must actively 'watch', rather than passively view, the 'event' of cultural production introduces ideas of temporal fluidity that are sympathetic to my arguments. Where she sees a continuity between the taking of the photograph and our subsequent encounter with that image, so I will assert that there is a continuity between specific phases of the Troubles and their ongoing intersection with ideas of capital. Azoulay also insists that, in her more fluid conception of photography, the meaning of each image is continually negotiated. As such, her work can also help to unfix the experience of boredom (those moments of uncontested or absent meaning) in ways that are germane to the critique of capital.[117] After all, boredom does not only describe life under the capitalist spectacle, it also serves to separate those experiences which 'come to us fully coded' from those that depend upon our own, personal, contingencies.[118] Here we might move away from the 'total domination of the spectacle' so as to, in Julian Jason Haladyn's phrase, 'go beyond the limitations of boredom' itself.[119] In other words, boredom can become what Walter Benjamin has memorably called 'the dream bird that hatches the egg of experience'.[120] That is, boredom as a productive experience in which something new is born. Framed in this way, our engagement with the politics of boredom, our ability to make known its enervating effects, is to make room for something different: a means of 'hatching' an alternative to occupy its place.

There is, then, much to be gained from an act of cultural and historical retrieval that takes boredom as its point of departure. Indeed, as Haladyn argues, boredom can become 'a key motivating factor in the social and political critique of capitalism'.[121] Since the late 1990s, a more enabling conception of boredom has been advanced by critiques of the political economy. The French collective Tiqqun, for example, have advanced ideas of slowness, boredom and fatigue as a means of resisting the aggressive manoeuvres of what they term 'cybernetic capitalism'. As they write in *The Cybernetic Hypothesis* (2001): 'speed upholds institutions. Slowness cuts off flows.'[122] Yet for all the emphasis this places upon ennui as being 'at the core ... of struggles against capital', there is an underlying condition that limits such potential.[123] This is something Heidegger's conception of boredom helps us to comprehend. Like so many philosophical engagements with the subject, Heidegger perceives boredom as an individual and internal condition – 'the very opposite of a possible ground for politics', as Peter Osborne writes in relation to Heidegger's work.[124] Despite this, however, Heidegger still discerns a utopian potential within the experience of boredom, one in which 'the possibility of whatever is possible is precisely intensified'.[125] The point here is that boredom does not possess an agency in and of itself. Rather boredom only contains the opportunity for 'possibility'. Boredom can highlight the need for alterity, it can – in Heidegger's phrase – 'intensify' the desire for change. But even in this more utopian guise, boredom simply does not have the energy to resist capital in the way Tiqqun describe.

As this reminds us, 'boredom is not simple'. Its formation can provide an index of privation and malcontent, but its inert demeanour offers no solutions. It is an act of repression that can give way to moments of startling revelation – what Goodstein calls 'the disaffection with the old that drives the search for change' – but boredom is also an empty experience that claims not to warrant our attention.[126] In Chapter 2 I explain how the poetry of Derek Mahon is particularly concerned with what he describes as this 'presageless' condition.[127] Written from a Protestant perspective, Mahon's work helpfully situates boredom's dialectics within the broader traditions of Northern Ireland's identity politics. This is not to endorse what Tom Nairn has memorably termed the 'pseudo-Marxist theory of "anti-imperialist" struggle in Ireland'. As Nairn conceives it, this theory suggests that under the weight of capitalist oppression sectarian conflict could 'be transmuted into war for socialism'.[128] However, to advance such an argument is to neglect the peculiar features of boredom itself – that is to say, boredom's elusive 'lack of quality'.[129] It is boredom's neutrality – its 'presageless' condition – that allows it to bypass what Mick Wilson calls the 'tireless logic' of an identity politics that views Northern Ireland as 'racialised' purely 'in terms of Catholic/Nationalist and Protestant/Loyalist'.[130] Boredom does not possess the energy to subvert these divisions, but it can work through them – giving us access to the alternatives these divisions might actually contain.

In this sense, *Northern Ireland and the politics of boredom* works against some of the foundational tenets of modernisation theory as it is figured in Irish studies, particularly in the work of Lloyd. While Lloyd has been invaluable in identifying Ireland's ability to question the narrative of capitalist rationalisation, the source of that challenge is often rooted in a Nationalist dynamic. This is perhaps most evident in his figuration of the clachan as a recurrent example of an anti-capitalist sensibility. For Lloyd, this land-holding pattern is crucial not because of its geographical arrangement so much as for the Gaelic orality it engenders. It is this unmistakably Irish soundscape that is, he argues, pivotal in the 'breaking down' of a British modernity.[131] Conversely, the moments of non-capitalism I identify are notable for their deracinated complexion – for their neutrality in the context of difference and for their ability to transcend strictures of division. In Chapter 1, for example, I document the construction of a boring geography that unsettles Unionist as much as Nationalist sensibilities. The anti-urbanism that hereby emerges is not tied to a particular 'tribe'. Instead it is formed out of an almost inherent desire to resist the fixed capital that is coming to modernise the North. The structure of this book, which moves from a spatial to a temporal conception of boredom, is designed to unfold the possibilities of this more uncommitted mode of disruption. Acknowledging Northern Ireland's inherently divided terrain, I shift into a timescape where these neutral moments of non-capitalism can be more carefully examined.

Understood in these terms, boredom is a critical tool that comes laden with a clear imperative: a need to identify the various means by which the possibility of alterity can be made explicit. It is for this reason that the following chapters are particularly concerned with boredom's relationship to cultural production. After all, as Haladyn has suggested, because the creative capacities of art are pivotal in 'challenging' the collective will of the spectator, it is via aesthetics that we can best comprehend the more enabling perspectives offered by the experience of boredom. Advancing such an argument, Tom McDonough has suggested that there is 'a great split between those who suffer boredom as a burden to be lifted and those who face boredom as itself an aesthetic experience with critical and transformative potential'.[132] However, like boredom's 'critical' potential, our ability to negotiate this 'split' must be managed with care. Too often a desire to distinguish between the realms of so-called 'high' and 'low' art has meant that the monotony of capital has been at best displaced, at worst ignored. During the twentieth-century 'there has been considerable reluctance', notes Haladyn, 'to examine commercial objects and works of art through similar aesthetic theories'.[133] Yet if art – and its cognates of literature, film and architecture – are to engage critically with life under the banality of capital, it must account for its own proximity to such procedures. Rather than perceiving art as inherently immune from the workings of the market, we must draw these spheres together through an understanding of cultural practice and capitalist monotony as engaged in a dialectical relationship of mutual aggression, confrontation or, as Jacque Rancière would term it, 'critical dissensus'.[134]

In Northern Ireland the need for such an 'agonistic recuperation of disagreement' is particularly pressing.[135] Here the sphere of cultural production has been increasingly nullified by the logic of capitalism as a conduit of peace. In the post-Agreement context this has meant that, as Graham writes, a 'note of warning, at its most banal a "don't rock the boat" threat, is central to the ways in which all forms of cultural expression now emerge'.[136] Titanic Belfast's occlusion of Northern Ireland's sectarian history testifies to this condition. Here culture is viewed through a corporate lens – a marketing of a complex history that supresses persistent divisions on the one hand, and quietuses their continued inequalities on the other. In our current moment there is, then, a tangible sense in which cultural practice in and about Northern Ireland has become a vacuous enterprise: a creative act by which the dominant order can shroud and conceal the scars and wounds it continues to impart.

At issue in this book, then, is a desire to reinvigorate our understanding of Northern Irish culture. In this, I echo Declan Long's belief that we should 'stress a certain power of *instability* and *indeterminacy* in art's appeals to politics and public representation'.[137] More specifically, I prioritise cultural texts that are alive to the machinations of capital and conflict, and use this awareness to, in Azoulay's phrase, 'renegotiate' the politics of boredom so prevalent in the North.[138] By way of an illustration, Martin Parr's image 'Titanic Belfast' – from the photographic series *Welcome to Belfast* (2016) (Plate 1) – sets Northern Ireland's nascent tourist industry in dialogue with the politics of pacification that tries to keep the peace. Carrying the quotidian qualities of a holiday snap, Parr's image is highly conscious of its own proximity to the commercial language of photography. Indeed, in his limp arrangement of faceless bodies, Parr is seemingly engaged with what Julian Stallabrass has termed 'the frivolities and cool eccentricities' of photography as mass media. For Stallabrass, it is this 'frivolity' that has denuded our ability to produce 'images of extraordinary political and aesthetic concentration'.[139] And yet there is something incredibly concentrated in Parr's composition. For all its informality, Parr's photograph is squarely focused on the steel sign that 'announces', according to its designers, 'Titanic Belfast to the world'.[140] 'Capitalism red in tooth and claw' might be responsible for photography's ever delimited 'critical function',[141] but, in Parr's displaced attention to the architectonics of Titanic Belfast, he also uses photography to scrutinise capitalism's 'technology of allure'.[142]

Much of Parr's work is concerned with social interaction (key influences being Diane Arbus, Tony Ray Jones and Robert Frank). In this image, however, his attention to the built environment is also redolent of the New Topographics and its practitioners Robert Adams, Lewis Baltz and Stephen Shore.[143] Chapter 3 discusses how this genre of landscape photography lends itself to the anti-capitalist potential in Northern Ireland's sectarian space. At this point, though, it is worth highlighting how that movement's insistence on the 'prominence of the ordinary' allows Parr to comprehend the erosive properties of Titanic Belfast as a structure.[144] The seductive glamour of the building is evident in the trajectory of those figures that line the photo's foreground; their bodies are bent towards the building's shimmering façade. But the image's compositional insistence on the steel Titanic logo also means that much of the allure is obscured, its glamour cropped and left, as it were, off screen. In this way, Parr suggests something of the emptiness that subtends Titanic Belfast as a spectacle – an absence carried not only by the hollowness of its sign but also by the backward portrait of its principal spectators. Like the identity politics of the Agreement and the fetish-ised labour on display inside this building, capitalism's co-option of Northern Irish politics precludes the possibility of knowing what individuality might look like. What is the face of the global citizenry Titanic Belfast is designed to greet? On the basis of this image, it is a question that is difficult to answer.

Writing about capitalism's influence on cultural production, the theorist Mark Fisher has suggested that capital tends to operate 'like a pervasive *atmosphere*, conditioning not only the production of culture, but also the regulation of work and education, and acting as a kind of invisible barrier constraining thought and action'.[145] In Fisher's schema, it is not that cultural production fails to articulate alternatives to capitalism's diminution of identity, rather that these alternatives remain consistently occluded – hidden behind a screen. To experience this impasse is to touch on the frustrations that motivate much of my writing in this book. One way forward, I will suggest, is to make visible the 'barrier' of capitalism's construction and, in so doing, to apprehend those fleeting alterna-tives capitalism serves to shade. Parr's photograph captures something of the complexity of this task. He acknowledges capitalism's co-option of Northern Irish space, yet in recentring his image Parr simultaneously foregrounds the emptiness of that endeavour. In Fisher's attempt to puncture late capitalism's pervasive assemblage, he also suggests that an attempt to reorientate our perspective might expose capital as an occlusive presence. For Fisher this operation is often at its most pronounced when examining disordered feelings, emotions and affects. 'Affective disorders', he contends, 'are forms of captured discontent; this disaffection can and must be channelled outwards, directed towards its real cause, Capital'.[146] Boredom, this book argues, is precisely such a disorder. Cultural practice, despite or perhaps because of its subservience to the capitalist spectacle, is an activity which contains the seeds for boredom's politicisation.

Notes and references

1   Roland Barthes, *The Pleasure of the Text*, trans. by Richard Miller (London: Jonathan Cape, 1976), p. 25.

2   Paul Cattermole, *Building Titanic Belfast: The Making of a Twenty-First-Century Landmark* (Belfast: Titanic Belfast Publications, 2013), p. 51.

3   'Titanic Belfast – Facts and Figures' http://titanicbelfast.com/Explore/ The-Titanic-Belfast-Building/Facts-Figures/.

4   Cattermole, *Titanic Belfast*, p. 77, p. 1.

5   Brian Kelly, 'Neoliberal Belfast: Disaster Ahead?', *Irish Marxist Review*, 1.2 (2012), 55.

6   Cattermole, *Building Titanic Belfast*, p. 49.

7   Nigel Thrift, 'The Material Practices of Glamour', *Journal of Cultural Economy*, 1.1 (2008), 10. At the time of writing, the admission price for an adult to Titanic Belfast is £18.

8   Kelly, 'Disaster Ahead?', p. 56.

9   Marc Augé, *Non-Places: Introduction to an Anthropology of Supermodernity*, trans. by John Howe (London: Verso, 1995).

10 Lars Svendsen, *A Philosophy of Boredom*, trans. by John Irons (London: Reaktion Books, 2008), p. 30.

11 Elizabeth Goodstein, *Experience without Qualities: Boredom and Modernity* (Stanford: Stanford University Press, 2005), p. 174.

12 *Ibid.*, p. 99.

13 Geoff Waite, 'On the Politics of Boredom (A Communist Pastiche), 1992', in *Boredom* ed. by Tom McDonough (Cambridge, MA: MIT Press, 2017), p. 168.

14 Fredric Jameson, *A Singular Modernity: Essay on the Ontology of the Present* (London: Verso, 2011), p. 13.

15 Saikat Majumdar, *Prose of the World: Modernism and the Banality of Empire* (New York: Columbia University Press, 2013), p. 15.

16 See Blaise Pascal, *Pensées*, trans. A.J. Krailsheimer (London: Penguin, 1966), p. 148, no. 414; Immanuel Kant, *Anthropology from a Pragmatic Point of View*, trans. by Robert B. Louden (Cambridge: Cambridge University Press, 2006), pp. 43, 128–130;

Martin Heidegger, *The Fundamental Concepts of Metaphysics: World, Finitude, Solitude*, trans. by William McNeill and Nicholas Walker (Bloomington: Indiana University Press, 1995); and Søren Kierkegaard, *Repetition and Philosophical Crumbs*, trans. by M.G. Piety (Oxford: Oxford World Classics, 2009), p. 38.

17   Majumdar, *Prose of the World*, p. 15.

18   Barack Obama, 'Remarks by President Obama and Mrs. Obama in Town Hall with Youth of Northern Ireland', 17 June (2013) http://iipdigital.usembassy.gov/st/english/texttrans/2013/06/20130617276442.html#axzz3Pdgnslqn [accessed 24 July 2017].

19   Obama, 'Remarks by President Obama'.

20   John Major, 'Mr. Major's Speech at the International Investment Forum', 14 December (1994) www.johnmajor.co.uk/page2268.html [accessed 24 July 2017].

21   Obama, 'Remarks by President Obama'.

22   Colin Coulter, 'Under Which Constitutional Arrangement Would You Still Prefer to Be Unemployed? Neoliberalism, the Peace Process, and the Politics of Class in Northern Ireland', *Studies in Conflict and Terrorism*, 37.9 (2014), 765.

23   Coulter, 'Neoliberalism, the Peace Process, and the Politics of Class', 765.

24   David Lowe, '14 Years after Good Friday Agreement, Belfast is still divided', *Sun*, 6 April 2012, p. 23.

25   Richard Kirkland, 'Visualising Peace: Northern Irish Post-Conflict Cinema and the Politics of Reconciliation', *Review of Irish Studies in Europe*, 1.2 (2017), 14.

26   Northern Ireland Economic Council, *Through Peace to Prosperity: Proceedings of the Peace Seminar Hosted by the Economic Council* (Belfast: Northern Ireland Economic Development Office, 1995), p. 92.

27   Daniel Jewesbury, 'Nothing Left', in *Where Are the People? Contemporary Photographs of Belfast 2002–2010* ed. by Karen Downey (Belfast: Belfast Exposed Photography, 2010), p. 39.

28   John McGarry and Brendan O'Leary, *Explaining Northern Ireland: Broken Images* (Oxford: Blackwell, 1995), pp. 76–78.

29   Louis Althusser 'On the Reproduction of the Conditions of Production', in *Lenin and Philosophy and Other Essays*, trans. by Ben Brewster (London: NLB, 1971), pp. 124–129. My emphasis.

30   Arend Lijphart, *Democracy in Plural Societies: A Comparative Exploration* (New Haven: Yale University Press, 1977), p. 135. See also John McGarry and Brendan O'Leary, *The Northern Ireland Conflict: Consociational Engagements* (Oxford: Oxford University Press, 2004).

31   John McGarry and Brendan O'Leary, 'Conclusion', in *The Future of Northern Ireland* ed. by John McGarry and Brendan O'Leary (Oxford: Clarendon Press, 1990), p. 283.

32   Arend Lijphart, *Patterns of Democracy: Government Forms and Performance in Thirty-Six Countries* (New Haven: Yale University Press, 2012), p. xviii.

33   Roy Mason, *Paying the Price* (London: Robert Hale, 1999), p. 21.

34   'Opposition MPs plan to "carpet" O'Neill', *Belfast Telegraph*, 10 May 1969, p. 1.

35 'New Belfast Maritime Trail Is Launched' www.ulsterscotsagency.com/news/article/201/new-belfast-maritime-trail-is-launched/ [accessed 24 July 2017]. NIB
36 Guy Debord, *The Society of the Spectacle*, foreword by Martin Jenkins, trans. by Ken Knabb, 2nd edn (Eastbourne: Soul Bay Press, 2012), p. 114.
37 See, for example, Joe Cleary, *Outrageous Fortune: Capital and Culture in Modern Ireland* (Dublin: Field Day Publications in association with University of Notre Dame, 2007); Mary Daly, *Sixties Ireland: Reshaping the Economy, State and Society, 1957–1973* (Cambridge: Cambridge University Press, 2016); and David Lloyd, *Irish Times: Temporalities of Modernity* (Dublin: Field Day, 2008).
38 Lloyd, *Irish Times*, p. 3.
39 See Aaron Kelly, 'Geopolitical Eclipse: Culture and the Peace Process in Northern Ireland', *Third Text*, 19.5 (September 2005), 553; Colin Graham, '"Let's Get Killed": Culture and Peace in Northern Ireland', in *Irish Postmodernisms and Popular Culture* ed. by Wanda Balzano, Anne Mulhall and Moynagh Sullivan (Basingstoke: Palgrave Macmillan, 2007), p. 181; Birte Heidemann, *Post-Agreement Northern Irish Literature: Lost in a Liminal Space?* (Basingstoke: Palgrave Macmillan, 2016); and Richard Kirkland, *Identity Parades: Northern Irish Culture and Dissident Subjects* (Liverpool: Liverpool University Press, 2002).
40 Conor McCabe, *The Double Transition: The Economic and Political Transition of Peace* (Belfast: Irish Congress of Trade Unions and Labour After Conflict, 2013), p. 7.
41 *Ibid.*, p. 19.
42 James Connolly, 'Labour and the Proposed Partition of Ireland', *Irish Worker*, 14 March 1914, p. 2.
43 John Major, 'Mr Major's Speech to the Institute of Directors in Belfast', 21 October (1994) www.johnmajor.co.uk/page1961.html [accessed 24 July 2017].
44 Coulter, 'Neoliberalism, the Peace Process, and the Politics of Class', 764.
45 Eddie O'Gorman, 'Peace ranks high as North and US get down to business', *Irish Times*, 13 December 1994, p. 17.
46 Major, 'Speech at the International Investment Forum'.
47 Tony Blair, 'Speech by Tony Blair to the Royal Agricultural Society Belfast', 14 May (1998) http://cain.ulst.ac.uk/events/peace/docs/tb14598.htm [accessed 24 July 2017].
48 Kelly, 'Disaster Ahead?', pp. 44–45. Over two-thirds of the project was funded publicly and it failed to generate the tasked 25 apprenticeships and 15 jobs for Belfast's long-term unemployed.
49 'David Cameron's speech at the Northern Ireland Investment Conference', 11 October 2013 www.gov.uk/government/speeches/david-camerons-speech-at-the-northern-ireland-investment-conference [accessed 24 July 2017].
50 Roger Mac Ginty, *International Peacebuilding and Local Resistance: Hybrid Forms of Peace* (Basingstoke: Palgrave Macmillan, 2011), p. 20.
51 Roland Paris, 'Saving Liberal Peacebuilding', *Review of International Studies*, 36.2 (April 2010), 346.
52 *Ibid.*, 361.

53 David Chandler, 'The Uncritical Critique of "Liberal Peace"', *Review of International Studies*, 36 (2010), 139.

54 *Ibid.*, 144.

55 *Ibid.*, 145.

56 Mark Duffield, *Global Governance and the New Wars: The Merging of Development and Security*, 2nd rev. edn (London: Zed Books, 2014), p. xix.

57 See, for example, Roger Mac Ginty and John Darby, *Guns and Government: The Management of the Northern Ireland Peace Process* (Basingstoke: Palgrave, 2006), pp. 123–138.

58 John Stuart Mill, *Principles of Political Economy: With Some of Their Applications to Social Philosophy* ed. by J.M. Robson (Toronto: University of Toronto Press, Routledge & Kegan Paul, 1965), p. 594.

59 *Ibid.*, p. 594.

60 See Norman Angell, *The Great Illusion* (New York: Putnam, 1933), pp. 103–107; Thomas Paine, *Rights of Man, Common Sense, and Other Writings* ed. by Mark Philip (Oxford: Oxford University Press, 1995), pp. 265–266. Thomas Friedman, *The World Is Flat: The Globalized World In the Twenty-First Century* (London: Allen Lane, 2005), pp. 580–607; Erik Gartzke, 'The Capitalist Peace', *American Journal of Political Science*, 51.1 (January 2007), 166–191; Patrick J. McDonald, *The Invisible Hand of Peace: Capitalism, the War Machine and International Relations Theory* (Cambridge: Cambridge University Press, 2009).

61 Mill, *Principles of Political Economy*, p. 594.

62 *Ibid.*, p. 594.

63 Debord, *Society of the Spectacle*, p. 114.

64 *Ibid.*, p. 114.

65 Heather Stewart, 'Eurozone boost of €1.1tn in "shock and awe" plan by Central Bank', *Guardian*, 22 January (2015) www.theguardian.com/business/2015/jan/22/ecb-boosts-eurozone-mario-draghi-kickstart-growth [accessed 24 July 2017].

66 Karl Marx and Frederick Engels, *Manifesto of the Communist Party*, trans. by Samuel Moore (Moscow: Progress Publisher, 1967), p. 47.

67 Denis O'Hearn, 'Peace Dividend, Foreign Investment, and Economic Regeneration: The Northern Irish Case', *Social Problems*, 47.2 (May 2000), 182–183.

68 Seamus Deane, *Strange Country: Modernity and Nationhood in Irish Writing since 1790* (Oxford: Oxford University Press, 1997), p. 163.

69 Joe Cleary, 'Introduction: Ireland and Modernity', in *The Cambridge Companion to Modern Irish Culture* ed. by Joe Cleary and Claire Connolly (Cambridge: Cambridge University Press, 2005), p. 3.

70 Karl Marx, *Grundrisse*, trans. by Martin Nicolaus (London: Penguin, 1993), p. 410.

71 Lloyd, *Irish Times*, p. 28.

72 'Behind the glitter of spectacular distractions, a tendency toward *banalization* dominates modern society the world over' (Debord, *Society of the Spectacle*, p. 47).

73 Deane, *Strange Country*, p. 163.

74 Marx, *Grundrisse*, p. 410.

75   Harcourt Developments, *TQ: Titanic Quarter – Regenerating Belfast* (London: Fox International, 2007), p. 37.

76   Phil Ramsey, '"A Pleasingly Blank Canvas": Urban Regeneration in Northern Ireland and the Case of Titanic Quarter', *Space and Polity*, 17.2 (2013), 173–174.

77   Cattermole, *Building Titanic Belfast*, p. 101.

78   John Nagle, 'Potemkin Village: Neo-Liberalism and Peace-Building in Northern Ireland?', *Ethnopolitics*, 8.2 (June 2009), 185. Quoting Peter Shirlow, 'Belfast: The "Post-Conflict" City', *Space and Polity*, 10.2 (2006), 97–107.

79   'Safeguards', *The Agreement: Agreement Reached in the Multi-Party Negotiations* (Good Friday Agreement, 1998), Paragraphs 5.d.i–ii, www.gov.uk/government/uploads/system/uploads/attachment_data/file/13665 2/agreement.pdf.

80   Adrian Little, *Democracy and Northern Ireland: Beyond the Liberal Paradigm?* (Basingstoke: Palgrave Macmillan, 2004), p. 29.

81   Chris Gilligan, 'Peace or Pacification Process? A Brief Critique of the Peace Process', in *Peace or War? Understanding the Peace Process in Northern Ireland* ed. by Chris Gilligan and Jon Tonge (Aldershot: Ashgate, 1997), p. 30.

82   Kelly, 'Geopolitical Eclipse', 547. Quoting Fredric Jameson, 'Cognitive Mapping', in *Marxism and the Interpretation of Culture* ed. by Cary Nelson and Lawrence Grossberg (Chicago: University of Illinois Press, 1988), pp. 349–350.

83   Kelly, 'Geopolitical Eclipse', 545–546.

84   *Ibid.*, 547.

85   *Ibid.*, 547–548.

86   Slavoj Žižek, 'Multiculturalism, Or, the Cultural Logic of Multinational Capitalism', *New Left Review*, 225 (September–October 1997), 46.

87   *Ibid.*, 44–46.

88   Thom Gorst, 'Maritime Myths and Meanings', *Architecture Today*, 228 (May 2012), 59.

89   James Alexander, 'Titanic Belfast – City of Experience: Belfast's Titanic Signature Project', in *Relaunching Titanic: Memory and Marketing in the New Belfast* ed. by William J.V. Neill, Michael Murray and Berna Grist (London: Routledge, 2014), p. 91.

90   Pauline Hadaway, 'Re-imagining Titanic, Re-imaging Belfast', In *Relaunching Titanic: Memory and Marketing in the New Belfast* ed. by William J.V. Neill, Michael Murray and Berna Grist (London: Routledge, 2014), p. 61.

91   Cattermole, *Building Titanic Belfast*, p. 84.

92   Hadaway, 'Re-imagining Titanic', p. 61.

93   Kierkegaard, *Repetition* and *Philosophical Crumbs*, p. 38.

94   Mark M, 'Boring Visit' www.tripadvisor.co.uk/ShowUserReviews-g186470-d2322884-r466732377-Titanic_Belfast-Belfast_Northern_Ireland.html#REVIEWS [accessed 26 April 2017].

95   Alexander, 'Titanic Belfast – City of Experience', p. 91.

96   Gilles Deleuze and Félix Guattari, *Anti-Oedipus: Capitalism and Schizophrenia*, trans. by Robert Hurley et al. (Minneapolis: University of Minnesota Press, 2000), pp. 240–241.

97   Alexander, 'Titanic Belfast', p. 94.
98   *Ibid.*, p. 92.
99   Adam Curtis, 'Now Then', BBC Blogs (25 July 2014) www.bbc.co.uk/blogs/adam curtis/entries/78691781-c9b7-30a0-9a0a-3ff76e8bfe58 [accessed 24 July 2017].
100   Gilles Deleuze, 'Postscript on the Societies of Control', *October*, 59 (Winter 1992), 3–7.
101   Daniel E. Martinez, 'Beyond Disciplinary Enclosures: Management Control in the Society of Control', *Critical Perspectives on Accounting*, 22.2 (February 2011), 204.
102   Deleuze, 'Postscript', 5.
103   Martinez, 'Beyond Disciplinary Enclosures', 208.
104   David Lloyd, *Irish Culture and Colonial Modernity, 1800–2000: The Transformation of Oral Space* (Cambridge: Cambridge University Press, 2011), p. 180.
105   Svendsen, *A Philosophy of Boredom*, p. 29.
106   Brendan C, 'Boring', www.tripadvisor.co.uk/ShowUserReviews-g186470-d2322 884-r477807434-Titanic_Belfast-Belfast_Northern_Ireland.html#REVIEWS [accessed 24 July 2017].
107   Aislingdove, 'Disastor [*sic*]', www.tripadvisor.co.uk/Attraction_Review-g186470-d2322884-Reviews-or20-Titanic_Belfast-Belfast_Northern_Ireland.html/BackUrl #REVIEWS [accessed 24 July 2017].
108   Svendsen, *Philosophy of Boredom*, p. 30.
109   Little, *Democracy and Northern Ireland*, p. 28.
110   Pauline Hadaway, 'Introduction', in *Where Are the People? Contemporary Photographs of Belfast 2002–2010* ed. by Karen Downey (Belfast: Belfast Exposed Photography, 2010), p. 8.
111   Graham, '"Let's Get Killed"', p. 173.
112   Aaron Kelly, 'Introduction: Troubles with the Peace Process: Contemporary Northern Irish Culture', *Irish Review*, 40–41 (2009), 4.
113   Charles Taylor, 'The Politics of Recognition', in *Multiculturalism: Examining the Politics of Recognition* ed. by Amy Gutmann (Princeton: Princeton University Press, 1994), p. 25.
114   Maurice Hayes, *Whither Cultural Diversity?* (Belfast: Community Relations Council, 1993), p. 9.
115   Joseph Ruane and Jennifer Todd, *The Dynamics of Conflict in Northern Ireland: Power, Conflict and Emancipation* (Cambridge: Cambridge University Press, 2000), p. 9.
116   Stuart Hall, 'Conclusion: the Multi-cultural Question', in *Un/Settled Multiculturalism: Diasporas, Entanglements, 'Transruptions'* ed. by Barnor Hesse (New York: Zed Books, 2000), p. 210.
117   See Ariella Azoulay, *The Civil Contract of Photography* (New York: Zone Books, 2008).
118   Svendsen, *Philosophy of Boredom*, p. 31.
119   Julian Jason Haladyn, *Boredom and Art: Passions of the Will to Boredom* (Alresford: Zero Books, 2015), p. 138.
120   Walter Benjamin, 'The Storyteller', in *Illuminations* ed. by Hannah Arendt, trans. by Harry Zohn (London: Fontana Press, 1992), p. 91.

121   Haladyn, *Boredom and Art*, p. 139.
122   Tiqqun, 'X', in *The Cybernetic Hypothesis* https://theanarchistlibrary.org/library/tiqqun-the-cybernetic-hypothesis [accessed 24 July 2017].
123   *Ibid.*
124   Peter Osborne, *Anywhere or Not At All: Philosophy of Contemporary Art* (London: Verso, 2013), p. 183.
125   Heidegger, *The Fundamental Concepts of Metaphysics*, p. 153.
126   Goodstein, *Experience without Qualities*, p. 1.
127   Derek Mahon, 'Subsidy Bungalows', *Icarus*, 32 (December 1960), 22.
128   Tom Nairn, *The Break-Up of Britain* (London: New Left Books, 1977), pp. 231–232.
129   Svendsen, *Philosophy of Boredom*, p. 14.
130   Mick Wilson, 'Preface', in Sarah Tuck, *After the Agreement: Contemporary Photography in Northern Ireland* (London: Black Dog Publishing, 2015), p. 8.
131   Lloyd, *Colonial Modernity*, p. 151.
132   In McDonough, *Boredom*, p. 14.
133   Haladyn, *Boredom and Art*, p. 124.
134   Jacques Rancière, 'Comment and Responses', *Theory and Event*, 6.4 (2003), para. 4.
135   Wilson, 'Preface', p. 7.
136   Graham, '"Let's Get Killed"', p. 176.
137   Declan Long, *Ghost-Haunted Land: Contemporary Art and Post-Troubles Northern Ireland* (Manchester: Manchester University Press, 2017), p. 8.
138   Azoulay, *The Civil Contract of Photography*, p. 13.
139   Julian Stallabrass, 'Sebastiao Salgado and Fine Art Photojournalism', *New Left Review*, 223 (May–June 1997), 134.
140   Cattermole, *Building Titanic Belfast*, p. 138.
141   Stallabrass, 'Fine Art Photojournalism', 133–135.
142   Thrift, 'Material Practices of Glamour', 10.
143   Val Williams, *Martin Parr* (London: Phaidon Press, 2002).
144   Colin Graham, *Northern Ireland: 30 Years of Photography* (Belfast: Belfast Exposed, 2013), p. 16.
145   Mark Fisher, *Capitalist Realism: Is There No Alternative* (Winchester: Zero Books, 2009), p. 16.
146   *Ibid.*, p. 80.

1

Geographies of boredom and the new city of Craigavon

On paper, the new city of Craigavon could have changed the face of Northern Ireland. Planned between 1963 and 1966 and undergoing a period of intense construction from 1967 to 1977, Craigavon was heralded as 'a major symbol of regeneration', which would transform the North's industrial and social landscape.[1] The drawings that depicted the new city are charged with the energy and optimism of the enterprise (Plates 2 and 3). Here, sleek sports cars race futuristic shuttles towards a horizon filled with the promise of a new metropolis. This would be a city of desire and desirability, an arena of enticement and seduction. In many ways, Craigavon was a radically new endeavour: one that would propel Northern Ireland's stagnating postwar economy towards the bright lights of economic regeneration, multinational capital and lavish consumerism. But despite its promise, the project struggled and never managed to attract the levels of industry or residency originally anticipated. Instead, Craigavon became an urban environment punctuated by abandoned junctions and ghost estates, representing a clear disunity between what we might call capitalism's fixed and mobile counterparts. In this sense, Craigavon proved to be an early symbol of the complexities of capitalist planning in twentieth-century Northern Ireland, with its underdevelopment providing a potent example of state-sponsored capitalism encountering 'barriers in its own nature'.[2] Consequently, if a cultural and historical reading of the new city can uncover the circumstances behind its ruptured urban form, then perhaps it might be possible to comprehend how Craigavon came to embody something close to what David Harvey has described as capitalism's potential for 'geographical inertia'.[3]

New towns have often been the subject of deprivation and decline – with their failure to create 'social support networks', encouraging them to be associated with a sense of boredom, banality or, as it is popularly dubbed, 'New Town Blues'.[4] But far too often these failings have meant that the social reality which produced them is consciously overlooked or disregarded. As Newton Emerson noted in his 2007 documentary about the new city, 'Craigavon is just a black-hole in people's knowledge of this part of the country'.[5] Even during its worst years, the reasons for Craigavon's failure were relatively unknown. As Madge Steele asserts in her poem about life in the new city's vacuous landscape, 'no officials take the time, to know it as they should'.[6] Yet if Craigavon is considered as the product of a capitalist contradiction, rather than a misguided urban experiment better off forgotten, then the new city's changing fortunes can serve an important function. In its unfortunate evolution, Craigavon can open a gateway on to the peculiar qualities of Northern Ireland's geography – providing us with a unique insight into the North's embedded political schisms, while also becoming a fragile marker of how capitalism has struggled to paper over such divides.

Craigavon was a top-down imposition of town planning upon a landscape riddled with its own internal difficulties. On the one hand, Craigavon was a site of considerable fixed capital investment, energised by a desire to modernise and monetise the North's precarious political economy. On the other hand, however, Craigavon's development needs to be seen in the context of a struggle between the wishes of a Unionist government, localised opposition, and the hopes and fears of those few working-class citizens who, in Steele's phrase, moved to the new city 'the seeds of life to sow'.[7] Those who found themselves living in Craigavon were often unfortunate victims of circumstance. But they also came to shape their own circumstances, using the new city's underdeveloped landscape to generate a politics of co-operation that countered prevailing attitudes in the North. As I will go on to argue, the literature of these residents illustrates something of the being-in-common that can be facilitated by a breakdown in the gyrations of capital. Ultimately, such cohesion would prove short lived, yet traces still remain, offering signs of hope against the backdrop of Northern Ireland's often uncertain future.

The competing national and local impulses which dominated Craigavon's development rarely wedded and, as they clashed, they came to create a landscape that was frequently petrified by its own instabilities. As Harvey has noted, 'fixed capital embedded in the land may facilitate ease of movement for mobile capital but loses its value when mobile capital fails to follow the geographical paths such fixed capital investments dictate'.[8] My argument will insist that it was precisely because of the inability for mobile capital to follow its fixed counterpart that Craigavon became replete with its own peculiar forms of geographical ennui. Central to this inertia is the intersection of capitalism and ethnic–national division, and it is ultimately through the spectre of plantation – the ominous origin of state-sponsored capitalism in Ulster – that Craigavon's troubled history can be best understood. The divisive historical residues which lie deep within the geography of Craigavon's designated area refused to be effaced by the imposition of the new city's modernity. Instead, anxieties about external interference in the context of a settler culture stoked the flames of a fierce resistance, the combative language of which illustrated the violent animosity that can be aroused in response to the manipulation of Northern Irish space. The conception of Craigavon predated the Troubles, but the militant rhetoric that formed in response to the plans anticipated much of the bitterness that would dominate that conflict: talk of 'not an inch', 'Brits out' and 'Ulster says no'.

Encircled by such fractious spatial relationships, Craigavon struggled to establish its own meanings within the geography of Northern Ireland. Instead of being the 'city of people's dreams', it became an alien environment – a city haunted by insignificance and boredom. As I discussed at the outset of this book, while boredom has assumed different forms across a diverse range of critical commentaries, 'all agree that boredom involves a loss of meaning and can be metaphorically described, in [Lars] Svendsen's words, as a "meaning withdrawal"'.[9] The geographical significance of this observation stems from the fact that it can rub against the foundational principle by which 'places' are generally thought to be conceived – namely that, as Tim Cresswell defines it, 'places must have some relationship to humans and the human capacity to produce and consume meaning'.[10] An absence of meaning can not only create the conditions for boredom, it can also destroy a sense of place. For Hubert de Cronin Hastings, long-term editor of the *Architectural Review*, this was the new towns' fundamental problem. The lack of a fruitful exchange between planners and population meant that such projects tended to become 'non-events': 'absolutely meaningless' environments which were always 'failing to come alive'.[11]

A cultural and geographical analysis based on boredom is, nevertheless, complicated by the fact that – in the convergence of place and empty meaning – the terms of this analysis seemingly direct us towards the manifestation of 'non-places'. That is to say, homogeneous regions which, in Edward Relph's phrase, 'not only look alike but feel alike and offer the same bland possibilities for experience'.[12] For Justin Carville, Craigavon's repetitive road-schemes epitomise the sense of 'placelessness' Relph has theorised. 'There is no time or space to dwell in this particular location', Carville writes.[13] But as I shall go on to argue, Craigavon's design did, in fact, reproduce a distinctly Irish settlement pattern – albeit one rendered in a startling modern form. As such, it was because Craigavon's attendant population failed to congeal around this architecture that the new city came to be punctuated with a sense of emptiness and desertion. Rather than geographies of boredom being the product of a placeless design, it is because of the ways in which those designs were imposed that such geographies became enmeshed with a peculiar sense of ennui. As the Northern Irish photographer Victor Sloan has stated in relation to Craigavon's troubled gestation:

'people want a structure and meaning in their environment that will reflect, and in part create, a structure in their lives. Craigavon has completely failed to provide them with this.'[14] Through the photographs that Sloan would go on to produce in response to Craigavon's uneven development, we get perhaps the clearest sense of how the disjunction between its fixed and mobile capital came to reflect this wider social disruption. Sloan's photography would eventually come to challenge the perception that Craigavon was little more than a static and soulless locale. None the less, it is through his lens that we can perhaps most fully comprehend how the new city embodied a planned environment that was broken, disrupted and devoid of meaning.

Today, Craigavon's uneven topography is well known, but its initial – often unrealised – aspirations have long been forgotten and are worth revisiting. Planned to be large enough to incorporate the surrounding towns of Lurgan and Portadown, Craigavon was always envisaged as a new city rather than a new town, and it was one that would be filled with the latest innovations in urban living. Central heating and piped systems of radio, television and telephonic services were to form part of Craigavon's 'ultra-modern town units', and these would be connected to the new city's nucleus via a road/rail corridor which promised both speed and ease of access.[15] This mass transit system had the advantage of pulling people towards Craigavon's new attractions – its recreation forum, its PVC sports dome, its air-conditioned shopping centre, its artificial ski-slope and its balancing lakes.[16] But such a joined-up system of transportation also offered an opportunity for the almost seamless movement of industry to and from the new city's business parks and beyond (Plates 4 and 5). This would be a city built for celerity, and with such ambitions it soon became a source of considerable financial speculation. In 1973 construction of its recreation forum was costed at over £2 million alone, and the finance necessary for the develop-ment of the new city's industrial zones was even greater.[17] State subsidies of up to £200,000 per annum helped entice Goodyear Ltd to set up a £6.5 million factory in 1968, thereby establishing a formidable industrial presence in the area.[18] But the Stormont government cemented its own financial commitment to Craigavon through plans for a civil service training centre and a modern local area hospital.[19] By any measure, the amount of capital involved was impressive. In 1967 Craigavon had a starting budget of £140 million and,[20] as construction began, Craigavon's Development Commission soon succeeded in attracting additional funds amounting to a total somewhere nearer £500 million.[21] With so much capital to support its development, it seems that this was to be a landscape riddled with investment – a place in which astonishing amounts of infrastructure would be, to use Karl Marx's phrase, 'welded fast to the surface of the earth'.[22]

Craigavon was a bold venture in every way. Conceived as part of Robert Matthew's 1963 *Belfast Regional Survey and Plan*, it was originally anticipated that the new city would be ideally placed to 'attract industrial enterprise' – an ambition Craigavon's Development Commission was keen to encourage.[23] As stated in its 1967 report, *Craigavon New City*, one of its 'basic goals' was 'to provide a new major base for industry which could increase the attractiveness of the province to site seeking firms from Great Britain, Europe and the United States'.[24] It was a case of the city as growth machine and here, as elsewhere, Craigavon's development is freighted with the rhetoric of globalisation – the hope that its construction might revive a Northern Irish economy which had shrunk in the face of international competition. The condition of industry in postwar Northern Ireland was undoubtedly precarious. Shipbuilding and engineering had been in decline since the mid-1950s and, in Craigavon's designated area, the textile sector had seen employment drop 25.7 per cent between 1950 and 1959.[25] Placed in this context, Craigavon clearly formed part of what Tim Blackman has described as this period's broader attempt 'to "stabilise" Northern Ireland and set it on a course of "normal" capitalist development'.[26] That Craigavon attracted such significant levels of state subvention suggests that something more than 'normal' capitalist development was at stake.

Like most new towns, Craigavon was planned with a sense of social integration in mind. Where British new towns had aimed to embrace 'all classes of society',[27] Craigavon's planners 'attempted to socially engineer religious mixing by integrating social facilities and amenities'.[28] The public housing that would make up Craigavon was not to be split between Catholics and Protestants, and its residents were expected to share the innovative infrastructure and industry Craigavon hoped to offer. In many ways, such progressive reforms dovetailed with the political ambitions of Terence O'Neill, Northern Ireland's Prime Minister at the time. Ever anxious to hold together the increasingly fragile political edifice of Northern Ireland, O'Neill sought to strike a difficult balance between appeasing Catholic demands for equality on the one hand, and maintaining the dominance of Unionism on the other.[29] Craigavon might have been conceived as a centre for capital accumulation, but such prosperity could also create opportunities for tentative political reform. In Craigavon, notes Blackman, the 'state's strategy was to facilitate capitalism in the belief that the resulting economic growth would be of political benefit'.[30]

The nature of this 'political benefit' is, of course, open to question. While Craigavon held the seeds for social change, there is also no doubt that it afforded Unionism an opportunity to reassert its supremacy in the North's political landscape. Indeed, for the new city's first chief architect – Geoffrey Copcutt – the whole enterprise was far too constrained by sectarian motivations. Aware that 'the Stormont government would not countenance any scheme that would upset the voting balance between Protestants and Roman Catholics', Copcutt resigned in August 1964, claiming that he had been asked to 'engineer propaganda rather than design a new city'.[31] The new city's location between Lurgan and Portadown placed it well within the Unionist 'heartland', east of the River Bann.[32] And, with this area roughly 71 per cent Protestant at the time, Craigavon's construction was seen by many Nationalists as coming at the direct expense of the more underdeveloped, predominantly Catholic, west.[33] Alongside this, Catholics were also alienated by the decision to name the new city after Northern Ireland's first Prime Minister James Craig – a politician who had once infamously boasted that he oversaw a 'Protestant Parliament and a Protestant State'.[34] Craigavon appeared little different in this respect. Centred so firmly within a Protestant political geography, any Catholics who were to benefit from Craigavon would be able to do so only from within the Unionist hegemony itself. This was a point O'Neill would hint at in his notorious 1969 pronouncement that 'if you give Roman Catholics a good job and a good house they will live like Protestants'.[35] But, in the case of Craigavon, the details were more telling. By framing the new city's development through a broad economic prism of competing Protestant and Catholic demands, the O'Neill government simultaneously downplayed the importance of local and cultural attachments already present within Craigavon's designated area. Rather than a mere misjudgement of priorities, this strategy reflected a fundamental misunderstanding about how people construct a sense of place, and it was an oversight that would become all too apparent as Craigavon's construction got under way.

Although Craigavon was intended as a Protestant city, its development did not rest comfortably with the local Unionist population. The new city's heavy dependence upon British financial aid had, for example, raised fears that the British government would now show a greater interest in Northern Irish affairs, threatening what Martin McCleery has termed Unionism's 'grass-roots patronage'.[36] Indeed, it is partly for this reason that local opposition to Craigavon's development was initially framed in terms of its adverse effects upon the Lurgan–Portadown economy. 'If this city ever does materialise and industries are available', declared one local councillor, 'the people of both towns will be going to the city to shop and the only things they will sell in Lurgan will be spools of thread'.[37] Others would be more critical still. Faced with the loss of their land, local farmers staged a series of protests and blockades that slowed some of Craigavon's early construction, while the Ulster Farmers' Union voiced a general scepticism about the whole concept of the new city from the outset.[38] 'Would it not have been wiser to empty Lough Neagh and put the New City in it?' joked a local Union secretary, after seeing Craigavon's plans.[39] Yet, despite these outcries, the most doubtful would be those residents for whom Craigavon was actually intended, and it was their opinions that would prove to matter most.

Construction of the new city's housing began on 20 February 1967 with a modest ground-breaking ceremony involving Samuel J. McMahon, chairman of Craigavon's Development Commission. As McMahon told the press that day, the sod cutting marked 'not merely the inauguration of another new housing scheme, but rather a new epoch in the history of Co. Armagh in particular and of Northern Ireland in general'.[40] Such optimism notwithstanding, McMahon would soon be deeply uncertain about the viability of Craigavon. The new city's construction proceeded apace, with many of the first houses ready ahead of schedule, but McMahon became keenly aware that challenges still lay ahead. Four months after housing construction began, McMahon startled journalists by declaring that 'something more than planning is required' – adding with more than a touch of foresight:

> Unless the Commission can succeed in integrating the civic pride and that sense of belonging that already exists to a marked degree in both Boroughs, we shall have failed in one of the most important aspects of our function ... I believe that the creation of a proper sense of community has, like every other aspect of a development to be planned for and then carefully nurtured and built up, not just by a few enlightened souls imbued with a sense of mission, but by the involvement of every man and woman in the new city area. Every man and woman, irrespective of class or creed must become involved in the creation of the City, and must be prepared to contribute personally to the building up of good community relations.[41]

Despite the trace of condescension, these comments are significant because the 'sense of belonging' of which McMahon speaks would prove to be such a major obstacle to Craigavon's future growth.

While fixed capital can, in Harvey's phrase, 'appear as the crowning glory of past capitalist development', any future 'glory' will always be dependent upon an ability to attract mobile forms of capital which can revalidate its value.[42] To put this another way, if the factories, houses and facilities in Craigavon are to be effective, then they must be able to draw upon future labour, consumers and industry to amortise their worth.[43] As the population shortages that plagued Craigavon's existence would go on to illustrate, this would be a far from easy task, and it is partly for this reason that McMahon's wariness about 'the involvement of every man and woman in the New City area' appears to be so prophetic.

Perhaps because of these anxieties, Craigavon's planners showed a degree of sensitivity when it came to the new city's design. Craigavon was planned in the absence of public consultation and with an eye to attracting foreign industry, but it also sought to re-create a distinctly Irish mode of living – one that spoke to Ireland's architectural traditions at the expense of the 'city-in-the-sky' mentality, which otherwise preoccupied so much postwar planning. The brutality and inflexibility often associated with such high-rise developments would be demonstrated all too clearly by the troubled gestation of the Divis Tower in Belfast's Lower Falls. Constructed at the same time as Craigavon, it was as if the problems of this estate served as a constant reminder of the potential pitfalls surrounding the imposition of a foreign mode of living on to Ireland. Certainly an anxiety regarding architectural form preoccupied Craigavon's design team. When interviewed about his time as the new city's Deputy Chief Planning Officer, Robert Strang recalls how, even though the original plan had been to import 'the Corbusier approach', they quickly retreated from this idea because 'in the Irish culture it was such a foreign concept'. Instead, as Strang acknowledges, in Ireland 'people generally want a garden or a yard'.[44] In 1967 the *Craigavon New City* report acceded to this cultural preference, with the plan now promoting the establishment of a 'Rural City' – one that would be driven towards 'the establishment of village communities' and 'the close inter-relationship of urban and rural elements'.[45]

As a defining feature of this bucolic urbanism was a rejection of the foreign and a loyalty to what Strang has termed 'the local psyche', it is perhaps possible to read in Craigavon's design an early indication of the Ulster regionalism soon to be demanded by the North's architectural community.[46] Just as Craigavon's designers had rejected 'the Corbusier approach' in favour of local culture so, for example, would Hugh Dixon's *An Introduction to Ulster Architecture* (1975) come to stress the importance of 'conservation' in the face of 'international fashions'.[47] For Dixon, 'too many buildings erected in Ulster during the first three-quarters of the twentieth century' had 'overlooked the traditional local qualities'.[48] With Craigavon set to resurrect that sleepy 'rural housing' of which, for instance, C.E.B. Brett would soon fondly speak, it seems that when it came to contemporary design Craigavon – the 'Rural City' – was able to cast something of a backward glance.[49]

Through its plans to create a number of sequestered estates punctuated by shared open space, Craigavon could even be considered a modern version of the clachan. That is, as a peculiarly Irish settlement type which Estyn Evans has documented as persisting until the time of the Great Famine. Just as Craigavon was designed to establish 'separate and identifiable communities', so the clachan was a collection of 'houses loosely grouped in "towns" or "villages"'. These were, moreover, dependent upon an 'openfield system' of shared land – much like Craigavon's 'green lungs' – and 'held together by the ties of kinship and of mutual help and protection'.[50] Although not apparent to Craigavon's design team in the 1960s, the potential for 'protection' and communality afforded by this type of settlement would be integral to how Craigavon evolved during the Troubles and beyond.

The complexities of urban planning in 1960s Northern Ireland went further than looks and design, however. Memory and politics were also an issue, and it is out of this matrix that Craigavon's inert geography was ultimately produced. Alongside a top-down imposition of planning, the construction of Craigavon also involved statutory reform, largely in the shape of the 1965 Northern Irish New Town Bill. In principal this Bill was a 'legislative masterstroke'.[51] Once ratified, it would enable Stormont's Northern Irish Minister of Development to designate any area as a New Town, and to appoint a Development Commission that 'could take over any local authority they pleased'.[52] There were obvious and immediate reasons for these changes. For one thing, it ensured that the new city's development would not be, in Strang's phrase, abated by 'conflicts with an existing municipal authority'.[53] However, from the perspective of the local population, the Bill had more sinister implications. Not only did it ensure that the British government would 'not be obliged to give any reason' why they might substitute a local authority for a Development Commission but it also allowed that same Commission to then 'take over any land at any time', meaning 'the landowner would have no rights at all'.[54]

In keeping with their initial anguish about Craigavon, both Lurgan's and Portadown's Unionist councils greeted this New Town Bill with a mixture of frustration and despair. Described by councillor Richie Best 'as the most shocking thing he had ever read', both the Bill and the plans for Craigavon were held to be the product of a despotic regime.[55] Before the Bill had even been ratified by Parliament, Best had effectively written his council's epitaph, declaring that any Commission formed in the name of Craigavon would be 'absolutely ruthless', 'totalitarian', and would spell 'the end of democracy'.[56] More striking, however, is councillor George McCartney's response, which associates Craigavon's conception with the start of a military assault on mid-Ulster. According to McCartney, the Bill took his 'mind back about 23 years [to] when Hitler's armies were over running Europe',[57] with the government's plans for Craigavon denoting 'the concentration camps they intended building'.[58] Ultimately, in McCartney's opinion, had the project for Craigavon 'been attempted in Ulster 30 or 40 years ago, the people responsible would have been stood up against a wall and "plugged"'.[59]

While the ethnic-religious violence that subtends McCartney's analogies is all the more poignant given the Troubles that await the North, his rhetoric also exposes the residual tensions that can be triggered by town planning in Ulster. Craigavon might have glistened with the trappings of modernity, but, with its implementation placing an emphasis upon the importance of construction at the expense of local interests, the new city also replicated the more belligerent history of plantation. Certainly this was an association of which the local press was all too well aware. Even as early as the unveiling of Craigavon's plans, the *Portadown Times* was quick to point out that

> It is important to realise that a strong historical link exists already between the two towns [Lurgan-Portadown] and the proposed City, in that the towns date from the great plantation period of building in Ulster and were thus 'New Towns' of that period.[60]

By naming the new city's first (and only) housing sector Brownlow, after Lurgan's plantation family, Craigavon's planners cemented this connection – resurrecting the North's turbulent history with what Joe Cleary has called plantation's 'inception of a centuries-long attempt to render Ireland amenable to the imperatives of English and later transnational capital'.[61] Yet the importance of this 'strong historical link' is not its suggestion that the construction of Craigavon constitutes an act of legislative neocolonialism, even if, according to Fredric Osborn and Arnold Whittick, new town planners were 'descendants of the adventurous colonizers of the past'.[62] Instead, the connection is significant because it illustrates just how easily urban planning in Northern Ireland can become ensnared within Ulster's plantation legacy – a tendency Ian Nairn reinforces in his depiction of Derry as London's 'oldest, most distant and most individual New Town'.[63]

In Craigavon's designated area, the experience of plantation runs deep. The bridge at Portadown, for example, was the site of one of the more savage incidents during the 1641 rising against colonial settlers. Here Irish rebels drove over a hundred Protestant men, women and children into the water 'and those that could swym and come to the shore they either knockt them in the heads and soe after drowned them, or els shott them to death in the water', as Elizabeth Price recounts in her deposition of 1641.[64] These 'memories of plantation and revolt are preserved in local culture', notes Liam O'Dowd, and as such it is increasingly tempting for Craigavon to be identified by an attuned cultural imagination, with a hostile entity that should be, in McCartney's phrase, violently 'plugged'.[65] Certainly this is something the new city's planners came to realise. Looking back at his time in Craigavon's planning team, Strang recalls how there was something of 'a natural Irish resistance to planning', adding that: 'It may be trite to say so, but there is a natural tendency in Ireland to be against the government, no doubt, anyway, borne of four hundred years of somewhat painful experience'.[66]

Craigavon, then, weighs heavy with plantation's legacy. But its prevailing attitudes are also symptomatic of what Jane Burbank and Frederick Cooper have described as plantation's 'intermediaries'; that is, 'transplanted groups, dependent on linkages to home, [who] were expected to act in the imperial interests'. Yet, Burbank and Cooper go on to argue, the experience of plantation also 'unintentionally created subversive possibilities for intermediaries, who could circumvent imperial purposes by establishing alternative networks and allegiances'.[67] In this way, the 'natural Irish resistance' that surrounded Craigavon was not simply the result of concerted opposition, it was also the product of a longer – almost unconscious – mode of anti-imperialism, one that related to the 'painful' history of plantation and one which would ensure that Craigavon's future population reacted dialectically to the vast quantities of immovable capital that were coming to constitute the new city.

Where Craigavon's infrastructure spoke of modernisation and employment, the local population saw only deception and disruption; where its development created a prospect for circulating capital, its potential inhabitants responded with stasis and stagnation – a rootedness to their pre-existing environments and their established ways of being. 'By 1969', notes O'Dowd, 'the managing director of Goodyear was claiming major labour recruitment problems'. The factory had lost 254 employees in its first four months and went on to 'screen' the unemployed of Belfast, Strabane, Newry and Enniskillen 'with little success'.[68] At its height, Goodyear would come to employ 1,800, but its growth was always underpinned by generous levels of state support which served to mask larger failings. When the factory finally shut its doors in July 1983, it was losing about £700,000 a month, with losses for that year totalling £4.5 million, and this despite the fact that the British government had underwritten a £3 million expansion three years earlier. As the company's American chairman was forced to admit on the eve of its closure, 'the Ulster factory had never made a profit since it opened in 1967'.[69]

These industrial difficulties were compounded by ongoing complications within the new city's residential sector. While Craigavon's estates had won honours for their layout (with both the Moylinn and Old Rectory Park estates given Civic Trust Awards), the houses had been built at speed and so suffered some unfortunate defects.[70] Common problems included: doors and windows that failed to fit their frames; defective central heating; leaking roofs; banisters falling down; floors subsiding; faults in the piped TV system; and the fact that legions of field mice invaded many of the homes – one resident claiming to have 'destroyed as many as 36 in a week'.[71] As if these faults were not enough, the new city was also devoid of almost all its amenities following a planning decision to prioritise residential development ahead of such advanced development.[72] Craigavon did claim to have a city centre, but its construction was piecemeal and its location too distant for residents deprived of the mass transit system originally envisaged.[73] Nevertheless, these issues were nothing when compared to the bigger problem of enticing an indigenous population unwilling to resettle. As early as 1969, Craigavon was well behind its anticipated levels of growth, posting a population deficit of 3,400 less than three years into its construction. By 1976 the situation had not improved, and those overseeing Craigavon's development were faced with the frustrating situation of having '1200 on the housing lists in Portadown and Lurgan',[74] while in the new city area the waiting list was 'virtually nil'.[75] Repelling potential residents, Craigavon became a classic example of the city as a centrifugal force, with the local population almost compelled to resist Craigavon's new residencies so as to remain wedded to its outlying fringe.[76]

In the context of Northern Ireland, such intransience was not without precedent. Noting the persistence of small settlement patterns in Ulster, Evans remarks that one of the reasons for their endurance was the ways their inhabitants proved so reluctant to leave: 'even if they were moving only half a mile away "they were crying as if they were going to America"'.[77] With Craigavon's housing uptake stuttering from the outset, it seems that a similar line of resistance was in process. By 1976, even the new city's normally encouraging newspaper, *Craigavon Times*, was forced to confess the intractability of the situation:

> All acknowledge that it will take a hard sell to persuade families to move to Brownlow from the neighbouring towns. The reason is simple – Ulster people are renowned for their general refusal to be housed anywhere other than in the vicinity of the locality where they were born, or where their families have lived for generations.[78]

A government-based mobility grant scheme served only to exacerbate this problem. Although movement into the new city grew as new residents were offered 'a cool £700' upon arrival, the Northern reputation for rootedness still remained.[79] Many of those attracted by the grants simply collected the money before returning from whence they came – a phenomenon dubbed the 'moonlight flit', and one that left the new city's estates littered with a mix of vandalised housing, discarded furniture and stray dogs.[80]

Away from Craigavon, sweeping changes within the North's political economy were also having a tangible effect upon the new city's development. Following the outbreak of the Troubles, local government throughout the North underwent a major reorganisation which, in 1973, resulted in the abolition of Craigavon's Development Commission. Quite aside from the fact that this ensured there was no one to take overall responsibility for the new city's development, the Commission's termination also meant that Craigavon now had to compete with the interests of Lurgan and Portadown councils which, as O'Dowd notes, still remained 'highly sceptical of the new city'.[81] More damning, however, was the fact that the growth-centre strategy – upon which Craigavon was founded – had been gradually phased out and terminated. In 1975 this policy was replaced by plans to disperse development amongst 26 district towns of which Craigavon would no longer be a part. Such a shift clearly down-graded Craigavon, an urban area whose own dependency on multinational capital had been further hampered by the fact that the outbreak of the Troubles had also managed to coincide with a major downturn in the global economy.

Marginalised politically, resisted locally and housing a deracinated popula-tion, Craigavon became an alien environment – a nightmare of the unknown and the unknowable. Brownlow would eventually see the completion of 22 housing estates, but it never managed to attract the numbers originally anticipated. There were a range of factors contributing to this migratory quiescence, not least of which was the retreat into traditional heartlands caused by the sectarian violence of the Troubles. But Craigavon also seems to have been the victim of a broader contradiction – the fact that, as Harvey reminds us, 'the deeper mean-ings that people assign to their relationship to the land, to place, home and the practices of dwelling are perpetually at odds with the crass commercialisms of land and property markets'.[82]

Craigavon never became the new city of Ulster's dreams precisely because of the strong spatial commitments that constantly engulfed its development. From the aggressive, antagonistic rhetoric of local councillors keen to maintain their local jurisdiction to the equally protectionist agenda of the Troubles, Craigavon's progress was stunted by the divisive ideologies that can be triggered through a manipulation of Northern Irish space. By 1982, at the end of the new city's 'first stage of operations',[83] Craigavon's main residential district was thoroughly depleted, with the estates of Ridgeway, Rathmore and Legahory containing over five hundred empty homes.[84] Faced with these numbers, the new city struggled to justify itself as a profitable enterprise and – amidst the reorganisation of local and national government – much of its surplus housing stock was set for demoli-tion. Such degradation clearly marked a low ebb in Craigavon's fortunes and was, in many ways, a clear sign that the original concept of the new city had been abandoned. Instead of being at the vanguard of Northern Ireland's leap into the twenty-first century, Craigavon was now unwittingly ensnared in a remorseless cycle of misery and deprivation.

The dramatic nature of Craigavon's demise reiterated its hollowness as a planned environment: its inability to relate to its human population and its struggle to create a coherent landscape to which people could be drawn. It is through these tensions that the new city's geographical inertia emerged, a vivid symptom of which was a constant anxiety that Craigavon lacked a 'heart' – those communal rhythms and social networks ultimately responsible for bringing a city to life. Certainly this is the impression conveyed by Sloan's photographic responses to the new city during the early 1980s. Living and working in Portadown, Sloan experienced the disintegration of Craigavon directly, and in 1979 he started to photograph the new city's broken architecture, documenting what he felt to be Craigavon's discordant reality.[85] 'One could be forgiven for thinking no overall view was ever taken of Craigavon's development', states Sloan in conversation with Gerry Burns, 'some buildings here are interesting enough, as far as shape and design go, but they bear no relationship to the lives of people who live here'.[86] Across his intimate portraits of the new city, collected in the photographic series *Vietnamese Boat People* (1984), *Craigavon* (1985), and *Moving Windows* (1985), an apprehension of communal paucity is deeply connected to an understanding and knowledge of Craigavon's listless geography and its ongoing disintegration under the rhetoric of spatial animosity.

In Sloan's *Craigavon* series, perhaps his most substantial and sustained engagement with the new city's urban fabric, politics and place coalesce, though not in an obvious way. The content of these images, and the techniques by which they are modified (a subtle addition of coloured crayon circles), provide a wry commentary on the condition of the new city as it entered its cycle of decline. By the mid-1980s Craigavon had become a place of disconnection and paralysis and, for Sloan, the dormancy within this landscape was a constant source of fascination. Commenting on the 'ghostly' and 'almost necrophilic' atmosphere in these photographs, Burns notes how Sloan's 'images of Craigavon are like that of a town which has been embalmed'.[87] Craigavon might have been built for movement and for industry but it was rapidly becoming a space shrouded with inertia and inaction.

Sloan's early work plays with Craigavon's conception as a 'Rural City'. The ironically titled, 'City Centre (with Pony)' (Plate 6), for example, highlights the excessive space in which the new city was situated. The image presents not the centre of a thriving metropolis but rather an area of former farmland in which a city has barely taken root. Its composition suggests that the solitary building which sits, incuriously, in the centre of this grassland is the centre of the new city itself. Alongside this the presence of a pony in the foreground not only implies the persistence of the rural over the urban – the country over the city – but it also raises the question of how we should traverse this terrain. With no mass transit system to take us into Craigavon's centre, we are faced with an undulating, undeveloped geography in which antiquated modes of transport seem the only means of movement. In a later image, 'Craigavon Centre' from the *Moving Windows* series (Plate 7), Sloan highlights how, even for those driving to the new city, its central remits still seem off limits – as if Craigavon was some sort of inaccessible domain, nothing more than an unknown prospect forever lurking on the horizon. Photographs such as these, in which the point of focus is our approach to the new city's hub, are familiar enough from the publicity shots and graphics used to promote Craigavon to future residents. However, unlike those images, in which desire is dominant, Sloan's photography seems to resist rather than encourage enticement, deconstructing any sense of persuasion and seduction. In these parodic, often oblique, glimpses into the new city, Sloan alienates us from Craigavon, even though its infrastructure was designed with ideas of attraction in mind.

Looked at another way, Sloan simply wants to capture Craigavon's geographical inertia, highlighting the new city's tendency for constriction, when it should be encouraging momentum. In this sense, Sloan's photography gives us an insight into how this space – to use Henri Lefebvre's terminology – 'wreaks repression and terror' where once it was 'strewn with ostensible signs of the contrary (of contentment, amusement or delight)'.[88] In the photograph 'Road, Rathmore, Craigavon' (Plate 8), we are seemingly welcomed into one of the new city's housing estates. Yet antagonistic graffiti relating to the Troubles fills the tarmac, revealing the hostile languages that punctuate even the most mundane terrain. Certainly this is how critics have tended to view this image – a reading encouraged by the red circles Sloan adds with care and precision. 'The small red circles, added in crayon indicate bullet holes, and were borrowed from police reports', states Brian McAvera. They 'suggest the ominous events that lurk behind the ordinary texture of life', he concludes.[89] Craigavon's development has always been scarred by such strong spatial commitments: from the aggressive rhetoric of Lurgan's councillors (with talk of planners being 'plugged' and foreign invasions) to the equally protectionist agenda of the Troubles (and its competing ideologies of 'No Surrender' and 'Smash H-Block'). With such contexts in mind, this image seems to reinforce a broader reading of Sloan's photographic oeuvre, namely that, as Colin Graham puts it: 'Sloan's work is made out of a to-and-fro between the poles of the identity politics of his "place" – an understanding of and a revulsion from the militaristic and uncompromising nature of unionism'.[90]

I want to suggest something different, however. I want to insist that Sloan's photographic concern with 'his "place"' is inflected by ideas of socio-economic regeneration as much as the identity politics of the Troubles. If nothing else, the circles in 'Road, Rathmore, Craigavon' are also indicative of those forces that have helped prevent mobile capital from following the geographical paths Craigavon's fixed capital dictates. Indeed, Sloan's attention to the road emphasises this effect. This image should evoke movement – our eyes should trace this winding path from the bottom to the top of the frame – and yet we are stopped.

Our progress is blocked by the graffiti, leaving us with an experience of non-movement within movement. As such these circles create something of a visual lexicon – a vernacular which points to the underlying disconnect between fixity and motion crucial to the idea of the city as growth machine. Indeed, as Marx tells us, circulation is the defining feature of capitalism; his M-C-C-M formula is one of indefinite movement, where money becomes capital only for that capital to become money again.[91] Like the figure of the circle, capital is always returning unto itself, and such continual motion is precisely what Craigavon lacks.

Reading Sloan's images in this way helps to explain the suffocating stasis that pervades so many of his photographs of the new city. In addition to Rathmore's traffic-free road, Sloan's images present an urban environment scarred by circles caught in suspension – be they on deserted bus stops, parked minibuses or children buried in sand. Through their silence and immobility, Sloan's images carefully open out the capitalist contradictions that underpin the new city's failings. Here, as elsewhere, the new city is a space of discontinuity: a cityscape of desolate roads and long echoing distances, of disused housing and redundant infrastructure, all of which will soon feel the 'SMASH' of demolition. Catching sight of these circles amidst this ruin, we are encouraged not only to think of the deeply held spatial divisions at work in this terrain but also to reflect on the disintegrated state of a fixed capital still awaiting the forms of circulation it craves. Sloan's recognition of the static nature of this infrastructure – its susceptibility to sclerosis – is more important to the work, I would argue, than the sense that we are somehow witnessing the emergence of the Troubles from a dormant urban domain.

For all Sloan's emphasis on Craigavon's architecture, however, he is also keenly aware of how its geography came to be inhabited. In *Vietnamese Boat People*, Sloan engages with Craigavon as a lived environment and, in so doing, provides a commentary upon what Graham has described as a city's 'ideal' potentiality – 'its capacious humanity, its "gravity", its function as a site of refuge'.[92] In 1979 houses in Brownlow were offered to refugees who had taken flight from Vietnam following the American military withdrawal.[93] Many of those 'boat people' who came to Craigavon found the environment isolating and uncomfortable – a sickening mix of displacement and discrimination – an effect Sloan conveys through the oppressive lighting of these photographs. In his images of 'Moyraverty Community Centre, Craigavon' (Plate 9), notes Aidan Dunne, Sloan seems to capture the plight of 'disorientated individuals trapped in a soulless municipal environment'.[94] These refugees would soon be victims of racial harassment, and many, unhappy with the conditions in which they found themselves, would leave Northern Ireland altogether. Yet, as Graham reminds us, Sloan's images of these new arrivals 'are in a variety of modes, as he searches for a way to render their experience'.[95] In his photographs of the younger members of this Vietnamese community (Plate 10), for instance, Sloan counteracts the 'dark, eerie, sometimes disturbing' atmosphere critics have often commented upon in relation to this series.[96] Photographing this younger generation in black and white, Sloan ensures that their character and innocence add warmth and colour to Craigavon's dull canvas. In many ways, Sloan is again shadowing the new city's own publicity. But, in so doing, he infuses it with a distinct personality – a unique identity that at once recognises the ephemeral nature of these moments, while also gesturing towards the potential for cohesion and conviviality they describe.

All this provides a different, more enabling perspective on Craigavon's sinking infrastructure. But it is important to realise that such hope is manifested at yet another level: despite the apparent circularity of the new city's decline, much of Craigavon was largely unaffected by the 'cycle of violence' which characterised the Troubles. While the new city's location meant that technically it formed part of what many Catholics came to dub the 'North Armagh Murder Triangle',[97] its housing districts still 'gained a reputation as being relatively free from sectarian conflict'.[98] As the *Craigavon Times* reported, with a touch of pride, 'Brownlow for all its faults, and its inability at times to attract families into its new estates, is one of the few places in the province where there has been little sectarian strife'.[99] This, in itself, was not surprising. Craigavon's underpopulation dramatically reduced the opportunity for sectarian violence, and it was partly for this reason that a divisive housing pattern did not emerge when the Troubles first erupted. In fact, far more than any fiscal incentive, it was the new city's reputation for neutrality that ultimately encouraged people to commit to Craigavon in substantial numbers. As Blackman has noted, 'many of the arrivals to Craigavon from the late 1960s were predominantly catholic refugees from violence in Belfast'.[100] While this might have tilted the population towards a Catholic bias, the new city's publicity could still promote its comparative ecumenicity:

> Although Brownlow is adjacent to larger towns which have suffered a great deal in the civil disorders, the sector still maintained its record of good relationships between the vast majority of the people living in its estates.
>
> There has been little or no sectarian expression in Brownlow since families first began moving into the estates eight years ago, and this is considered highly encouraging by the authorities, especially as a large proportion of the families come from areas in Belfast and other centres where trouble was prevalent.[101]

Craigavon's female writing group, the Dolly Mixtures, help to reveal the largely invisible effects of this integration. Forming part of 'what they call

Northern Ireland's unheard voice', their dynamic compilation of short stories and poetry – *Troubles and Joys* (1992) – provides a rare insight into what these 'ordinary working class women' have been living through during the worst years of the Troubles.[102] While the anthology covers a range of topics from the hunger strikes to romances in Paris, what is telling about its dealings with life in Craigavon is the security it presupposes. As one member of the Dolly Mixtures, Roisin Anderson, has commented: 'it has a community spirit, you know the areas and you feel safe'.[103] This spirit permeates a story like Madge Steele's 'Innocent Victim'. Here the female protagonist, Deborah, is keen to remove her impressionable sons from the paramilitary enclaves in which they live, and so leaves her alcoholic husband to resettle with her children in Craigavon. The new city's underdeveloped landscape certainly lacked vibrancy but, in Steele's fictional account, this inert geography enables the security of observation. In the story's closing image we are told how, now ensconced in Brownlow, Deborah

> wandered over to the window and looked out, at least the sun was shining today. Maybe that was a good sign, from where she stood the place looked good, looks were not enough. She knew that she would have to wait and see … By the end of the month she would have a better idea of what life was like here, and if she had made the right move. She went downstairs and made coffee, opening the front door she stood with the coffee cup in her hand. She smiles, raised the cup to her lips and drank a toast to her 'New City'.[104]

The assurances of vision linger throughout this dénouement, capturing the sense of solace Craigavon could offer. By looking through her 'window' Deborah can comfort herself that the 'place looked good', that the outbreak of sun was a positive premonition. Of course, Deborah is understandably cautious about this new environment and knows such 'looks were not enough'. Yet it is still at the level of sight that the final affirmation of her security is figured. As the narrator tells us, 'she would just have to wait and *see*'. Steele further emphasises the importance of this need for visual familiarity through the rhyme between 'see' and 'coffee' which, as a drink that is antithetical to the alcoholic environment Deborah has left behind, can also serve as a metonym for safety. In the story's final line these connections are tightly enfolded. Standing on the threshold to her new home and shifting into the present tense of her new life, Deborah's sober 'toast' carries the symbolic significance of 'see' and 'coffee' into the very essence of 'her "New City"'.

For Steele, Craigavon's attraction comes from the fact that the New City offers 'a very mixed community'.[105] This is a view reinforced by Norma McConville's story 'Fear Turned Into Hope and New Life', where the 'arrival of the Jesuit Community' transforms a Craigavon estate into a more inclusive territory.[106]

In this, both these authors are gesturing towards the sensibilities which their writing group personifies as a whole:

> The all-woman writing group took for its title a local nickname for Craigavon. 'People came from all over to live in Craigavon when it was built and it became known as Dolly Mixture land because of that.'[107]

For those seeking refuge from the Troubles, this plurality had its own advantages – downplaying ethnic–national identities so as to prioritise a more inclusive sense of communality. 'We can live together, work together, eat together, sleep together', says Rose Mulholland, resident of the new city and long-term member of the Dolly Mixtures.[108] In an early section of Steele's 'Craigavon' poem, she captures traces of this atmosphere:

> For some few years, the times were good, and people pulled together.
> Colour mattered to them little, religion not one feather.
> All kinds of people jumbled up together, were as one.
> They worked and played, and socialised as they should have done.[109]

Although somewhat clichéd and tainted with nostalgia, this is rigid, reverberating verse, in which we glimpse the circumstances by which variety, difference and displacement are 'pulled together'. As she looks back at this moment of solace, Steele's rhymes and repetitions seem to reiterate the sense of stability she describes – ensuring her lines are grounded, like her poetry which always adheres to the fixity of a full stop.

Recognised in this way, the city of immobility and paralysis, of boredom and inertia, comes to emit an alternative sense of stasis – one supported by internal forms of cohesion and co-operation. Indeed, in its 'jumbled up' mode of living, Craigavon can perhaps be understood as replicating what David Lloyd has called 'the higgledy-piggledy arrangement' of the clachan and its 'pragmatic' modes of existence.[110] Craigavon had gestured towards such a settlement pattern in its original design, but in its subsequent underdevelopment the new city seems to have gained further correlations. In its vandalised condition, for example, Craigavon echoes the clachan's 'disordered' and 'untidy' design.[111] In its lack of amenities, Craigavon's sequestered housing estates replicate the clachan's own underdevelopment – what Evans has called its conscious ability to 'attrac[t] none of the elements of the true village, whether church, inn or shops'.[112] As the clachan was a settlement pattern that would counteract the capitalist impulses of colonial 'improvers', its emergence within Craigavon's devalued landscape is certainly symptomatic: yet another sign of the new city's apparent failure to be an urban growth machine.

Yet there are also limits to the new city's comparisons with the clachan. While both embody what Lloyd would term a 'non-modern' entity 'living on through and in relation to modernity', the clachan, in Lloyd's reading at least, remains rooted to a specific spatial history that belies Craigavon's broader anti-capitalist potential.[113] For Lloyd, 'the practices of the *clachan* were ... [a] means to survive the depredations of a colonial settlement', and were 'to become anathema to the economically rational British and their index of the obdurate contentment of the Irish'.[114] Craigavon differs crucially in this respect. Where Lloyd remains within the binary logic of planter and native, British and Irish, the role of Craigavon's 'imperial intermediaries' – that internal Unionist resistance – steers the new city towards a more pan-ethnic model of subversion. Craigavon's boring geography is, as the term Dolly Mixtures suggests, a more inclusive entity. It is an ecumenical landscape that opens out Lloyd's belief in Ireland's 'contagious defiance of capitalism' – incorporating ethnic–national identities that include those individuals formally associated with 'the economically rational British'.[115]

Understood in this way, Craigavon's non-modern rendering raises broader questions about Northern Ireland's disruptive positon within a globalising economy. More specifically, it raises questions about the alternative modes of living made possible when capital breaks down: the communality and being-in-common made possible when a city no longer functions under the auspices of accumulation. The stigmas surrounding Craigavon suppress these alternative perspectives, yet they are, I want to suggest, discernible within the cultural and creative responses to the new city. While the writing of the Dolly Mixtures lacks, in many important ways, the formal and linguistic complexity of literary writing, their aesthetic is none the less drawn from, and attached to, ideal modes of living. In their anthology of *Troubles and Joys*, they wonder where the optimism might be found within Craigavon's otherwise hollow terrain. Their writing might appear utopic, but its articulation is valuable for a minority culture that has few secure institutions for dissemination and development. Like Sloan before them, they push past Craigavon's failed urban experiments to search out the real city that could exist just beneath the surface. In this sense, their work (however populist) helps to guide Craigavon towards the key component of any place – what Cresswell calls its ability 'have some relationship to humans and the human capacity to produce meaning'.

Craigavon's successes were short-lived. Although the new city had become something of a haven from the Troubles, a combination of demolition, 'mothballing' and privatisation made the new city estates increasingly segregated and dangerous environments in which to live.[116] By the late 1980s, the housing nearest Lurgan had become 'overwhelmingly Catholic', while any Protestants in the area generally gravitated towards Portadown.[117] At this time Brownlow's central estates still remained mixed, but the ongoing clearances constantly reduced their size. As one community worker observed in the midst of all this destruction, 'I think that's going to create difficulties in the future – it could exacerbate sectarian difficulties of which there has not been much so far'.[118] In March 1991, central Craigavon suffered its first sectarian murder – the killing of two Catholic girls in a mobile shop on the Drumbeg estate.[119] This was followed by the detonation of a 2,000 pound bomb outside Craigavon's RUC station nine months later.[120] Throughout its history, Craigavon's politics had never really been those of Nationalism or Unionism, instead a collective of residential groups emerged and campaigned vehemently (if unsuccessfully) for social welfare reforms and an end to the new city's neglect.[121]

Terminating Craigavon's originally expansive ambitions, the turn to demolition also betrayed an acute lack of interest in the community work the new city's inert condition had otherwise managed to inspire. Instead, notes Blackman, the area now 'served a useful province-wide function as temporary housing (what critics called a "dumping ground")'.[122] Rather than supporting those strands of residential politics that remained, the Northern Irish Housing Executive now sought (with limited success) private developers willing to take over Craigavon's residual and decaying housing.[123] Denuded of its new city ambitions and assigned 'problem families' while it awaited the transformative effects of private investment, Craigavon became a resonate symbol of social neglect and deprivation or, as one state official put it, a 'collection of problem housing estates, located somewhere between Portadown and Lurgan'.[124]

As this suggests, the years which followed the new city's demolition were also its most traumatic. In the opening decade of the twenty-first century, Craigavon became a place renowned for its 'general lawlessness' – a space in which 'gun attacks have combined with arson attacks' to create 'a "Wild West" reputation', as the *Craigavon Echo* put it in 2002. Often a turf war between gangs and drug dealers, this anti-social behaviour – described as the work of 'mindless-thugs' by one of Craigavon's aldermen – also threatened to spill into more violent forms of political dissent.[125] A common tactic was the use of bomb scares, 'designed to draw security forces into areas where stones and petrol bombs could be thrown'. As Craigavon councillor Tony Elliott asserted in the aftermath of one such incident:

There is no doubt in my mind that these operations are orchestrated by dissidents who want to keep the pot boiling … The sad part is, they are using young impressionable youths to do their dirty work. The youths will eventually be caught by the PSNI [Police Service Northern Ireland] but the godfathers will get off scot-free.[126]

For those in Craigavon the consequences of this strategy could not have been more ominous. Since 2001, Brownlow has been subjected to sniper fire, rocket-propelled grenade attacks, viable devices and, in 2009, the fatal shooting of PC Stephen Carroll by the Continuity IRA – 'the first officer from the PSNI to die at the hands of paramilitaries'.[127]

A public meeting with Chief Superintendent Irwin Turbitt in 2003 placed at least part of the blame upon the neglect Craigavon had suffered during its construction. He observed that, while Craigavon's underdevelopment had protected its residents from 'paramilitary difficulties' in the past, this had also helped to create turbulent conditions in the present:

> One of the great problems has been that while police were focused on the difficulties associated with the 'Troubles' somewhere like Brownlow did not receive the priority it should have.[128]

Insulated from the violence of the Troubles, Craigavon's devalued landscape also avoided the interests of increasingly sophisticated forms of state surveillance which, as Chapter 4 will go on to illustrate, deployed the monotonous logic of capitalist temporalities to disable civilians in the most debilitating of ways. Consequently, what happened in Craigavon tended to have a regulation of its own; in the post-new-city years there were frequent stories of lives being destroyed amidst a growing climate of anarchy and disorder. As one resident told Turbitt during this 2003 meeting, 'I have seen the most incredible destruction in that community, where ordinary citizens are trying to go about their daily lives'; 'I have watched my own estate destroyed, with 40 houses demolished after being burnt out'; and 'we have been left to cope with it in whatever way we can'.[129] The new city's geographical ennui meant it was also an environment rendered meaningless to the forces putatively designed to combat such disorder. During its years of decline, Craigavon had become an unobserved fringe on the margins of society; as such, it was an environment that could descend into a state of abeyance without any direct intervention from the law.

Craigavon's future is still unfolding, but its cultural legacy consists of more than the failed urban experiment for which it is so often decried. Alongside the accounts of Craigavon's demise, there are counter-narratives, stories and images which illustrate how the new city fostered an alternative politics of co-operation and 'through-otherness'. Despite its uneven development, Craigavon's dilapidated environment was still a sanctuary for those wishing to escape the bruised realities of the Troubles elsewhere. Even amidst the social disorder of the early 2000s, something of this attitude has persisted. We should note, for instance, the photographic journal – *My Country Is Where I Am* (2009) – which was produced by women from a diverse range of ethnic backgrounds, now living in

Craigavon. Created as part of the borough council's 'Re-imagining Craigavon Programme', the photographs taken by these women 'present', in the words of the project's co-ordinator, 'a snapshot of their experience as families "at home" in our community'.[130] Often little more than casual portraits taken against the backdrop of a daily routine (meal times, car journeys, social interactions), the sheer banality of these photographs is often what makes them so effective. These images were taken at a time when Craigavon was renowned for its animosities and stark brutality – a '"hoodland" rife with violence, vandalism and drug-dealing', dramatised by Jonny Kerr and Nigel Steele in their short film *Craigavon Safari* (2006).[131] The content of this photographic journal presents an entirely different urban environment, however – one in which, to return to Steele, 'all kinds of people jumbled up together, were as one', where 'they worked and played, and socialised as they should have done'.

In spite of these resonances, the geography of the Dolly Mixtures is not actually present in any of the images from *My Country Is Where I Am*. The troubled Brownlow estates which were once the centrepiece of Craigavon are given no visual reference in the album, nor are any of the new city's devalued remains. Instead the photographs focus upon Portadown's built environment and historic features – the River Bann and the Portadown Bridge made so infamous by the events of 1641. The remnants of Craigavon's inert infrastructure are, then, effectively eradicated by the wider project of 'reimagining' in which these images are implicated. It is tempting to read this photographic journal as being motivated by the circulation of capital – reminding us how, in Harvey's words, 'if the geographical landscape no longer serves the needs of mobile capital, then it must be destroyed and built anew in a completely different configuration'.[132] But other connotations present themselves. In their grainy pixilation, subject matter and oblique, off-centre focus, these images also reproduce a critical aesthetic close to that developed in the art-photography of Sloan.[133]

Sloan was an active participant in this project, helping Craigavon's artist-in-resident Ann Donnelly compile and publish a catalogue of these photographs. In this, Sloan went some way to ensuring that this work was not only preserved but also disseminated. It is not difficult to understand why. Taken by a migrant community for whom Craigavon was never really intended, these images variegate and diversify the historic origins of mid-Ulster's fractious relationship with town planning – setting Craigavon's uncertain prospect of a multicultural future against the plantation traumas of its past. As such, the possible resonances from these photographs are powerful. Certainly, for the members of this multi-ethnic minority, soon to find themselves victims of the racial harassment that still rankles through the North, these images are nothing less than a call for inclusion – a reassertion of the hope and possibility to which Sloan's *Vietnamese Boat People* had helped give expression. The remnants of Craigavon's inert geography will be subjected to the creative destruction of further redevelopment. Yet what remains unclear are the class schisms such urban renewal can inspire.

Notes and references

1   Robert H. Matthew, *The Belfast Regional Survey and Plan* (Belfast: HMSO, 1963), para. 144, p. 38.
2   Karl Marx, *Grundrisse*, trans. by Martin Nicolaus (London: Penguin, 1993), p. 410.
3   David Harvey, *The Limits to Capital*, 2nd edn (London: Verso, 2006), p. 428. Harvey sees this inertia as arising when 'increasing quantities of fixed capital and longer turnover times on production check uninhibited mobility'.
4   Anthony Alexander, *Britain's New Towns: Garden Cities to Sustainable Communities* (London: Routledge, 2009), p. 102.
5   Newton Emerson, *The Lost City of Craigavon* (Double-Band Films, BBC NI, 2007).
6   Madge Steele, 'Craigavon', in *Troubles and Joys – An Anthology of Craigavon Women Writers* ed. by Philomena Gallagher (Lurgan: Ronan Press Limited, 1992), p. 7.
7   *Ibid.*, p. 7.
8   David Harvey, *The Enigma of Capital: And the Crises of Capitalism* (London: Profile, 2011), p. 191.
9   Barbara Dalle Pezze and Carlo Salzani, 'The Delicate Monster: Modernity and Boredom', in *Essays on Boredom and Modernity* ed. by Barbara Dalle Pezze and Carol Salzani (New York: Rodopi, 2009), p. 14.
10 Tim Cresswell, *Place: A Short Introduction* (Malden, MA: Blackwell, 2004), p. 7.
11 Ivor de Wolfe, 'Sociable Housing', *The Architectural Review*, 154.920 (October 1973), 204. When Hasting contributed to the *Architectural Review*, he did so under a pseudonym – usually Ivor de Wolfe (a printer's error that was allowed to stand).
12 Edward Relph, *Place and Placelessness* (London: Pion, 1976), p. 90.
13 Justin Carville, 'Place and Placelessness in Victor Sloan's Photographs of Craigavon', in *Victor Sloan: Drift* ed. by Justin Carville and Ken Grant (Banbridge: F.E. McWilliam Gallery, 2015), p. 11.
14 Victor Sloan and Gerry Burns, 'Craigavon: The Heart Is Missing', *Circa*, 5 (July–August 1982), 15.
15 'Image of city plan', *Portadown Times*, 11 December 1964, p. 18; 'Piped Radio, Television and Telephone!', *Ulster Commentary*, 310 (March 1972), 2.
16 'Focus on Craigavon', *Portadown Times*, 12 January 1973, p. 1; 'Ski Slope at Craigavon', *Ulster Commentary*, 331 (February 1974), 11.
17 '£2 million Recreation Forum Planned', *Portadown Times*, 5 January 1973, p. 25.
18 Emerson, *Lost City* (Double-Band Films).
19 'Craigavon's House-Building Target Is Eight Hundred Per Annum', *Ulster Commentary*, 279 (May 1969), 14.

20 'Craigavon strides out towards 2000 AD', *Portadown News*, 9 June 1967, p. 3.

21 Liam O'Dowd, 'Craigavon: Locality, Economy and the State in a Failed "New City"', in *Irish Urban Cultures* ed. by Chris Curtain, Hastings Donnan, and Thomas Wilson (Belfast: Institute of Irish Studies, 1993), p. 42.

22 Marx, *Grundrisse*, p. 740.

23 Matthew, *Belfast Regional Survey*, para. 142, p. 37.

24 Craigavon Development Commission, *Craigavon New City* in *The New Towns Record 1946–2002* www.idoxplc.com/idox/athens/ntr/ntr/cd1/html/txt/u1500303.htm [accessed 24 July 2017].

25 Tim Blackman, 'Housing Policy and Community Action in County Durham and County Armagh: A Comparative Study' (unpublished doctoral thesis, University of Durham, 1987), p. 79.

26 Tim Blackman, 'Craigavon: The Development and Dismantling of Northern Ireland's New Town', *Capital and Class*, 11.2 (Summer 1987), 119.

27 Peter Dickens, Simon Duncan and Mark Goodwin et al., *Housing, States and Localities* (London: Methuen, 1985), p. 214.

28 Blackman, 'Housing Policy', p. 295.

29 Martin Joseph McCleery, 'The Creation of the "New City" of Craigavon: A Case Study of Politics, Planning and Modernisation in Northern Ireland in the Early 1960s', *Irish Political Studies*, 27.1 (2012), 91.

30 Blackman, 'Housing Policy', p. 300.

31 'Stormont attacked over "new city"', *Irish Times*, 15 August 1964, p. 11.

32 Paul Bew, Peter Gibbon and Henry Patterson, *Northern Ireland 1921/2001: Political Forces and Social Classes* (London: Serif, 2002), p. 137.

33 Luther A. Allen, 'New Towns and the Troubles: Some Political Observations on Northern Ireland', *Town and Country Planning*, 50 (November–December 1981), 284.

34 Quoted in Jonathan Bardon, *A History of Ulster* (Belfast: Blackstaff Press, 2001), p. 539.

35 'Opposition MPs plan to "carpet" O'Neill', *Belfast Telegraph*, 10 May 1969, p. 1.

36 McCleery, 'The creation of the "New City"', 97, 107.

37 'Pro-city folk "told off", *Lurgan Mail*, 18 December 1964, p. 6.

38 McCleery, 'The creation of the "New City"', 106.

39 'Planners face the farmers', *Lurgan Mail*, 23 December 1964, p. 9.

40 'Craigavon – 4,500 houses by 1971', *Portadown News*, 24 February 1967, p. 1.

41 'More than planning is required', *The Portadown Times*, 9 June 1967, p. 23.

42 Harvey, *Limits to Capital*, p. 237.

43 Housing is not part of the production process and it is not strictly included in what Marx calls 'fixed capital'. Instead it is technically defined as being a feature of the consumption fund. However, as Harvey has argued, the rent paid in relation to property creates its own 'special case' of capital circulation: the interest gained through rent ensures that capital can accumulate and thus housing 'occupies strategic co-ordinating roles within the capitalist mode of production'. In this way, continues Harvey, housing is 'drawn into a pattern of broad conformity to that experienced by fixed capital'. (*ibid.*, pp. 236, 331).

44 Mark Strong, 'Interview with Robert (Bob) Strang, 1996', *The New Towns Record 1946–2002* www.idoxplc.com/idox/shibboleth/ntr/ntr/cd1/html/txt/w2ca0200.htm#b006c [accessed 24 July 2017].

45 Craigavon Development Commission, *Craigavon New City*, in *The New Towns Record 1946–2002* www.idoxplc.com/idox/shibboleth/ntr/ntr/cd1/html/txt/u1500601.htm [accessed 24 July 2017].

46 Strong, 'Interview with Robert Strang, 1996'.

47 Hugh Dixon, *An Introduction to Ulster Architecture* (Belfast: Ulster Architectural Heritage Society, 1975), p. vii.

48 *Ibid.*, p. vii.

49 C.E.B. Brett, *Buildings of Belfast 1700–1914* (London: Weidenfeld and Nicolson, 1967), p. ix. Brett was particularly proud of how Craigavon's designers 'showed themselves unusually enlightened in their attention to planting, landscaping, and the retention of historic buildings' (C.E.B. Brett, *Housing a Divided Community* (Belfast: Institute of Irish Studies, 1986), p. 34).

50 Estyn Evans, *The Personality of Ireland: Habitat, Heritage and History* (Cambridge: Cambridge University Press, 1973), p. 91.

51 A.H. Bannerman, 'Craigavon – the "rural city"', *Town and Country Planning*, 36.1–2 (January–February, 1968), 120.

52 'New towns bill gets a flaying', *Lurgan Mail*, 19 February 1965, p. 1.

53 Strong, 'Interview with Robert Strang, 1996'.

54 'New towns bill gets a flaying', p. 1.

55 'Plan is "rotten"', *Lurgan Mail*, 12 March 1965, p. 1.

56 *Ibid.*, p. 1; 'New towns bill gets a flaying', p. 1.

57 'Moira goes to town', *Lurgan Times*, 18 June 1965, p. 1.

58 'Engulfed', *Lurgan Mail*, 12 June 1965, p. 1.

59 'New towns bill gets a flaying', p. 1.

60 'Details of the city plan', *Portadown Times*, 11 December 1964, p. 17.

61 Joe Cleary, 'Introduction: Ireland and Modernity', in *The Cambridge Companion to Modern Irish Culture* ed. by Joe Cleary and Claire Connolly (Cambridge: Cambridge University Press, 2005), p. 3.

62 Fredric Osborn and Arnold Whittick, *The New Towns: The Answer to Megalopolis* (London: Leonard Hill, 1963), p. 114.

63 Ian Nairn, *Britain's Changing Towns* (London: BBC, 1967), p. 123.

64 Trinity College Dublin, '1641 Depositions Project', online transcript (January 1970) http://1641.tcd.ie/depositions.php?depID=836101r054 [accessed 24 July 2017].

65 O'Dowd, 'Craigavon', p. 52.

66 Strong, 'Interview with Robert Strang, 1996'.

67 Jane Burbank and Frederick Cooper, *Empires in World History: Power and the Politics of Difference* (Princeton: Princeton University Press, 2010), p. 14.

68 O'Dowd, 'Craigavon', p. 44.

69 Bob Rodwell, 'Goodyear closure costs 700 jobs in Ulster', *Guardian*, 26 July 1983, p. 1; 'Fears for Goodyear jobs in Ulster', *Guardian*, 4 March 1983, p. 17.

70   Mark Strong, 'Development Progress', *The New Towns Record 1946–2002* www. idoxplc.com/idox/athens/ntr/ntr/cd1/html/txt/w1ca0205.htm [accessed 24 July 2017].

71   'Meadowbrook – "a jungle"', *Portadown News*, 16 January 1970, p. 3.

72   Gerry Burns, 'Craigavon', in *Victor Sloan: Selected Works 1980–2000* (Belfast: Ormeau Baths Gallery, 2001), p. 11.

73   'Vital year ahead', *Craigavon Progress* (= *Craigavon Times*), 21 January 1976, p. 3.

74   '£70 million spent in the past five years but the next few months are crucial for Craigavon', *Craigavon Times*, 28 January 1976, p. 6.

75   'New hope for the home hunters', *Craigavon Times*, 12 January 1976, p. 1.

76   Gerald R. Pitzl, 'Centrifugal forces', in *Encyclopaedia of Human Geography* (Westport, CT: Greenwood Press, 2004), p. 28.

77   Estyn Evans, *Irish Folk Ways* (Mineola: Dover, 2000), p. 26.

78   'The task facing the housing chiefs in attracting people to move to Brownlow', *Craigavon Times*, 28 January 1976, pp. 6–7.

79   'A new roof over your head – and hard cash in your hand', *Craigavon Progress*, p. 7.

80   'Wanted – any type of house, barn or outhouse', *Craigavon Times*, 8 September 1976, p. 6.

81   O'Dowd, 'Craigavon', p. 44.

82   Harvey, *Enigma*, p. 192.

83   Alf McCreary, 'The creation of a city', *Belfast Telegraph*, 3 May 1965, p. 6.

84   Jim Cusack, '450 homes face demolition in "new city" of Craigavon', *Irish Times*, 7 July 1982, p. 9.

85   Gerry and Sloan, 'The Heart Is Missing', 13.

86   *Ibid.*, 15.

87   *Ibid.*, 15.

88   Henri Lefebvre, *The Production of Space*, trans. by Donald Nicholson-Smith (Oxford: Blackwell, 1991), p. 144.

89   Brian McAvera, *Marking the North: The Work of Victor Sloan* (Dublin: Open Air, 1990), p. 23.

90   Colin Graham, *Northern Ireland: 30 Years of Photography* (Belfast: Belfast Exposed in partnership with the MAC, 2013), p. 232.

91   Marx, *Grundrisse*, p. 626.

92   Graham, *30 Years of Photography*, p. 89.

93   'Photo standalone 1 – no title', *Guardian*, 18 September 1979, p. 4.

94   Aidan Dunne, 'A Broken Surface: Victor Sloan's Photographic Work', in *Victor Sloan Selected Works*, p. 40.

95   Graham, *30 Years of Photography*, p. 230.

96   Mairtín Crawford, 'Ambiguous Images', *Fortnight*, 393 (March 2001), 28.

97   Blackman, 'Housing Policy', p. 302.

98   O'Dowd, 'A failed "new city"', p. 44.

99   'Will anything worthwhile come from this trip to Holland?', *Craigavon Times*, 19 May 1976, p. 4.

100   Blackman, 'Housing Policy', p. 302.
101   'Vital year ahead', *Craigavon Progress*, p. 2.
102   David Sharrock, 'From bad to verse', *Guardian*, 22 August 1994, p. A11.
103   *Ibid.*, p. A11.
104   Madge Steele, 'Innocent Victim', *Troubles and Joys*, p. 121.
105   *Ibid.*, p. 121.
106   Norma McConville, 'Fear Turned Into Hope and New Life', p. 14.
107   Sharrock, 'From bad to verse', p. A11.
108   *Ibid.*, p. A11.
109   Steele, 'Craigavon', p. 7.
110   David Lloyd, *Irish Culture and Colonial Modernity 1800–2000: The Transformation of Oral Space* (Cambridge: Cambridge University Press, 2011), p. 68.
111   Evans, *Irish Folk Ways*, p. 30.
112   *Ibid.*, p. 31. In his eighteenth-century account of a clachan in Gweedore, Lord George Hill is particularly struck by this condition, reporting that 'The nearest market towns being nine, sixteen and twenty-eight miles distant; [residents] had thus far to go in order to purchase the smallest or commonest articles, such as iron to shoe a horse, boards and nails for a coffin, etc.' (Lord George Hill, *Facts From Gweedore*, with an introduction by E. Estyn Evans (Belfast: Queen's University of Belfast: Institute of Irish Studies, 1971), p. 29). As with Craigavon, this state of affairs led to a dependency upon mobile shops and passing trade.
113   Lloyd, *Colonial Modernity*, p. 6.
114   *Ibid.*, pp. 68–69.
115   *Ibid.*, p. 69.
116   Blackman, 'Housing Policy', p. 345.
117   O'Dowd, 'A failed "new city"', p. 52.
118   Quoted in O'Dowd, 'A failed "new city"', p. 52.
119   'A Chronology of the Conflict – 1968 to the Present' http://cain.ulst.ac.uk/othelem/chron.htm [accessed 24 July 2017].
120   Bardon, *A History of Ulster*, p. 813.
121   O'Dowd, 'A failed "new city"', p. 46.
122   Blackman, 'Housing Policy', p. 351.
123   *Ibid.*, p. 346.
124   Quoted in O'Dowd, 'A failed "new city"', p. 45.
125   'Crowe hits out at thugs', *Craigavon Echo*, 22 October 2003, p. 1.
126   'Dissidents blamed for recent bomb hoaxes', *Craigavon Echo*, 23 February 2005, p. 1.
127   Chris Buckler, 'Craigavon: City of Hope and Fear', 11 March 2009, http://news.bbc.co.uk/1/hi/uk/7938663.stm [accessed 24 July 2017].
128   'District commander questioned over police role in Brownlow estates', *Craigavon Echo*, 17 December 2003, p. 12.
129   *Ibid.*, p. 12.
130   Hetty Smith, 'Introduction', in *My Country Is Where I Am* ed. by Ann Donnelly and Victor Sloan (Craigavon: Arts Development, Craigavon Borough Council, 2009), n.p.

131 *Craigavon Safari*, directed by Nigel Steele, music by Jonny Kerr (YouTube, 2006) www.youtube.com/watch?v=mW8W1WA47tM [accessed 24 July 2017].
132 Harvey, *The Enigma of Capital*, p. 191.
133 For a discussion of this style in Sloan's photography see Colin Graham, 'A Persisting Anachronism: Luxus, a Collaboration by Victor Sloan and Glenn Patterson', *Source: Photographic Review*, 50 (Spring 2007), 57.

2

'Middle-class shits': political apathy and the poetry of Derek Mahon

'Wonders are many and none is more wonderful than man'
Who has tamed the terrier, trimmed the hedge
And grasped the principle of the watering can.
Clothes pegs litter the window ledge
And the long ships lie in clover; washing lines
Shake out white linen over the chalk thanes.

Now we are safe from monsters, and the giants
Who tore up sods twelve miles by six
And hurled them out to sea to become islands
Can worry us no more. The sticks
And stones that once broke bones will not now harm
A generation of such sense and charm.

Only words hurt us now. No saint or hero,
Landing at night from the conspiring seas,
Brings dangerous tokens to the new era –
Their sad names linger in the histories.
The unreconciled, in their metaphysical pain,
Dangle from the lamp-posts in the dawn rain;

And much dies with them. I should rather praise
A worldly time under this worldly sky –
The terrier-taming, garden-watering days
Those heroes pictured as they struggled through
The quick noose of their finite being. By
Necessity, if not choice, I live here too.   (Derek Mahon, 'Glengormley')[1]

Glengormley's postwar development was extensive. Lying to the north of Belfast, this sleepy suburban village grew rapidly during the 1950s and 1960s as attempts were made to ameliorate acute housing shortages within Belfast's central limits.[2] Little more than 'a small rural service centre'[3] before the Second World War,[3] by 1958 Glengormley had become an integral part of Newtownabbey – the third largest urban area in Northern Ireland at that time.[4] Evolving during a period of sustained postwar construction, Glengormley benefited from generous levels of British subvention. The 1945 Northern Irish Housing Act allowed the North's Unionist government to facilitate 'a large expansion of subsidized local authority housing'. Alongside these homes, Glengormley's transport links were also improved through an increase in funding for the Ulster Transport Authority.[5] Until this point migration from Belfast's inner regions had been an expensive undertaking, but, with the advent of affordable housing and an economical commute, areas like Glengormley became accessible to elements of the North's working class.[6] By the 1950s Glengormley could offer Belfast's cramped proletariat a better lifestyle. As the Northern Ireland Housing Trust would assert with some confidence at the height of Glengormley's expansion, 'working class tenants find these houses palatial compared with the very poor accommodation to which many of them are accustomed'.[7]

This social elevation was registered in unusually political ways. Unlike the heady mix of sectarianism and urbanism that came to envelop Craigavon, the secluded nature of Glengormley's geographical positioning meant its new estates were largely devoid of communal fixations or loyalties. At the time of Glengormley's integration into Newtownabbey, for example, there was little pomp or protest. Instead, as the *Larne Times* reported in 1958, 'a feeling of disinterest – of apathy even – towards the historic event they are to witness and to be part of exists among the 35,000 people who will make up the population of Ulster's new town'.[8] Such 'disinterest' signalled a broader shift, however. Revisiting this moment of urban migration, Henry Patterson observes that, 'while not displacing traditional fixations', the improvement in living standards 'drained them of some of their emotional centrality' and ultimately 'weakened traditional allegiances with the Unionist party'.[9] While the Unionist government had 'modified' Britain's postwar housing legislation 'for local conditions', these 'tactical concessions' were not wholly successful.[10] As Patterson notes, they still 'created much turbulence within unionism' and 'implicitly raised major questions about the future direction of the state'.[11] The repercussions of Glengormley's development ran deep. Indeed, at the risk of hyperbole, it can be argued that the story of Glengormley's transformation sheds important light upon cultural trends that have shaped the nature of Northern Ireland's contemporary political configuration.

Derek Mahon's 1965 poem 'Glengormley' captures the politics of this suburban development. His poem is keen to acknowledge the ways in which the ease and luxury of this new community (conveyed through the colloquial phrase 'in clover') are also tied to its apparent uninterest in Northern Ireland's historic conflicts – a transition triggered by the temporal shift ('now') which gives the verse its momentum. 'The long ships' of industrial Belfast are still present in Glengormley, but the materialism of this environment has also served to attenuate the vitriolic, Protestant, loyalties with which this industry has long been associated.[12] At the same time, however, Glengormley's material excesses – carried also in the washed-out guise of Belfast's 'linen' industry – similarly serve to mask 'over' the new social hierarchies ('thanes') that this social advancement creates. These changes produce a tension between the old and the new, and Mahon registers this effect through the uncertainty of his lyric voice. The dilemmas of his own persona emerge in the closing stanza to foreground the ways in which the banal comfort of Glengormley's 'worldly time' can only come at the direct expense of what has gone before. Having moved to Glengormley at the age of seventeen, Mahon is implicated in the 'we' of this complacent community.[13] Yet, rather than obscuring the power relations this social elevation has created, Mahon comes to adopt an 'unreconciled' position whereby Glengormley's gains can be registered only through another's relative 'pain'. As the final stanza opens, the reader will never know what 'dies with them' because the troubled terms of the poet's 'praise' have come to silence their response.

In many ways the image of the affluent worker haunts this narrative. But s/ he does so with a degree of discomfort. While this migratory moment might represent a proletarian shift towards what Friedrich Engels has famously called 'bourgeois "respectability"', it is important to realise the complexities this involves.[14] The political reality of Northern Ireland is considerably different from the English milieu of which Engels was writing. As this book is keen to illustrate, in the North, sectarianism distorts class divisions, adding a layer of friction to its formations. These abrasions, in turn, are not evenly distributed across that religious divide. Following Northern Ireland's 1947 Education Act, for example, the North's Nationalist working class would undergo their own form of social elevation – entering into what Seamus Heaney has dubbed 'the generic life of the newly upwardly mobile eleven-plus Catholic'.[15] By the 1990s this now Catholic middle class would find itself settling in Belfast's wealthy and largely Protestant enclaves.[16] Despite these material gains, however, their ethnic–national identity would not fracture in the manner that Mahon's 'Glengormley' describes. Instead for the North's Catholic population there is, as Rosie Lavan has suggested, an implicit 'loyalty owed to origins'[17] – something as true in 1947 as it was for those 'lawyers, teachers, business people and property owners' who responded to the Drumcree crisis of 1996.[18] Indeed, as we will see in Chapter 4, a writer like Seamus Deane can remain thoroughly wedded to a working-class Nationalism despite the upturn in his own social status. For Deane, Westminster's Education Act meant not only social aspiration but also a hardened sense of Nationalism. 'It was education that delivered the first serious injury to the unionists' blind bigotry', Deane recalls, 'advancement was now to be achieved on the basis of merit, not on sectarian affiliation'.[19]

Mahon narrowly missed an eleven-plus scholarship in 1952 but, in this new climate of educational advancement, his parents still took the decision to send him to the prestigious Royal Belfast Academical Institution. Founded by Protestant businessmen seeking to educate 'the "middling classes"', this school was an early influence on Mahon's own evolving class status.[20] It was here, for instance, that he first was introduced to a new socialist perspective which would initiate Mahon's withdrawal from the politics of his roots.[21] Consequently, if this chapter is to chart the construction of Northern Ireland's political apathy, arguably it will be best to proceed via Mahon's unsettled, Protestant perspective – that 'unreconciled ... pain' his 'Glengormley' describes. This will, of course, be far from a stable journey. It will not, to use Raymond Williams's formation, delineate a neat 'hierarchy' between classes.[22] Instead, it will expose a narrative punctuated with moments of resistance, accommodation and discomfort. Indeed, it is perhaps because of the alienation this involves, and the uncertainties it breeds, that changes within the politics of this class are worth revisiting and reframing. After all if, to invoke Warren Buffett's oft-cited phrase, it is 'the rich class' that is both making and winning the global class war, then there is much to learn in returning to those times and spaces where the confluence of capital and class were more contingent and contested.[23]

The politics of place are important to Mahon's work, and in his attention to Glengormley he provides an implicit examination of Northern Ireland's post-war modernity. However, Mahon's specific focus on the relationship between Glengormley's new materialism and Belfast's traditional industries situates the poem in a far more explicit socio-political moment than critics have hitherto acknowledged – a moment in which traditional allegiances and material realities clash.[24] Indeed, the strength of Mahon's poem stems from its ability to present Glengormley as a dialectical space: a neighbourhood in which new values were established and old attitudes effectively effaced. In this sense, Mahon's poem reveals a more socially specific understanding of Northern Ireland's post-war development. By moving to this suburb, Glengormley's residents could distinguish themselves from the working-class communities they left behind, while simultaneously gaining access to the values of those middle-class inhabitants whose migratory path they followed. Caught between these two social extremes, the contours of this new social class should be difficult to delineate and yet, as Mahon's poem demonstrates, at one level this transition is clearly marked by the apathy with which these residents viewed the North's divisive past. While this apathy is far from apolitical, its vacuous materialism and class composition have made it integral to the post-conflict politics of the North.

Class has come to occupy an increasingly important position in studies of Northern Irish literature and culture. While the onset of a protracted ethnic–national conflict served to diminish the apparent salience of social class in the North, critics have managed to reframe analyses of the Troubles in ways that illustrate the importance of class formations.[25] Much of this thinking has been animated by the North's uncertain status as a post-conflict society and the conspicuous ways in which this existence has been marked by what Aaron Kelly calls 'the occlusion rather than the inclusion of working class experience'.[26] Most notable amongst this occlusion, as Michael Hall has documented, is the way in which members of the Protestant working class perceive themselves as marginalised, not only by the reconciliatory rhetoric of Northern Ireland's post-conflict dispensation but, more specifically, by the peculiar absence of the Protestant middle class from such discussions. As one of the participants in Hall's work has stated:

> it's not really about Protestants and Catholics, it's to do with us being poor. But whenever you tried to challenge the Protestant middle class, it was 'get down, youse are all anarchists, youse are all gay, youse are all dope-smokers.' In fact, if we had started talking to Catholics, *seriously* talking, and we all then started doing something together, the powers-that-be would have been really frightened. They would have created a body to *prevent* 'community relations' in that situation![27]

The frustrated terms of this account present its own dilemmas. Compelled to forge connections with an apparently antagonistic ethnic–national group, such 'relations' are then seemingly precluded by the potential class conflicts they could inspire. As a result, the possibility of establishing any serious conversations *between* Protestants and Catholics is effectively foreclosed, while a sense of alienation *within* these denominations is seemingly exacerbated.

It is partly for this reason that the politics of post-conflict Northern Ireland appears so hollow, depleted and apathetic. In a political order predicated upon agreement, there is little room for dialogue or debate. Instead we are offered two narrowly defined 'communities' which are, in turn, rendered 'static and unchanging' by their constant need to share power.[28] Constructed on these terms, the Good Friday Agreement 'over-simplifies the wide range of conflicts that politicians need to deal with by suggesting that *the* division is the *only* major schism that needs to be addressed'.[29] Excluded from consociationalism's elite negotiations, the citizens of Northern Ireland are hereby forced to experience a scenario close to what Theodor Adorno has called 'the most compelling reason for apathy': 'the by no means unjustified feeling of the masses that political participation … can alter their actual existence only minimally'.[30] That we should find this experience in a consociational arrangement is unsurprising. As Arend Lijphart outlined in an early theorisation of this power-sharing model, it is layered with 'fragility' that means 'popular apathy and disinterest in politics and its apparent dullness have a positive value'.[31] For Adorno, however, the opposite is true. His discussion of political apathy highlights its debilitating affects in ways that are pertinent to my arguments in this book. As he writes, apathy's 'well founded or indeed neurotic feeling of powerlessness is intimately bound up with boredom'. 'Boredom', Adorno contends, 'is objective desperation'.[32]

It is at this intersection between boredom and apathy that we get a clear insight into the stasis that surrounds Northern Ireland's post-conflict politics. For Kelly this meeting has culminated in 'mainstream politics in the North', having hereby forgone 'the capacity to disagree'.[33] In many ways this breakdown helps us to define the political itself, with the contrast between disagreement and agreement operating almost as an axis around which politics can rotate. Indeed, as Jacques Rancière has argued, politics is an entity that hinges upon such a distinction – the difference between what he terms 'dissensus' and 'consensus'.[34] On the one hand, a politics based on 'consensus' is a vacuous enterprise, in which 'there is no contest on what appears [or] on what is given in a situation and as a situation'; on the other hand, an invigorated sense of politics is that which is based on 'dissensus', and in which 'there is a debate on the sensible givens of a situation … on how it can be told and discussed'.[35] Building upon this distinction, Kelly argues that 'Rancière's notion of disagreement or dissensus offers a means of challenging the reiterative consensus and agreement demanded by the Peace Process'.[36]

Realising this ambition, however, is not a simple matter. While there is much to be gained from a politics of 'dissensus', the apathetic conditions of political 'consensus' have become so entrenched that they appear almost impossible to displace. Indeed, as Mark Fisher has suggested, one of the ways in which we might comprehend the complex assemblage of contemporary capitalism is through its proclamation that 'politics itself has been "disappeared"'.[37] The poignancy of that image within the context of Northern Ireland is not insignificant. Taking its lead from Adorno's intersection between apathy and boredom, this chapter defines the contours of this disappearance and illustrates, moreover, how politics has become increasingly difficult to unearth. By casting this backward glance, I argue that it is possible to ascertain the fragments of something different; a language of 'dissensus' that has, in its fleeting appearances, the capacity to expose the contingencies within the 'capitalist peace' of post-conflict Northern Ireland.

Faced with the inert, institutionalised sectarianism of the power-sharing executive, there has often been a desire to naturalise the North – to replace its constricted governance with a more 'normal' mode of politics. Sociologists like Colin Coulter and Michael Murray have suggested that, rather than our speaking of an ethnic–national divide, Northern Ireland should be spoken of as a place which 'exhibits all of those inequalities and injustices that are the essential trait of all capitalist societies'.[38] Important as this may be, there is a danger in this impulse to essentialise the region. As this book will demonstrate, the long history of capitalism's imposition upon the North's ethnic–national division creates its own debilitating effects, and it is arguably for this reason that Northern Ireland struggles to be recognised as analogous to 'all capitalist societies'. Indeed, as Mahon's poem has illustrated, the convergence of postwar materialism and historically violent divisions produces a form of political apathy peculiar to the socio-economic landscape of Northern Ireland itself.

The torpid nature of this apathy makes it particularly difficult to discern. Indeed, for all its fraught consequences, it tends to remain a rather nebulous and insignificant condition – a point Mahon invokes in another, early poem ('Subsidy Bungalows') about the North's postwar housing expansion:

> And so the hillside holds a new harvest,
> With new methods of spring cleaning. And I,
> Knowing that this is not the last word, trust
> Five other senses to the flowering sky
> That dimly blooms about me now and snows
> Rain, rain presageless, on the open earth
> Where they are building subsidy bungalows,
> And on the hillside heaving before birth.[39]

In many ways this dim, 'presageless' condition has helped to obscure the social significance of the new apathetic class that these bungalows would help to create. In fact, it has only really been in Coulter's earlier work – which charted the contentment of the Unionist middle class during the years of direct rule – that the consequences of such apathy have been comprehended.[40] Consequently, to borrow from these arguments, there is still 'a pressing need to map out the political beliefs and practice' of this apathetic class.[41] In the post-conflict period, this need has been made all the more pressing by the erosion of Unionism's 'cultural capital'.[42] For Patterson the corollaries of this situation could not be more significant because, 'as Northern Ireland faces a decade of commemorations, inquiries and inquests that will focus predominantly on the actions of the Security Forces during the Troubles, Unionism's intellectual and ideological weaknesses have the capacity to become its Achilles' heel'.[43]

Writing with an intimate knowledge of Northern Ireland's evolving Protestant middle class, Mahon's poetry has much to offer this analysis. Critics of his work, however, have been reluctant to advance such readings. Rather than viewing his poetry as a response to the socio-economic background against which it was written, readers have tended to approach his work with what we might call a New Critical idiom – or, as Gail McConnell puts it, 'the academic practice of reading the well-made lyric poem as a self-contained verbal icon'.[44] Much of this approach stems from Deane's landmark assertion that 'Mahon's poetry expresses a longing to be free from history' – that 'his urbanity helps him to fend off the forces of atavism' which otherwise dominate the politics of Northern Ireland.[45] Hugh Haughton's more recent assessments have tried to reorientate this perspective by stressing Mahon's 'strongly developed "historical sense"'. Yet Haughton is unwilling to locate this history within the North itself. Emphasising the 'inherently intertextual and international' nature of Mahon's verse,[46] Haughton actually comes to invigorate Mahon's cosmopolitan flair. In this, Mahon's poetry has continued to reinforce the New Critical belief 'that language', in W.J. McCormack's phrase, can 'come through the bombs and bombast miraculously unscathed'.[47]

The cumulative effect of this critical practice has been to develop a framework that supresses the significance of Mahon's poetic interventions in the North, particularly as they relate to the socio-economic nature of the Troubles. As McConnell argues perceptively, 'the critical suppression of Mahon's violent poetics for a contrary emphasis on redemption, plurality and humanism masks the logic of sectarianism in Northern Ireland … much as the logic of entrepreneurial aspiration has been forged in the wake of the Belfast Agreement'.[48] In contrast to this position, McConnell concludes her study by tentatively suggesting that Mahon's 'violent poetics' might actually critique the pervasions of 'the free market … and the economic disparities it produces'.[49] It is the purpose of this chapter to develop this important contention: to delineate Mahon's critical engagement with the tumult of Northern Irish modernity by grounding his poetic techniques in the systemic violence from which they emerge. The deep reading this requires means I have room to discuss only a handful of poems. But through this approach I aim to develop a broader understanding of Mahon's formalism and the complex cultural conditions they invoke. As such, the mode of literary analysis undertaken in this chapter ultimately subscribes to Seb Franklin's broad awareness that 'methods of surface or form-centric reading … must be paired with a second stage of analysis that locates the concrete, extra-textual implications of the formal and conceptual structures that constitute a given surface'.[50] After all, only by attending to how Mahon's poetic techniques are also enmeshed with the North's evolving social and economic contexts will we ever attain a fuller sense of the political 'dissensus' that underpins so much of his verse.

As I shall go on to discuss, Mahon's work owes perhaps its greatest structural debt to the early poetry of W.H. Auden. For both writers, the contradictions and complacencies of a middle-class audience find common ground in a mutually frustrated attempt to challenge the apathy of their audience. With this in mind, it is telling that Auden's influence on Mahon has been occluded by a critical predilection for the putatively apolitical example of Louis MacNeice. 'Mahon does not reproduce MacNeice's struggle with political and historical impera-tives', asserts Edna Longley. 'Rather, he distill[s] its meaning – an *engagé* but unillusioned liberalism – and move[s] on'.[51] Where, for Longley, MacNeice's 'unillusioned liberalism' allows Mahon to retreat into the confines of a well-made poem, I will contend that Auden's Marxism allows Mahon to wed his formalist approach with the abstracter socio-economic contexts of his period. My aim, in this, is to read Mahon dialectically – to merge form and formlessness so that I can, in Carolyn Lesjak's phrase, 'hold together the visceral, affective, and local textures of experience and the global, virtual, derivative-driven flows of capital'.[52] As my analysis of 'Glengormley' has already come to suggest, such a practice is vital not only if we are going to comprehend the complexities of Mahon's poetry but also if we are going to apprehend how the interplay of apathy and boredom has become a such ingrained presence in the politics of the North.

To comprehend apathy as the preserve of a particular social class is, in many respects, to subscribe to Pierre Bourdieu's conception of class distinction. In his *Distinction: A Social Critique of the Judgement of Taste* (1984), Bourdieu explains how social classes can be designated via the concept of class 'habitus', or, as Elliot Weininger describes it, through 'a socially constituted system of *dispositions*'.[53] For Bourdieu these dispositions are imprinted upon an individual according to the particular conditions that characterise their given social space. As such, class divisions can be established through lifestyle choices rather than a purely economic positioning. The advantage of this model is that it allows for a degree of flexibility around conceptions of the middle class. While, as Weininger observes, a strictly Marxist class analysis can become restricted in its scope by viewing the middle class purely 'in terms of ownership of and/or con-trol over the means of production', Bourdieu's model 'encompasses the entirety of the occupational division of labour' so as to account for those positions which straddle the 'canonical division between "owners" and "workers"'.[54]

A sense of this flexibility can be discerned in Bourdieu's discussion of 'legiti-mate culture'.[55] Referring to those elements of culture universally recognised as worthy, different modes of living then compete to become as proximate as possible to this cultural marker. According to Bourdieu this is a competition fought most fiercely between the petty bourgeoisie and the dominant class, 'with each faction seeking to elicit recognition from the others of the superiority of its own way of living'.[56] As this suggests, the middle class are a social stratum that is constantly in flux, contested and porous – accessible to anyone who is able to engage in the battle for cultural legitimacy. The development of Glengormley encapsulated this process of embourgeoisement: its expansion allowed sections of the working class to enter its bourgeois arena and thus to compete in the struggle for legitimate values. Indeed, the geographical distribution of Glengormley's new estates brought this process into a startling perspective. As James Johnson has noted in his discussion of the changing settlement patterns within the suburb, 'the spread of this new building after the war incorporated into the settlement certain existing superior residences, which were formerly distinct'.[57] Little wonder, then, that members of Northern Ireland's established middle class would spend much of the 1950s demanding the denationalisation of public transport and the termination of the working-class route into these new suburban vistas.[58]

As compelling as Bourdieu's analysis is, however, it struggles to account for any such opposition. For Bourdieu, 'the dominant class is able to impose its lifestyle as the legitimate standard of judgement by sheer force or "symbolic violence"' and, because 'this arbitrary act of violence is hidden from view', it is invariably 'accepted by the victims themselves'.[59] There is, in other words, little opportunity to expose or challenge the 'legitimate' standards that the ruling classes have imposed. Such a rigid conception of class conflict is, as David Gartman has observed, largely because Bourdieu's theory is ahistorical and thus struggles to capture the 'specificity' and 'changing relations' posed by different societies and different periods.[60] With this awareness, an application of Bourdieu's model to Northern Ireland raises certain subtexts which require acknowledgement. As Glengormley was also developed in an attempt to avoid an extension of Belfast's city boundary – an extension which the then Unionist Prime Minster, Basil Brookeborough, feared 'might increase the number of Nationalist seats'[61] – this population redistribution can be understood also as an attempt to bolster support for the Unionist government and its belief that such political domination required, in Kelly's phrase, 'no justification other than the tautological fact of its own power'.[62] As this suggests, postwar Northern Ireland was a period in which the state could be quite explicit in its endorsement of sectarian activities. Yet, it is important to realise that, far from being a persistent bias, such sectarianism was, as Paul Bew, Peter Gibbon and Henry Patterson have argued, 'a set of institutions and practices which acquired significance in the context of the state's relations with the Protestant working class'.[63] With the Unionists' governing majority dependent upon the votes of working-class Protestants, the essential basis for the government's sectarian action was one that was invariably motivated by a 'sensitivity to the political impact on the Protestant working class of changes in their material conditions'.[64]

In this context, apathy emanating from Glengormley would have been a paradoxically threatening phenomenon. In contrast to apathy's torpid composition, its occurrence amongst these new residents had the potential to weaken relations between the state and elements of the Protestant working class, and to do so in a manner that could also jeopardise the sectarianism with which the Unionist state had tended to reinforce its right to rule. 'The concept of apathy is not a static concept', wrote Tony Cliff in 1969. 'At a certain stage in its development it can turn into its opposite, swift mass action.'[65] By distancing themselves from the North's divisive allegiances, Glengormley's residents represented more than just the emergence of a new class willing to compete in a struggle for Unionism's legitimate culture; rather, the apathy with which they greeted that culture provided a fundamental challenge to the very legitimacy of the Unionist status quo. It was, in this strange way, an apathy charged with Rancière's sense of 'dissensus', a mode of disengagement that could engineer 'a debate' on the sectarian structure of the Northern Irish state. In many respects this challenge was realised in the 1958 election, when the Unionist party lost four of its Belfast seats to the Northern Irish Labour Party. While the reasons for this defeat were various, a key determinant was that this was a period in which 'the heartlands of proletarian Unionism began to lose population to new housing estates in which the party had failed to establish a presence'.[66] This was a time in which the Unionist 'leadership was particularly worried about the position in Belfast which it believed was threatened by ... apathy amongst traditional Unionist voters'.[67] But the manifestation of this anxiety also enabled it to be resisted and redressed. Indeed the arrival of an alternative participant within Bourdieu's game of distinction could allow Unionism to become a more fluent tongue – one able to neutralise Rancière's sense of 'dissensus' by invoking that broader structure of 'consensus'.

Perhaps the most startling sense of the pressures with this emergent class position arose during the civil rights marches that heralded the Northern Irish Troubles. In themselves, notes cultural anthropologist Allen Feldman, the civil rights protests were devised to agitate for 'an ethnically neutral jural subject'.[68] And yet, as Bew, Patterson and Gibbon have asserted, in the North of Ireland marches invariably 'meant, and still mean, the assertion of territorial claims'.[69] As this suggests, despite the ostensible neutrality of the Northern Irish Civil Rights Association, its protests were always in danger of degenerating into a set of 'territorial transgressions' that could lead to what Bew, Patterson and Gibbon have called 'the creation of "militant areas"'.[70] What are less apparent, however, are the class positions that underpin this transformation. This is a phenomenon that Feldman has described directly:

> The hostility of the Northern Ireland state to the formal equivalence of civil space, the claiming of an emergent and idealized civil space by the largely Catholic middle-class leadership of the civil rights demonstrations, and the residual cultural valuations of space in Protestant and Catholic working-class communities formed a syncretistic cauldron of available and contradictory political frames. Within this admixture, crowd violence and its repression emerged as 'articulatory practices' between and within adversarial blocs.[71]

Identifying three strands within this 'syncretistic cauldron' – the state, the Catholic middle class and a collection of working-class communities – Feldman's analysis reveals an important condition behind the North's transition from civil rights to civil war. While these three parties clashed over their divergent 'cultural valuations of space', the influence of the North's Protestant middle class is notable only through its absence. As such, what is significant is not so much their disengagement but, more importantly, the fact that this apathy poses absolutely no challenge to the sectarian actions of the state itself. Apathy may not be a static concept, but at this particular moment it certainly seems to present an impotent and ineffective brand of politics. 'Repelled by traditional loyalties and taking the attitude "a plague on both your houses"', writes Jonathan Bardon, the Protestant middle class saw these protests as an opportunity to 'avoi[d] politics altogether'.[72]

The February 1969 election, which followed much of the civil rights agitation, saw an increase in the Unionist vote amongst suburban constituencies like Glengormley.[73] As these districts had previously registered disaffection with the Unionist government through a defection to the Northern Irish Labour Party, such gains were significant. At the very least, they indicated the extent to which this bourgeois apathy had lost its threatening edge, becoming enmeshed within the broader framework of the Unionist hegemony and embodying, thereby, a Rancièrian sense of 'consensus' instead. It is possibly because of this entanglement that members of the Protestant middle class appeared to be so ignorant of the hostilities that the civil rights movement invigorated. '1969 – how it took me by surprise', recalls Mahon in an interview with Eamonn Grennan.[74] Detached from the vitriolic contestations that had come to dominate Northern Irish politics and unable to countenance an intervention, some elements of the Protestant middle class would respond to the unfolding violence with a strange sense of culpability – what Mahon describes as feeling 'as perhaps a hit-and-run driver must feel when he wakes up the next morning'.[75]

Mahon's 'Derry Morning', a poem first published in 1980, emphasises this remorse and, in so doing, uncovers some obscurer reasons behind the North's descent into sectarian war:

> The mist clears and the cavities
> Glow black in the rubbled city's
> Broken mouth. An early crone,
> Muse of a fitful revolution
> Wasted by the fray, she sees
> Her *aisling* falter in the breeze,
> Her oak-grove vision hesitate
> By empty dock and city gate.
>
> Here it began, and here at last
> It fades into the finite past
> Or seems to: clattering shadows whop
> Mechanically over pub and shop.
> A strangely pastoral silence rules
> The shining roofs and murmuring schools;
> For this is how the centuries work —
> Two steps forward, one step back.[76]

That which had the potential for change is presented as being prematurely 'wasted by' its contact with a broader conflict, or 'fray', the shape of which is conveyed via the competing nationalisms with which Mahon frames his verse. As Haughton has noted, the structure of 'Derry Morning' is a hybridisation of the English, Protestant eight-line Marvellian stanza and the Aisling genre 'associated with the Irish-language poetry of the eighteenth century'.[77] What is less clear, however, is why this national dimension has been allowed to corrupt that revolutionary 'muse' so that any promise it carried can be sensed only in a state of decay ('crone'). As Mahon's 'pastoral' allusion suggests, this is a poem whose social comments will be allegorically revealed, and in the final stanzas of this verse these opening dilemmas are answered metaphorically:

> Hard to believe this tranquil place,
> Its desolation almost peace,
> Was recently a boom-town wild
> With expectation, each unscheduled
> Incident a measurable
> Tremor on the Richter Scale
> Of world events, each vibrant scene
> Translated to the drizzling screen.

What of the change envisioned here,
The quantum leap from fear to fire?
Smoke from a thousand chimneys strains
One way beneath the returning rains
That shroud the bomb-sites, while the fog
Of time receives the ideologue.
A Russian freighter bound for home
Mourns to the city in its gloom.[78]

The final six lines describe a conflict played out between 'smoke' on the one hand – that which is redolent of the conditions of industry and unified in its movement 'beneath' a higher power – and 'rains' on the other which return, 'strain' and, ultimately, extinguish the fervour below. Viewed in this way, 'Derry Morning' presents a particularly bleak reading of the class cleavages created by the movement for civil rights. The 'bomb sites' that these 'rains' now 'shroud' seemingly refer to how those disengaged from the conflict also serve to mask its fleetingly jural origins. The precise positioning of the meteorological and embroidering term 'drizzling' in the preceding stanza encapsulates the details of this fabrication – illustrating how the vibrancy of a revolutionary potential is translated, through the secure distance and material luxury of the television screen, into other forms, namely the contrasting nationalities around which this poem is formally composed. The 'Russian freighter bound for home' crystallises this betrayal. Returning to what was then the USSR, the freighter's departure suggests that a Marxist sense of revolution – based upon an exposure of the normally 'veiled civil war' between the bourgeoisie and the proletariat – has now all but disappeared from the streets of Derry.[79]

Read in these terms, Mahon's approach gestures towards the poetic method of W.H. Auden's early verse – a period in which Auden also tried to write against society's political placation by 'vulgar success'.[80] Auden's approach was to produce a poetics that challenged these attitudes by drawing his reader through a series of sharp transitions from the particular to the universal, the certain to the unclear. As John G. Blair has argued in his classic study of Auden's verse, his poetic method was built around a sense of irresolution, one that could nudge the reader into 'their own personal self-examination'.[81] Auden is arguably most engaged with this technique during the 1930s, a time when his poetry operated with an elliptical syntax that we can see Mahon beginning to replicate in his own verse. Consider, for example, how the rapid interplay of aerial perspectives and grounded detail in Mahon's 'Derry Morning' is indebted to the cinematic quickness of Auden's 1932 poem 'The chimneys are smoking':

The chimneys are smoking, the crocus is out in the border;
The mountain ranges are massive in the blue March day;
Like a sea god the political orator lands at the pier;

(W.H. Auden, 'The Chimneys Are Smoking')[82]

Smoke from a thousand chimneys strains
One way beneath the returning rains
That shroud the bomb-sites, while the fog
Of time receives the ideologue.

(Derek Mahon, 'Derry Morning')

Just as Auden's punctuation arranges his verse in what Robert Bloom calls 'the most kinetic, if not the best, order', Mahon's enjambment ('strains / One way'; 'rains / That shroud') produces a similar sense of 'linguistic urgency'.[83] In both texts we transit from a specific, material landscape towards a more abstract, political condition – one in which an extremity of motion suggests a dawning of finality.

In 'Derry Morning', Mahon's particular skill is to conclude with a symbol whose vivid particulars could not be anticipated at the outset of the poem: 'A Russian freighter bound for home / Mourns to the city in its gloom'. Reading these final lines we cannot but question the incongruous presence of this 'Russian freighter' – to wonder, with Haughton, why the poem should end 'with no clear vision of resolution'.[84] Shrouded in confusion, we leave Mahon's poem with a need to reassess its meaning, to think through its opaque 'truth' by reconsidering the relationship between the closing Soviet image and the frenetic enjambment that preceded its arrival (and departure). We are thus asked to relate the poem's 'truth' to our own interpretative agendas and, specifically, to our understanding of Northern Ireland's 'quantum leap from fear to fire'. We are, in other words, encouraged to engage in what Patricia Palmer has termed 'the microcosm–macrocosm analogy on which allegory rests' – moving from the specific images of Mahon's poem towards the more abstract reading of the Troubles it communicates.[85] There is an uncertainty in this process, what McConnell has characterised as Mahon's proclivity to do 'violence to [his] textual body and to [his] reader'.[86] But the irresolution offered by 'Derry Morning' also acts as something of a stepping stone – a crossing by which we might move from the consensual realm of political apathy and occlusion towards the dialogue and debate of a Rancièrian 'dissensus'.

If, as I have suggested, the self-reflexive allegorical 'truth' carried by Mahon's Russian freighter is a Marxist reading of the Troubles, then its departure from the poem also signals that it is a 'truth' that cannot be maintained. Mahon, in this respect, is arguably returning us to a tension that has preoccupied Irish poetry since Philip Sidney – what Palmer has called allegory's ability to be 'ground to a standstill by a violence rooted in conquest and dispossession'.[87] Yet, in the context of Northern Ireland's postwar modernisation, Mahon is also alive to the ways in which this poetic 'standstill' is connected to the changing contours of political apathy. In many ways, Mahon is developing his interest in the inertia that arises when new attitudes intersect with archaic divisions, some-thing a poem like 'Glengormley' distilled so acutely. The significance of 'Derry Morning', however, is that it is far more severe in the conclusions it draws: the closing image of 'the fog / Of time' leaves little promise of future redemption or historical retrieval. Such intensification is no accident. As we have seen, the credence which a bourgeois apathy gives to sectarian behaviour can induce a strong feeling of compunction, particularly in the context of heightened state militancy and reactive violence. The challenge Mahon faces, however, is in translating his personal sense of guilt on to his broader middle-class community – a middle-class community whose apathy has the potential to leave them per-petually ignorant of its perversely political effect.

Facing a similar predicament following the onset of the Troubles, Michael Longley has stated the case accordingly:

> The crisis for me was ignorant and complacent and self-satisfied, that as a middle-class Protestant I'd always thought this sort of thing could never happen, and here it was – it had happened.
>   I think most middle-class Protestants in the North should have felt like that. In conversation with people of my own class and religion, I would say that most of them certainly haven't felt like that and this is part of the problem.[88]

In this account, Longley sees the privatism[89] of the Protestant bourgeoisie not simply as the Bourdieusian 'habitus', or disposition, of their class position but also as a means for their protection – an attitude that could insulate them from the debate and dialogue of a politics of 'dissensus'. It is arguably for this reason that there is a fundamental disconnect in much of Mahon's poetic handling of the Troubles. As Mahon has stated, my 'poems on the surface are not about the North ... But they are about the North because I'm choosing to use my own per-sonal dilemmas as metaphors for the Northern situation.'[90] Viewed in this way, the innocuous metaphors of rain and smoke in a poem like 'Derry Morning' can also be attributed to Mahon's desire to implicate a middle-class audience in the grim realities of a conflict that has remained, as Mark Brennock puts it, 'out of sight and, to a large extent, out of mind'.[91]

Nevertheless, while Mahon insists upon a personal engagement with the Troubles, the indirectness of this approach has enabled critics to downplay the critical charge in his Northern Irish verse. Haughton's use of Heaney when assessing three Northern poems from Mahon's volume *The Hunt by Night* (1982) is a representative example of this broader displacement:

> These poems draw on the dark autobiographical capital generated by his return to his native province in the late 1970s, but view it from elsewhere. Like *The Snow Party*, *The Hunt* casts its net much more widely than Northern Ireland or the poems he wrote there. Heaney, who thought it his 'most exuberant and authoritative volume', suggested 'some creative tremor has given him deepening access to his courses of power … as if the very modernity of his intelligence has goaded a primitive stamina in his imagination'.[92]

As with many critical readings of Mahon's poetry, Haughton emphasises – via Heaney – the international dimension of Mahon's work: his decision to 'cas[t] the net more widely than Northern Ireland', 'to view it from elsewhere'. The 'modernity' of Mahon's verse is hereby located in a larger framework, and one which is consciously positioned away from Northern Ireland. Indeed, as Haughton states earlier in his study, Mahon's 'attempt to draw upon his personal sense of cultural exile [is] a template for mapping a crisis of self-identification and knowledge that goes far beyond the North and seems to be implicated in modernity itself'.[93] 'Modernity', in other words, is a domain accessible only once the poet has moved 'far beyond the North'. Caught in this dominant critical frame, Mahon's Northern poems become little more than a staging post – a hurdle that must be overcome if he is to reach the glittering prospects of a modernity that lies elsewhere.

Such conclusions are perhaps unsurprising given the cosmopolitan nature of Mahon's later verse – epistolary poems where Auden's influence is restricted to what John Redmond calls the 'mostly limited' form and tone of the verse letter.[94] Yet, in the desire to view Mahon's work in this global context, critics such as Haughton are in danger not only of misreading Mahon's engagement with modernity but also of misunderstanding the poetic and political frustrations this engagement can engender. Take Mahon's poem 'North Wind: Portrush', for example, a poem in which Mahon is, for Haughton, 'shadowed by an acute historical awareness of violence':[95]

> I shall never forget the wind
> On this benighted coast.
> It works itself into the mind
> Like the high keen of a lost
> Lear-spirit in agony
> Condemned for eternity
>
> To wander cliff and cove
> Without comfort, without love.

It whistles off the stars
And the existential, stark
Face of the cosmic dark.
We crouch to roaring fires.[96]

Here the 'agony' of Northern Ireland is far more than a haunting, shadowy
presence. Instead the prospect of violence is part of the speaker's persona – a
'madness' to which that 'I' is 'condemned for eternity'. Like Lear, the poetic
voice endures the anguish of a partitioned state: the darkening of a boundary, a
border and a 'coast'.

As 'North Wind' progresses, it begins to replicate this process – searching
for that sense of release to which critical readings are so often drawn. Yet rather
than achieving that longed for escape, Mahon's 'North Wind' remains rooted
within the Northern landscape. Instead of attaining exile, its speaker can only
entertain a fantasy of 'elsewhere' – a moment of contrast whose seductions
cannot be sustained:

So best prepare for the worst
That chaos and old night
Can do to us: were we not
Raised on such expectations,
Our hearts starred with frost
Through many generations?

Elsewhere the olive grove,
Naked lunch on the grass,
Poppies and parasols,
Blue skies and mythic love.
Here only the stricken souls
No springtime can release.[97]

Here 'elsewhere' is little more than an illusion, a 'mythic' realm whose juxtaposition serves to insulate rather than internationalise the North. That this insula-
tion has a political bent is something suggested by an earlier image of Ulster's
'wrapped-up bourgeoisie / Hardened by wind and sea'. In keeping with 'Derry
Morning', Mahon's focus is again on an indigenous middle-class audience – the
'we' and 'us' who have inured themselves against the ravages of the North.
Sheltered from the Troubles, the relative comfort of their 'benighted' perspective (carried by the cloying rhyme between 'bourgeoisie' and 'sea') strikes
a clear contrast with the turbulent imagery of the poem's opening tempest.
Despite this, however, Mahon's jolt into the plaintive pleasures of 'elsewhere'
is also layered with a paradoxical sense of discomfort. Its syntax is fraught,

not effortless – littered with an omission of articles ('poppies and parasols'), missing conjunctions ('love. / Here') and absent pronouns ('souls / No'). In the urgency this creates, Mahon unsettles the tranquil image of being safely sequestered elsewhere – a discomfort exacerbated by his intertextual echo of Auden's 1933 poem 'Out on the lawn'. Here Auden creates a similar point of contrast so as to attack, through an equally bucolic image, the 'gentle' – or genteel – class who do not ask: 'what doubtful act allows / Our freedom in this English house, / Our picnics in the sun'.[98] In 'North Wind', Mahon leans upon this Marxist element in Auden's poetry to emphasise the political 'dissensus' of his own verse.[99] Surrounded by a storm that 'is here to stay', the seductions of a pastoral escape are simultaneously undercut by a poet frustrated with the middle class's complacent 'habitus' – to use Bourdieu's terminology – towards a conflict of which they are, in fact, inextricably a part.[100]

Mahon's critique of Northern Ireland's modernity lies in these contradictions: his anxiety in the face of pleasure, his restlessness amidst the certainty of form. Yet, despite the predominance of these contrary positions, critical readings still discern a salvific potential in his depictions of the North. 'Perhaps', argues Stephen Enniss in relation to 'North Wind', 'the poem suggests, one really can start anew'.[101] Combining personal dilemmas with intricate poetic techniques, Mahon's desire to move his reader from the specific to the general – from an indulgent individualism to a critical class-consciousness – is a process that opens itself to misinterpretation. Enniss, for example, reads 'Derry Morning' – a poem written while Mahon was battling with alcoholism – as a work which 'equates the uncertain progress towards peace in the North with [Mahon's] personal struggle towards recovery'.[102] That this misses the poem's complex distillation of the intersections between the Troubles and Northern Irish class conflict is evident enough. But, in making this point, Enniss also suggests how Mahon's conflation of the personal and political can unwittingly create a teleological trajectory – one that downplays the irresolution of his poetry and its potential for 'dissensus'. Just as biography can claim to be a narrative of progression, so any political parallels can be tilted towards a consensual language of reform. As Enniss writes:

> Mahon's best poems are those that put suffering to constructive use, those that probe his past of fracture and of loss while working through that human condition towards some longed-for recovery.[103]

What that 'constructive use' may be is never fully explored; instead a vague and indeterminate sense of 'longed-for recovery' becomes the poem's ultimate destination. In this, Mahon's work mutates into a 'hoped-for' act – moving our attention away from the 'suffering' and 'fracture' implicit in the verse.[104]

As this reading suggests, the notion that Mahon's poetry could politicise its reader through the discord of 'dissensus' is an idea that has not received sustained critical attention. Instead critics have tended to view Mahon's work as a poetry stabilised by the apparent polish of his verse. Deane and Longley, for example – although writing from ideologically opposed positions – both concur that there is a redemptive force at work in Mahon's oeuvre. 'Because of its clean emptiness', argues Deane, Mahon's poetry represents 'a new beginning',[105] one which creates, in Longley's phrase, 'socially redemptive symbols'.[106] Underpinning this approach is an insistence on Mahon's poetic 'freedom', a belief that his 'craft' can counteract 'the subservience of poetry to ideology or history'.[107] That this insistence upon the bounded, apolitical neutrality of poetry might be far from Mahon's own poetic sensibility is something made clear by his 1979 version of *The Sea in Winter*. Chastising the belief that poetry inhabits an sequestered domain, while simultaneously acknowledging the difficulty of inspiring social transformation through art, Mahon concedes that 'these lines carefully set down' are 'all farts in a biscuit tin, in truth – / Faint cries, sententious or uncouth'.[108]

Reading Mahon's work alongside the context from which it was produced, these anxieties are not entirely surprising. Since the onset of the Troubles, Mahon's Protestant middle class had retreated further from public life. With the imposition of direct rule from Westminster in 1972, moreover, that class was effectively liberated from having to support any brand of indigenous politics at all – a situation compounded by the fact that direct rule could encourage a selfless pursuit of material interests. Believing that the Troubles were a situation best resolved through fiscal benevolence, the generous levels of public provision which came to characterise this period of government also ensured that, in Mahon's phrase, the North could support 'a prosperous middle class out of all proportion to its real assets'.[109] The steady flow of capital from the British exchequer also served to insulate the Northern Irish bourgeoisie from the shocks and consequences of global financial crises. Far from making Northern Ireland 'the most socialist region in the United Kingdom', as some commentators have suggested, this constant stream of subsidy ensured that wealth largely accrued at one pole and not the other.[110] By 1992 'the disposable income available to the wealthy' in Northern Ireland was, as Bill Rolston has noted, 'higher than almost anywhere else in the UK'.[111]

Despite these substantial economic corollaries, it was at the level of attitudinal values, to return to Bourdieu, that the middle class's social distinction was most forcefully maintained. While direct rule allowed the Protestant middle class to express, in Coulter's phrase, a 'profound political apathy' with Northern politics, they were entirely dependent upon the political structures that had

come to govern the North. As Coulter suggests, this was a 'contradictory experience'.[112] By professing a political attitude of non-intervention, this stance not
only represented another moment of political inconsistency, it also represented
yet another stage in the evolution of the Protestant middle class. Much like
Unionism's nullification of postwar apathy, the mechanics of direct rule were
now also ensuring this new apathetic attitude could become ever more impotent
and intractable. Whatever the socio-political consequences of London's Irish
policy, the affluence it bestowed upon the Northern bourgeoisie meant it would
remain largely unchallenged by members of that class. 'Rather than reflect upon
the problematic nature of their political environment', writes Coulter, 'the
unionist middle class preferred instead to cast their considerable energies into
the rather more rewarding task of accumulating wealth'.[113]

This was not a smooth transition, however, and the depletion of a bourgeois
political culture did not occur in isolation. In many respects, it was accom-
panied by an increase in deprivation, inequality and what Rolston has termed
'the politicisation of the marginalised'.[114] Indeed, if anything, the absence of a
bourgeois political conscience made this inequality all the more pronounced,
something the Opsahl Report on Northern Ireland touched upon in 1993:

> The poor are not listened to; the extraordinary silence of the centre more than
> anything else highlights the special nature of this conflict and underscores the necessity
> to bring the professional, business, and middle classes back into the political process.
> Until they can be convinced of their *civic* responsibility to play a role and of the *neces-
> sity* to find a solution, it is unlikely that the accommodations, which a settlement will
> require, will be made.[115]

To a large extent this represents an uneasy co-existence of two extremes –
an affluent silent centre rubbing alongside a conflictual deprived margin. The
inability of one attitude to replace the other – the poor will not be 'listened to',
just as the rich refuse to speak – means that the North must persist in a state of
irresolution. In this respect, it is a scenario which returns us to the 'unreconciled' tensions that Mahon's 'Glengormley' has carefully described.

Mahon's poetry is an important resource when attempting to comprehend the apathy of Northern Ireland's bourgeoisie. Since such early poems as
'Glengormley', 'Spring in Belfast' and 'Ecclesiastes', Mahon has been deeply
engaged with the tensions that can exist between an individual awareness and
the broader pulls of communal belonging. Alive to such divisions, his work
frequently constructs a narrative whereby an imagined, if tentative union
between self and society is established, before then being pointedly undercut.
Certainly the number of Mahon poems that end with a displaced sense of
self – 'I know too much / To be anything any more' – is striking,[116] and yet

it is arguably through this method that he is best able to express the 'solitude and community' which he has come to call his poetic 'subject'.[117] Rather than the coherence with which literary critics have characterised Mahon's verse, his work actually represents something of a contradiction: offering a perspective that is at once able to criticise the apathetic values to which he reluctantly ascribes while simultaneously revealing their inner, attitudinal appeal. This is a scenario encapsulated in Mahon's own description of how he experienced much of the Troubles:

> our peculiar upbringing as middle-class, grammar-school-educated, liberal, ironical Protestants allowed us to think of ourselves as somehow not implicated. I told myself that I had more important things to do. Which were going to London, getting on with my own literary career as I had now started to conceive of it, marrying Doreen, getting myself together, discovering a sense of purpose. And writing directly about those conditions in the North was not part of that purpose.[118]

Couched in regret, such a recollection cannot circumvent the disengagement it seeks to chastise. After all, once he was 'allowed' to disengage from the North, the prospect of a return seemingly offered only obstruction and distraction. Conditions in the North were undoubtedly a source of guilt, but they were also an impediment: a potential barrier to Mahon's unfolding life events.

It is in the contradictions of this ironic attitude that Mahon's critique of capitalism and conflict lies. In contrast to critical readings that avow the measure and control of his verse, Mahon's poetry is riddled with an uncertainty that, remembering McConnell's perceptive phrase, does 'violence to its textual body and to its reader'.[119] A poem such as 'Afterlives', for example, finds itself descending into a state of frustration that allows for a strident evaluation of bourgeois apathy while also producing some problematic conclusions:

> I wake in a dark flat
> To the soft roar of the world.
> Pigeons neck on the white
> Roofs as I draw the curtains
> And look out over London
> Rain-fresh in the morning light.
>
> This is our element, the bright
> Reason on which we rely
> For the long-term solutions.
> The orators yap, and guns
> Go off in a back street;
> But the faith doesn't die

That in our time these things
Will amaze the literate children
In their non-sectarian schools
And the dark places be
Ablaze with love and poetry
When the power of good prevails.

What middle-class shits we are
To imagine for one second
That our privileged ideals
Are divine wisdom, and the dim
Forms that kneel at noon
In the city not ourselves.[120]

Again, what is presented as an innocuous violation – a voyeuristic intrusion upon the bustle of London – becomes, in its translation onto the broader and more complex terrain of the Northern Irish Troubles, a depraved set of 'ideals'. What seemed a 'bright / Reason' is now flawed not only for its dismissal of rational motivation – the North's complex pieties diluted to a state of 'yap' and oratory – but also because it renders 'divine' its own, more irrational, interpretation of the Troubles: the abstract belief that the conflict can be cured simply by 'the power of good'. 'Divine', in this respect, serves a double function: at once stressing how the disengagement of the middle class – 'look out over' – gives them the power and freedom to control interpretations, while also highlighting how their own 'solutions' tend to be presumptive, rather than based on an exact and intimate knowledge of events.

As so often in Mahon's work, the idea of communal cohesion buckles under the weight of a personal sense of crisis. But, in this case, it is a crisis that professes a state of ambivalence. Mahon's outburst ('what middle-class shits we are') is clearly intended to be abrasive, but it also marks a point of depletion – a realisation that the poem's metaphors will never actually alter the situation they chastise. In this way the fourth stanza represents a form of abdication: it reiterates (and is perhaps complicit in) the warped realities created by a divisive middle class privatism, but it is also unwilling to offer any 'solutions' other than the act of criticism itself. As Mahon will demonstrate in the second part of this poem, he has benefited through this ability to distance himself from the painful realities of the Troubles; in many respects, this is what has allowed him to avoid needing to learn 'what is meant by home'.[121] Damnable yet attractive, the apathy of the Protestant bourgeoisie seems to have become an increasingly intractable perspective. For all its 'dissensus', Mahon's poetry is seemingly powerless in the face of the consensual, attitudinal values that are becoming increasingly entrenched within the middle class politics in the North.

Since such early poems as 'Glengormley', the content of Mahon's verse has been delivered through the most technically precise and visually compact of forms. The cautious appearance and traditional shape of Mahon's poetry has often rendered his work compliant with various assumptions about how it should be read and what it should convey. Riven through critical assessments of Mahon's work is an underlying belief that his poems are compliant with what McConnell has termed a 'readerly faith in the stability and endurance of the communicative capacities of poetic language'.[122] In other words, readings of Mahon's poetry have tended to reinforce an aesthetic understanding of form, such that form is denied any political agency. That a critic can praise Mahon's poetry for its ability to record 'a triumph of style over content' not only attests to this tendency but also highlights how effortlessly Mahon's invective narratives can be obscured.[123] Readers of Mahon must, therefore, follow Caroline Levine's lead in expanding an understanding of form: moving it away from an aesthetic reading in which it miraculously transcends the specificities of history, and towards a definition that conceives of form as a broader 'arrangement of elements – an ordering, patterning, or shaping'.[124] To do so is to see form not as an escape from politics but as a mode of politics. After all, if, as Rancière has taught us, politics pivots around a distinction between consensus and 'dissensus', then form as 'patterning' is precisely that which enables a movement between these terms. As Levin writes, 'if the political is a matter of imposing and enforcing boundaries, temporal patterns, and hierarchies on experience then there is no politics without form'.[125]

The various ideologies that underpin Auden and, indeed, Marvell's poetry help to corroborate this politics of form. In my analysis of Mahon's work, however, I have also tried to buttress form's politicisation by following Lesjack's cue and reading his poetry dialectically – attending to the 'perverse rather than obvious' so as to comprehend the nexus of text and context that destabilises so much of Mahon's verse.[126] The significance of this approach should not be understated, given the apolitical and ahistorical reading practices that surround critical discussions of Mahon's work. Drawn to the New Critical method of insulating literary texts from their deeper social-political contexts, Mahon's critics avow that while he 'laments and rebukes the impotence of art' he simultaneously disavows 'any kind of "committed" poetry'.[127] In contrast, my analysis of 'Afterlives' asserts that it is precisely because of the commitment to his socio-political contexts that Mahon then comes to rebuke the effectiveness and relevance of his art.

In light of the critical propensity to displace the dissensus that undergirds Mahon's formalism, his profound change of style in *The Hudson Letter* (1995) and *The Yellow Book* (1997) – following a prolonged poetic hiatus in the late 1980s and early 1990s – carries resonances pertinent to the argument of this chapter. If, for Peter McDonald, the 'loose form' of both these collections 'suggests

... an indiscriminate impatience and intolerance', then by the same token it is possible to read such irritation as an unshackled version of the contempt and commitment that have always been the subject of Mahon's work.[128] McDonald, in this sense, is finally coming to experience the derision that Mahon tried to communicate in his earlier depictions of the middle class. Yet as McDonald's tone indicates and as he admits early in his review, the problem with such polemical poetry is that Mahon's bourgeois audience end up 'disliking these poems' and become 'bored' by their content.[129] In this Mahon is erring towards what Auden termed 'propagandist' poetry: 'us[ing] his powers over words to persuade people to a particular course of action'.[130] Yet rather than contradicting McDonald, Mahon will go on to reiterate this sense of ennui – describing 'my boring little provincial home-fixation as, paradoxically, one of [*The Hudson Letter*'s] big themes'.[131] As these comments suggest, it seems that the materialistic atomisation of the Protestant middle class has again evolved to ensure that an apprehension of Northern Ireland's ethnic–national divisions – no matter how forcefully evoked or how 'big' a theme – can still remain 'little' in comparison. At the same time, however, and as Mahon's recurrent engagement with the Troubles has implied, Northern Ireland's ethnic–national conflict has never been too insignificant for the poet to ignore.

In its play with hegemonic forces – with the various modes of governance promoted by Unionist and British governments – the apathy of the middle classes has become an almost irreversible entity in the North. Emerging as a strangely threatening phenomenon from Glengormley's new estates, the political 'dissensus' offered by embourgeoisement of the Protestant working class was subsequently translated into a mode of political 'consensus' through the agility of the Unionist elite and the onset of the Troubles. Rather than eroding this stance, the outbreak of ethnic–national violence ensured that the political impotence of such apathy was reinforced, becoming impervious to what Mahon has called the demand that the Troubles require 'our serious, grown-up attention'.[132] Mahon's poetry is particularly valuable not least because – in its ability to unpick the contingencies and conflicts within this political withdrawal – we are given access to the personal instabilities that such political apathy generates, as well as the unsettled class positions it conceals.

With direct rule ensuring apathy could become further ingrained – or, returning to Bourdieu, legitimised – it is relatively unsurprising that this attitude should find additional ideological momentum in post-conflict Northern Ireland. In many respects this energy derives from the ways in which many members of the Protestant middle class have been able to use apathy as a camouflage for their politics. While such figures have proved perennially apathetic towards the governance of Northern Ireland, they have been far from static in the pursuit of their own political desires. Indeed, as Coulter has argued, much of their success has been enabled by the civil and commercial language with which their politics is framed. As Coulter states:

> The measures and values advanced by various professional organisations have been portrayed not as an articulation of the particular interests of the more elevated strata within Northern Irish society but rather as the tenets of universally beneficial common sense to which all can subscribe.[133]

Far from diminishing such tactics, the Peace Process has provided fertile ground for their continuance. The consociational nature of the Agreement has meant that the governance of Northern Ireland is still preoccupied with ethnic-national division – a situation encapsulated most succinctly in the 'parallel consent' required for 'key decisions' at Stormont.[134] Alongside this, however, the unity that consociationalism requires also means that the seemingly apolitical and universal principles of bourgeois ideology are well placed to suture these ethnic–national differences. 'Popular apathy and disinterest in politics', lest we forget, 'have a positive value' in the context of consociationalism's inherent 'fragility'.[135] As a result, and precisely because the language of bourgeois ideology is misconstrued as apolitical, the paucity of Northern Ireland's post-conflict politics is almost unsalable.

Faced with this situation, Coulter goes on to demand the changes from the Peace Process outlined earlier in this chapter. However, as this chapter has illustrated, an irresolution underlies this desire to make the North signify as a space which 'exhibits all of those inequalities and injustices that are the essential trait of all capitalist societies'.[136] This is not because such change is unforthcoming, but rather because this is a region in which the principles of sectarianism and capitalism can only ever be held in tension. Although this is an abstract condition, it is one given a tangible shape in the form and content of Mahon's verse. For this reason it is revealing that two poems at the forefront of this process – 'Derry Morning' and 'Afterlives' – have been anthologised under the rubric of aspiring towards 'healing, peace [and] normality' in Frank Ormsby's collection of Troubles poetry *Rage for Order* (1992).[137] As I have discussed, the contradictions that beset these poems also encapsulate the tense relationship between the North's ethnic-national divisions and capitalism's restless drive towards an atomistic individualisation. That these poems are also held to be representative embodiments of the 'peace' and 'solutions' to which they tentatively, and, at points, ironically aspire, illustrates just how intimately the conception of a politically stable Northern Ireland has come to depend upon the intersection of two contradictory positions. For all the poise of a poem such as 'Derry Morning', it is unable to imagine anything other than a tense intersection between sectarian division and materialist desires, the irresolution of which indicates how the prospect of a peaceful Northern Ireland is to experience a future structured around the 'unreconciled ... pain' that Mahon's 'Glengormley' described all those years ago. To escape this irresolution will require, I suggest, a different approach – one that demands a re-examination of those atavistic logics that underlie Northern Ireland's deep sectarian divisions.

Notes and references

1   Derek Mahon, 'Glengormley', *New Collected Poems* (Oldcastle: The Gallery Press, 2011), p. 16. All poems are taken from this edition unless otherwise stated. Reproduced by kind permission of the author and The Gallery Press, Loughcrew, Oldcastle, County Meath, Ireland.

2   Between 1937 and 1951 Glengormley more than doubled its population (401 persons – 1,107 persons) and housing (121 houses – 325 houses). This was a striking expansion compared to a neighbouring area like Randalstown which increased only minimally in the same period (1,331 persons – 1,374 persons and 331 houses – 381 houses). ('Table 5: Population, Houses, and Accommodation' in Government of Northern Ireland, *Census of Population of Northern Ireland 1951: General Report* (Belfast: HMSO, 1955), p. 60).

3   James H. Johnson, 'The Geography of a Belfast suburb', *Irish Geography*, 3.3 (1956), 150.

4   F.W. Boal, 'Contemporary Belfast and Its Future Development', in *Belfast: The Origin and Growth of an Industrial City* ed. by J.C. Beckett and R.E. Glasscock (London: BBC, 1967), p. 178.

5   Henry Patterson, *Ireland since 1939: The Persistence of Conflict* (London: Penguin, 2006), p. 121.

6   Jonathan Bardon, *A History of Ulster* (Belfast: Blackstaff Press, 2001), p. 389.

7   Eric Leslie Bird, *The Work of the Northern Ireland Housing Trust* [Reprinted from *The Journal of the Royal Institute of British Architects*] (London: Hudson and Kearns, 1950), p. 6.

8   'Newtownabbey means little to its citizens-to-be', *Larne Times*, 27 March 1958, p. 8.

9   Patterson, *Ireland since 1939*, p. 182

10   *Ibid.*, p. 118.

11   *Ibid.*, p. 117.

12   Probably the best example of the shipyards' intimacy with Protestant loyalties can be found in the myth that 'the registration number of Titanic if held up to a mirror revealed the slogan "No Pope"' (John Wilson Foster, *The Titanic Complex* (Vancouver: Belcouver Press, 1997), p. 77).

13   Paul Durcan, 'The World of Derek Mahon', *Magill*, 8.5 (Christmas 1984), 43.

14   Karl Marx and Frederick Engels, *Selected Correspondence 1846–1895*, trans. by Dona Torr (London: Lawrence and Wishart, 1943), p. 461.

15 Neil Corcoran, *The Poetry of Seamus Heaney: A Critical Guide* (London: Faber, 1998), p. 19.

16 Mark Brennock, 'Guess who's coming to Belfast 9?', *Irish Times*, 23 March 1991, p. 1.

17 Rosie Lavan, 'Explorations: Seamus Heaney and Education', *The Irish Review*, 49–50 (Winter–Spring, 2014/2015), 58.

18 Stephen Douds, 'All Croppies Together', *Fortnight*, 353 (September 1996), 18.

19 Seamus Deane, 'The Famous Seamus', *The New Yorker*, 20 March 2000, p. 62.

20 Stephen Enniss, *After the Titanic: A Life of Derek Mahon* (Dublin: Gill and Macmillan, 2014), p. 19.

21 Unusually for a Protestant Institution, Mahon's tutor John Boyle 'took a particular interest in Irish labour history' and Mahon has subsequently credited him with 'introducing him to a new political perspective'. Enniss, *A Life of Derek Mahon*, p. 26. See also Lucy McDiarmid and Michael Durkan, 'Q. and A. with Derek Mahon', *Irish Literary Supplement*, 10.2 (Fall 1991), 27.

22 Raymond Williams, *Keywords: A Vocabulary of Culture and Society* (London: Fontana Press, 1988), p. 65.

23 Cited in David Harvey, *Rebel Cities: From the Right to the City to the Urban Revolution* (London: Verso, 2012), p. 161.

24 Though critics have commented upon Glengormley's relationship to the modernisation programme initiated by Terence O'Neill, they have not been specific or detailed about how this modernisation affected Glengormley directly nor how Glengormley's development encapsulated a wider socio-economic shift. See, for example, Hugh Haughton, *The Poetry of Derek Mahon* (Oxford: Oxford University Press, 2010), pp. 35–36.

25 See, for example, Liam O'Dowd, 'Social Class', in *Social Attitudes in Northern Ireland* ed. by Peter Stringer and Gillian Robinson (Belfast: Blackstaff Press, 1991), p. 49.

26 Aaron Kelly, 'Geopolitical Eclipse: Culture and the Peace Process in Northern Ireland', *Third Text*, 19.5 (September 2005), 547.

27 Michael Hall, *A Question of 'Community Relations': Protestants Discuss Community Relations Issues*, Island Pamphlets No. 32 (Newtownabbey: Island Publications, 2000), p. 12.

28 Adrian Little, *Democracy and Northern Ireland: Beyond the Liberal Paradigm?* (Basingstoke: Palgrave Macmillan, 2004), p. 28.

29 *Ibid.*, p. 29.

30 Theodor W. Adorno, *The Culture Industry: Selected Essays on Mass Culture* ed. by J.M. Bernstein (London: Routledge, 1991), p. 166.

31 Arend Lijphart, *The Politics of Accommodation: Pluralism and Democracy in the Netherlands* (Berkeley: University of California Press, 1968), p. 138.

32 Adorno, *The Culture Industry*, p. 166.

33 Aaron Kelly, 'Introduction: Troubles with the Peace Process: Contemporary Northern Irish Culture', *Irish Review*, 40–41 (2009), 2.

34 Jacques Rancière, 'Comment and Responses', *Theory and Event*, 6.4 (2003), para. 4.

35 *Ibid.*

36   Kelly, 'Troubles with the Peace Process', 4.
37   Mark Fisher and Jeremy Gilbert, 'Capitalist Realism and Neoliberal Hegemony: A Dialogue', *New Formations*, 80–81 (Winter 2013), 90. In Northern Ireland the term 'disappeared' refers to people believed to have been murdered and secretly buried during the Troubles.
38   Colin Coulter and Michael Murray, 'Introduction', in *Northern Ireland after the Troubles: A Society in Transition* ed. by Colin Coulter and Michael Murray (Manchester: Manchester University Press, 2008), p. 22.
39   Derek Mahon, 'Subsidy Bungalows', *Icarus*, 32 (December 1960), 22.
40   The continued relevance of Coulter's earlier arguments is confirmed by the republication of his essay 'Peering in from the Window Ledge of the Union: The Anglo-Irish Agreement and the Attempt to Bring British Conservatism to Northern Ireland', *Irish Studies Review*, 21.4 (2013), 406–424.
41   Colin Coulter, 'The Culture of Contentment: The Political Beliefs and Practice of the Unionist Middle Classes', in *Who Are 'the People'?: Unionism, Protestantism and Loyalism in Northern Ireland* ed. by Peter Shirlow and Mark McGovern (London: Pluto Press, 1997), p. 114.
42   Henry Patterson, 'Unionism after the Good Friday and St Andrews', *The Political Quarterly*, 83.2 (April–June 2012), 254.
43   *Ibid.*, 254.
44   Gail McConnell, *Northern Irish Poetry and Theology* (Basingstoke: Palgrave, 2014), p. 232.
45   Seamus Deane, *Celtic Revivals: Essays in Modern Irish Literature 1880–1980* (London: Faber, 1985), p. 156.
46   Haughton, *The Poetry of Derek Mahon*, p. 3.
47   W.J. McCormack, *The Battle of the Books* (Mullingar: Lilliput Press, 1986), p. 18.
48   McConnell, *Northern Irish Poetry and Theology*, p. 234.
49   *Ibid.*, p. 233.
50   Seb Franklin, 'The Context of Forms', *World Picture*, 11 (Summer 2016), 10, www.worldpicturejournal.com/WP_11/pdfs/Franklin_WP_11.pdf.
51   Edna Longley, 'Looking Back from *The Yellow Book*', in *The Poetry of Derek Mahon* ed. by Elmer Kennedy-Andrews (Gerrards Cross: Colin Smythe, 2002), pp. 29–48; p. 38.
52   Carolyn Lesjack, 'Reading Dialectically', *Criticism*, 55.2 (2013), 264.
53   Elliot B. Weininger, 'Foundations of Pierre Bourdieu's Class Analysis', in *Approaches to Class Analysis* ed. by Erik Olin Wright (Cambridge: Cambridge University Press, 2005), p. 91.
54   *Ibid.*, p. 86.
55   Pierre Bourdieu, *Distinction: A Social Critique of the Judgement of Taste*, trans. by Richard Nice (London: Routledge, 1984), p. 28.
56   Weininger, 'Bourdieu's Class Analysis', p. 98.
57   Johnson, 'The Geography of a Belfast Suburb', p. 155.
58   Henry Patterson and Eric Kaufmann, *Unionism and Orangeism in Northern Ireland since*

1945: The Decline of the Loyal Family (Manchester: Manchester University Press, 2007), p. 23.

59 Quoted in David Gartman, *Culture, Class and Critical Theory* (London: Routledge, 2013), p. 36.

60 *Ibid.*, p. 34.

61 Patterson, *Ireland since 1939*, p. 186.

62 Aaron Kelly, *Twentieth-Century Irish Literature: A Reader's Guide to Essential Criticism* (Basingstoke: Palgrave Macmillan, 2008), p. 48.

63 Paul Bew, Peter Gibbon and Henry Patterson, *Northern Ireland 1921/2001: Political Forces and Social Classes* (London: Serif, 2002), p. 106.

64 *Ibid.*, p. 105.

65 Quoted in Chris Harman, 'Thinking It Through: Out of Apathy', *Socialist Review*, 219 (May 1998) http://pubs.socialistreviewindex.org.uk/sr219/harman.htm [accessed 24 July 2017].

66 Patterson, *Ireland since 1939*, p. 142.

67 Patterson and Kaufmann, *Unionism and Orangeism*, p. 17.

68 Allen Feldman, *Formations of Violence: The Narrative of the Body and Political Terror in Northern Ireland* (Chicago: Chicago University Press, 1991), p. 22.

69 Bew et al., *Northern Ireland 1921/2001*, p. 147.

70 *Ibid.*, p. 147.

71 Feldman, *Formations of Violence*, p. 22.

72 Bardon, *A History of Ulster*, p. 644.

73 Patterson, *Ireland since 1939*, p. 208

74 Eamonn Grennan, 'Derek Mahon, The Art of Poetry', *The Paris Review*, 154 (Spring 2000) www.theparisreview.org/interviews/732/the-art-of-poetry-no-82-derek-mahon [accessed 24 July 2017].

75 *Ibid.*

76 Mahon, 'Derry Morning', p. 99.

77 Haughton, *The Poetry of Derek Mahon*, p. 161.

78 Mahon, 'Derry Morning', p. 99.

79 Karl Marx and Frederick Engels, *Manifesto of the Communist Party*, trans. by Samuel Moore (Moscow: Progress Publisher, 1967), p. 59.

80 John G. Blair, *The Poetic Art of W.H. Auden* (Princeton: Princeton University Press, 1965), p. 67.

81 *Ibid.*, p. 77.

82 W.H. Auden, 'The chimneys are smoking' in *The English Auden* (London: Faber, 1986), p. 116. All poems are taken from this edition.

83 Robert Bloom, 'The Humanization of Auden's Early Style', *PMLA*, 83.2 (May 1968), 446.

84 Haughton, *Derek Mahon*, p. 162.

85 Patricia Palmer, *The Severed Head and Grafted Tongue: Literature, Translation and Violence in Early Modern Ireland* (Cambridge: Cambridge University Press, 2014), p. 77.

86 McConnell, *Northern Irish Poetry and Theology*, p. 234.

87   Palmer, *Severed Head*, p. 92.

88   Eavan Boland, 'The Northern writers' crisis of conscience: Part 2', *Irish Times*, 13 August 1970, p. 12.

89   I borrow this phrase from Mark Clapson's discussion of embourgeoisement (Mark Clapson, *Invincible Green Suburbs, Brave New Towns: Social Change and Urban Dispersal in Postwar England* (Manchester: Manchester University Press, 1998), p. 8).

90   Eavan Boland, 'The Northern writers' crisis of conscience: Part 3', *Irish Times*, 14 August 1970, p. 12.

91   Brennock, 'Guess who's coming to Belfast 9?', p. 1.

92   Haughton, *The Poetry of Derek Mahon*, p. 154.

93   *Ibid.*, p. 61.

94   John Redmond, 'Auden in Ireland', in *The Oxford Handbook of Contemporary British and Irish Poetry* ed. by Peter Robinson (Oxford: Oxford University Press, 2013), p. 435.

95   Haughton, *The Poetry of Derek Mahon*, p. 154.

96   Mahon, 'North Wind', p. 91.

97   *Ibid.*, p. 92.

98   Auden, 'Out on the lawn I lie in bed', p. 137.

99   For a discussion of the Marxist trajectory of Auden's 'Out on the lawn' see John Lucas, 'Auden's Politics: Power, Authority and the Individual', in *The Cambridge Companion to W.H. Auden* ed. by Stan Smith (Cambridge: Cambridge University Press, 2005), pp. 158–159.

100   Mahon, 'North Wind', p. 92.

101   Ennis, *After the Titanic*, p. 152.

102   *Ibid.*, p. 151.

103   *Ibid.*, p. 5.

104   *Ibid.*, p. 5.

105   Deane, *Celtic Revivals*, p. 158.

106   Edna Longley, *Poetry in the Wars* (Newcastle: Bloodaxe, 1986), p. 204.

107   *Ibid.*, p. 205.

108   Derek Mahon, *The Sea in Winter* (Dublin: The Gallery Press, 1979), n.p.

109   Derek Mahon, 'The Coleraine Triangle', in *Journalism* ed. by Terence Brown (Oldcastle: Gallery Press, 1996), p. 219.

110   John McGarry and Brendan O'Leary, *Explaining Northern Ireland: Broken Images* (Oxford: Blackwell, 1995), pp. 76–78. Understood in these terms, the subvention of the Northern economy bears a striking similarity to Marx's description of 'The General Law of Capitalist Accumulation': 'accumulation of wealth at one pole is, therefore, at the same time accumulation of misery ... at the opposite pole' (Karl Marx, *Capital Vol. I*, trans. by Ben Fowkes (London: Penguin, 1990), p. 799).

111   Bill Rolston, 'The Contented Classes', *Irish Reporter*, 9 (1993), 7.

112   Colin Coulter, 'Direct Rule and the Unionist Middle Classes', in *Unionism in Modern Ireland: New Perspectives on Politics and Culture* ed. by Richard English and Graham Walker (Basingstoke: Macmillan, 1996), pp. 177–178.

113   *Ibid.*, p. 178.

114 Rolston, 'The Contented Classes', 9.

115 *A Citizen's Inquiry: The Opsahl Report on Northern Ireland* ed. by Andy Pollak (Dublin: Lilliput Press, 1993), pp. 12–13.

116 Mahon, 'Lives', p. 46.

117 Grennan, 'Derek Mahon'.

118 *Ibid.*

119 McConnell, *Northern Irish Poetry and Theology*, p. 234.

120 Mahon, 'Afterlives', p. 57.

121 *Ibid.*, p. 58.

122 McConnell, *Northern Irish Poetry and Theology*, p. 51.

123 William Wilson, 'A Theoptic Eye: Derek Mahon's *The Hunt by Night*', *Éire-Ireland*, 25.4 (Winter 1990), 127.

124 Caroline Levine, *Forms: Whole, Rhythm, Hierarchy, Network* (Princeton: Princeton University Press, 2015), pp. 15–16.

125 *Ibid.*, p. 16.

126 Lesjack, 'Reading Dialectically', 251.

127 Longley, 'Looking Back from *The Yellow Book*', p. 38.

128 Peter McDonald, 'Incurable Ache', *Poetry Ireland: Review* ed. by Frank Ormsby, 56 (Spring 1998), 118.

129 *Ibid.*, 117.

130 W.H. Auden, 'Introduction', in *The Poet's Tongue* by W.H. Auden and John Garrett (London: G. Bell & Sons, 1935), p. ix.

131 Grennan, 'Derek Mahon'.

132 *Ibid.*

133 Coulter, 'The Culture of Contentment', 132.

134 'Safeguards', Paragraphs 5.d.i–ii, *The Agreement: Agreement Reached in the Multi-Party Negotiations* (Good Friday Agreement), 1998, www.gov.uk/government/uploads/system/uploads/attachment_data/file/13665 2/agreement.pdf.

135 Lijphart, *The Politics of Accommodation*, p. 138.

136 Coulter and Murray, 'Introduction', p. 22.

137 *A Rage for Order: Poetry of the Northern Ireland Troubles* ed. by Frank Ormsby (Belfast: Blackstaff Press, 1992), p. xix.

3

Double negative: the psychogeography of sectarianism in Northern Irish photography

In Northern Ireland sectarianism is typically defined by its 'destructive patterns of relating'.[1] As a mode of speech it preaches hate and division, as a physical action it produces violence and devastation. It poses a threat to social harmony and jeopardises the well-being of a population. As such, sectarianism is little desired and greatly despised. The Good Friday Agreement, for example, 'seeks to remove' sectarian symbols and the divisions they serve to propagate.[2] And yet, sectarianism still endures. Its divisive structures haunt Northern Irish society through flags and murals, parades and bonfires, yet also via ethnic–national voting structures, consociational arrangements and segregated schools. Taken as a whole, such persistence speaks not only to the weight of Northern Ireland's historic divisions but to something more fundamental – a deeper question about how people forge relationships with the places they inhabit and the communities they embody. After all, as Peter Geoghegan has suggested, sectarianism is perhaps at its most pronounced when it is spatially conceived – producing 'boundaries' and 'markér[s]' that create a sense of 'group identification' through 'physical separation'.[3]

Understood in terms of a more constructive pattern of relating, sectarianism becomes a tricky concept. While its destructive consequences are to be rejected, its communality points to something more enabling and protective. In this uncomfortable sense, the imperative to efface sectarianism is a process that can also impinge upon the networks through which a sense of collectivity is forged. The impulse to move beyond sectarianism is, then, a fraught and difficult process – a task which might militate against a geography of belonging and the personal sense of identity, or hereness, this can breed. As if aware of this inherent complication, John Duncan's 2008 photograph of a Loyalist bonfire on Belfast's Shore Road is virtually devoid of people (Plate 11). The community this symbol putatively embodies is entirely absent from the image, with any sense of their collective identity displayed, instead, by the inanimate and intricate architecture of the bonfire. Framed between two luminous traffic bollards, Duncan's image presents this spatial marker as both a toxic hazard and an immovable object – a structure that is no longer acceptable and yet cannot be effaced. The only solution, this image seems to say, is to cordon off this symbol – to isolate it from the people it supposedly represents.

If sectarianism's destructive patterns of relating ultimately depend upon human actions – 'what goes on in people's hearts and minds' as Joseph Liechty and Cecelia Clegg define it – then dehumanising its expressions is perhaps one way in which these disruptive consequences might be contained and even diminished.[4] But with its collectivism dehumanised we must also ask why these symbols recur and who, moreover, is responsible for their construction. Duncan's image is thoroughly grounded in the North's post-conflict moment. His decision to photograph the bonfire prior to its burning suggests that the fierce fire of sectarian destruction might now have subsided, but in so doing he foregrounds tensions that would be missed were we just to witness the inferno. Gazing upon this denuded structure, we might ascertain how, in Pauline Hadaway's phrase, the North's consociational framework has managed to drain of meaning its 'two diametrically opposed' traditions, 'leaving only their outer shells intact'.[5] The hollowness of this particular bonfire is replicated across Duncan's entire *Bonfires* series, where his relentless and repetitive focus reproduces these wooden structures with the regularity of mass production. The photographic typologies of Bernhard and Hilla Becher are an immediate and obvious influence in this respect. But Duncan does not simply adopt their style, he also adapts their aesthetic. His *Bonfires* series projects the Becher's interest in industrial homogeneity on to a Northern Irish landscape. In so doing, Duncan crystallises how, in a post-Agreement context, 'the notion of community', to cite Colin Graham, 'has been reified, hollowed out and repackaged'.[6]

Discussing Duncan's 'Shore Road' photograph, Graham notes that 'on the right-hand side of the image Lidl's signage stands in unknowing mockery of the Union flag on top of the bonfire'.[7] Yet, as 'unknowing' as it may be, this mirroring raises a number of important points. Firstly, there is, of course, a parallel between the 'repackaged' sense of community carried by the bonfire's pallets on the one hand, and the prepackaged produce that the budget supermarket Lidl distributes on the other. But, secondly, in Lidl's creeping incursion, we have a sense of how consumer culture may also be responsible for the bonfire's precarious position within the urban landscape. 'On the Shore Road', Graham continues, 'the geography of redevelopment has pushed the bonfire onto the footpath, as if it had nowhere else to go'.[8] Viewed in this way, Duncan's image makes a broader intervention – one that invokes the spectacle of consumer capital and, perhaps more tentatively, what Guy Debord has termed its 'weapons' of urban change.[9]

Debord's sense of violence is significant because it helps to expand the frame of social disruption so as to incorporate capitalism's own inherent aggressions, the 'creative destruction' that David Harvey has helped to theorise.[10] Looked at with this in mind, the luminous bollards in Duncan's image suggest a structural doubling: a warning that two hazards exist within this landscape, coming from opposite directions and pitched at opposite extremes. If, as Karen Downey and David Chandler have argued, Duncan's photograph describes 'how public space is disrupted by the familiar and long-established form of the bonfire', then it is also important to realise that it mimics the ways in which that same public space has been disrupted by the equally familiar and long-established concept of capital.[11] In its hurried construction and rudimentary vernacular, the bonfire is as incongruous as those retail zones and studio apartments that have come to characterise Stormont's post-conflict insistence on being, in Conor McCabe's phrase, 'a facilitator of private market initiatives'.[12] Indeed, in this context, it would not be too crude to read the bonfire in Duncan's image as a makeshift barrier: a wooden screen by which Belfast's terraced housing can be protected from the placeless reconstruction that lingers on its margins. Duncan does not provide an answer as to what these sectarian expressions represent. But, by repeatedly photographing these divisive structures, he serves to emphasise their underlying uncertainties. In the case of 'Shore Road', notes Graham, Duncan captures the anxieties that emerge when 'the psychogeography of home [is] altered by forces beyond one's control or even comprehension'.[13]

In Graham's remarkable study *Northern Ireland: 30 Years of Photography* (2013), he suggests that critical assessments of Northern Irish photography have been particularly buoyed by the discomfiture of peace. Graham describes how he became 'impatient' with the North's literary tradition during this period: 'the Troubles had worn a conceptual and ideological path which Northern Irish writing (poetry, novels and drama) had difficulty leaving'. This path, he continues, was typified by 'a middle ground that disavowed sectarianism and looked [instead] towards a "shared" future (or a shared past)'. The Peace Process gradually shattered this conceptual avenue because, as Graham puts it, 'sectarianism had won out'. The Good Friday Agreement 'gave up on the insistence of reaching a shared vision and instead managed the acrimony of Northern Ireland through contingent political structures'.[14] Graham is quick to point out that it is now possible to see how Northern Irish literature has evolved to broach these new imperatives. But his initial impatience with literature and his concomitant turn towards photography also suggests that visual – rather than written – arts are perhaps better at comprehending and examining the North's embedded (and ongoing) divisions. Graham does not pursue this point, yet, as my reading of Duncan's photograph has suggested, Northern Irish photography is alive to the complexities within sectarianism as an expression of belonging. As this chapter will demonstrate, Northern Irish photography has proved particularly adept at scrutinising these divisive structures intensely and directly.

Alongside and connected to this issue is the question of photography as a strand of the visual arts. The photography under consideration is, as Graham reminds us, an 'art photography': a cultural form that questions the assumed authenticity or truth of the photojournalism to which it is simultaneously indebted.[15] As Chapter 1 suggested, the work of Victor Sloan has been crucial in the development of this genre. Sloan's decision to interfere with his images helped him to, in Graham's phrase, 'turn documentary photography into a potentially symbolic semantics, an image which pushes towards a meaning without allowing final meaning to accrue'.[16] For this reason, Northern Irish photography also intersects with what John Tagg has described as a broader 'discussion of *the prerequisites of realism*'; that is 'the relationship of photography to reality' and its complication by the 'processes and procedures' of the capitalist state.[17] Central to these prerequisites is a tension between photography as being both mimetic *and* aesthetic or, as Roland Barthes has put it, both '"objective" and "invested", natural and cultural'.[18] On the one hand, photography is a medium that claims to capture the world as it really is; on the other hand, it claims to be a critical tool, one that aims to view the world with an agenda in mind. While this debate is unresolved, Northern Irish photography has proved particularly adroit at negotiating this double-bind. Indeed, as I will go on to explain, this negotiation is at its most pronounced when connected to a psychogeographic practice, a practice that turns our attention to the photographic process in ways that contradict, or undermine, the content of the image.

Before such an argument is made, however, we need to understand how this bifurcated view of photography speaks to a bigger schism within the field. For those who write about photography, the camera is an inherently deceptive tool. Operating within a capitalist society, photography is often held as a technology which simply buttresses that economic reality. Just as capitalism 'requires', to use Susan Sontag's phrase, 'a culture based on images', so photography becomes an obvious and immediate medium for perpetuating this ideologically freighted imaginary. As a visual technology, photography is arguably indebted to the capitalist spectacle and can thereby furnish, as Sontag writes, 'vast amounts of entertainment in order to stimulate buying and anaesthetise the injuries of class, race and sex'.[19] Indeed, even when the photograph casts a critical eye upon capitalism's human injustices, it can still be held as a critically blunt instrument. After all, as Julian Stallabrass has wryly asserted, such a critically motivated photography 'is in no position to presume to speak for the people depicted'.[20] Indeed, such photography could even be accused of further disempowering its subjects, leaving them powerless to respond to the circulation of their suffering in what Jessica Evans has described as 'the capitalist culture of images'.[21]

Evans deployed this phrase when writing about *Camerawork*, a Marxist collective whose writings on photography were unable, ultimately, to displace the belief that photography was always already 'colonised by the beast of "dominant ideology"'.[22] Yet, having surveyed the impasses that led to *Camerawork*'s demise, Evans calls for a change in perspective. 'Could we shift our starting point', she asks, 'so far as to think of the audience or users of photography as having a life outside the text'.[23] This is an important speculation because it is through the mechanics of spectatorship that we might enter into a discussion more suited to what Ariella Azoulay has titled *The Civil Contract of Photography* (2008). In this work Azoulay argues that the photograph 'extends beyond the photographer's action' such that the image becomes independent of meaning, 'an object in the world'. 'Even when it seems possible to name correctly in the form of a statement what it shows – "This is X" – it will always turn out that something else can be read in it', Azoulay writes. As her vocabulary suggests, we must encounter the image in a new way, one that prioritises a change of action: 'to stop looking at the photograph and instead start watching it'. We must, in other words, think of our spectatorship as entailing 'dimensions of time and movement that need to be reinscribed in the interpretation of the still photographic image'. In this sense, Azoulay asserts, the photograph can become 'an object in the world, and anyone, always (at least in principle), can pull at one of its threads and trace it in such a way as to reopen the image and renegotiate what it shows'.[24]

There is much that appeals in Azoulay's conception of photography. For one thing, her insistence that we must 'renegotiate' photographic meaning can become, in turn, a means of countering the meaninglessness upon which the experience of boredom depends. But there are also questions raised by Azoulay's schema. Her parenthesised '(at least in principle)' is particularly revealing, acknowledging, as it does, that there are also always blockage points in the desire to unfix meaning, to 'watch' the photograph. Even with this more emancipatory approach, there are still anxieties that something – what Azoulay goes on to call 'the phantom picture' – might 'take part in the stabilization of what is seen'.[25] Azoulay ultimately locates this threat in advertising photography, an entity that implicitly returns us to a discussion about the camera's role in the capitalist spectacle. Helpfully, however, Northern Irish art-photography – a genre caught between photojournalism, on the one hand, and an artistic practice, on the other – pushes and pulls around this dilemma.

From its earliest inception in the work of Bill Kirk to the more recent outputs of Mary McIntyre, the category of Northern Irish art-photography has pivoted around these competing ideas. It is, as Graham has argued, 'both documentary and art at the same time'.[26] As such, gallery-based photography from Northern Ireland has proved particularly adept at moving its audience between a meaning that appears both predetermined and contingent. Certainly, Duncan's *Bonfires* suggests this duality. Across this photographic series, each of his images points towards a specific reading of these sectarian symbols, yet each of these images also fails to draw any firm conclusions. In this sense, notes Graham, Duncan's photographs leave us with a series of 'sculptural question marks' rather than a collection of full stops.[27]

Understood in these terms, Duncan's work raises another important question about Azoulay's extended ontology of the photograph. While the *Bonfires* series (and its photographic influences) relate to how humans have manipulated the landscape, Azoulay's conception of photography as civil contract is, in contrast, very much concerned with people themselves. For Azoulay, the critical challenge of photography relates to 'photographed persons' and the question of 'citizenship' that lies therein.[28] Alongside this, ideas of gender and, specifically, 'the shape of women's narrowed living space' – their '*impaired civic* status' – are key motivators in Azoulay's approach.[29] This has produced invaluable insights, particularly concerning sexual violence, but Azoulay's broader conception of the photograph also has much to offer to photographs of depeopled terrains – especially those banal landscapes marked only by their psychogeographic effects. For a writer such as Stallabrass, the 'ennui' that subtends this strand of landscape photography means it is 'hardly conceivable' that such photographs could inspire anything but 'the distanced, anaesthetic' experience of life under capital.[30] Monotonous and uneventful genres of landscape photography are, in other words, ostensibly immune to the insights Azoulay has advanced. Certainly those audiences who first encountered Berndt and Hilla Becher's banal industrial landscapes found these photographs alienating, and thus the very opposite of images that demanded the empowered spectatorship Azoulay describes. 'I don't like this at all', remarked one early viewer of the Bechers' work. 'They're dull and flat. There's no people, no involvement, nothing.'[31]

The Bechers were not alone in propagating this banal aesthetic. Indeed their influence upon a photographer like Duncan is due, in part, to their inclusion in the now infamous exhibition that reconstituted conceptions of landscape photography – *New Topographics: Photographs of a Man-Altered Landscape* (1975). The unabashed urbanism celebrated in this exhibition has had a profound effect upon the shape of Northern Irish photography as it has evolved since the 1980s. Key figures here are Lewis Baltz, Nicholas Nixon, John Schott and Stephen

Shore, and, as these names suggest, this was a photographic movement pre-
dominately male in both influence and inheritance. The absence of women
is, perhaps, another reason why writings about this genre have neglected
Azoulay's insights.[32] Graham's book on Northern Irish photography, for example, makes no mention of Azoulay's work. But such an absence should not
mean that Azoulay's thinking can have no critical purchase in discussions of
this aesthetic. In what follows I examine two prominent Northern Irish photographers, Paul Seawright and Willie Doherty, both of whom have adapted
the New Topographic aesthetic in ways that are alive to Azoulay's ideas about
'renegotiating' the photographic image. Central to this effect, I argue, is the
juxtaposition of word and image, an interplay that is particularly pronounced
in Seawright's photographic series *Sectarian Murder* (1988) as well as a range
of phototexts Doherty has produced since the 1980s. Viewed with Azoulay in
mind, I argue, these works help us visualise the tensions between capital and
conflict that are central to this book.

   While Seawright and Doherty do not make any explicit claim to engage
with Northern Ireland's political economy, their manipulation of word and
image none the less negotiates the bind between fixing and unfixing meaning
that is central to the experience of boredom under capital. As I have been
insisting throughout this book, the constrictive and more enabling perspectives this negotiation bestows on boredom as a product of meaning withdrawal
are fundamental to our understanding of capitalism's 'creative destruction'
in the context of ethnic–national division. By attending to these experiences
in the work of Seawright and Doherty it is also possible, I suggest, to see
their work as an updated response to the ideologies that underpinned the
New Topographic venture as a whole. As John Rohrbach has argued, despite
their diverse make-up, the New Topographics all shared a visual attention
to the displacement caused by 'a culture defined more by corporate commerce than community'.[33] It was this concern which led to their mutual
engagement with uneventful terrains that had been, in Wendy Cheng's telling phrase, 'previously cropped out of American landscape photographs: the
"spaces in between", such as parking lots, industrial buildings, grain elevators,
tract developments, shopping malls, freeway underpasses, and the like'.[34] As
Seawright and Doherty adapt this style against the backdrop of the Troubles,
they also animate its features with sectarian ideologies which recalibrate, in
turn, that broader play of commerce and community. Consequently, if we are
to apprehend how these forces have now managed to reconfigure so much of
Northern Ireland we must revisit these earlier visualisations of the Troubles.
The Good Friday Agreement insists that we can 'best honour' the 'tragedies
of the past' through a 'fresh start'.[35] This book, in contrast, seeks to return to

that traumatic history and to apprehend within it a fuller sense of the North's post-conflict predicament.

While tracing the 'spatial formations of violence' created by the outbreak of the Troubles, Allen Feldman concludes his analysis of Belfast's sectarian composition with the following observation:

> Crowd violence colonized and inscribed anomalous social space with sectarian codes. In this dynamic, topography ceased to function as a thing. It was much more than a passive template for the inscription of violence or an object to be manipulated in order to create political representations. Space became a power and an animated entity.[36]

Although sectarian spaces are formed through an inscriptive moment of human agency – in this case 'crowd violence' – Feldman is keen to acknowledge the spatial 'power' that these actions can also instigate. Once a space is sectarianized, argues Feldman, it is changed utterly: no longer an insensate backdrop, it becomes 'an animated entity'. The automatism that subtends this process stems from the fact that, following their ethnic–national conversion, sectarian spaces come to possess a new referent by which they might influence future events. Now personifying specific ideologies, any future incidents that occur within these sectarian topographies will find that their meaning is manipulated according to the new doctrines of that environment. Indeed, it is through such semantic destruction that sectarian effects tend to be asseverated. To return to Liechty and Clegg's definition: 'if the outcome entails the developing of, or the augmenting of, one or more destructive patterns of relating, then the speech or action can be judged sectarian'.[37]

It is for this reason that Feldman argues that a sectarian space can no longer be considered simply 'a passive template'. Armed with 'sectarian codes' through which spatial assessments will now be judged, sectarian spaces have the ability to counteract any challenges to their divisive tenets. If an interpretation is ambiguous, then the space's 'sectarian codes' will begin to determine its meaning; if it is threatening, then they will contest its significance. In fact, so potentially constrictive is sectarianism's spatial power that the landscape it creates is one that echoes, in certain respects, the spatial consequences of the Debordian 'spectacle' – the performance by which consumer capitalism attains a 'totalitarian domination of all aspects of life'.[38] Just as Feldman describes sectarian violence as having 'colonized' social space, so Debord writes of how the spectacle succeeds in 'colonizing social life'.[39] Where Feldman sees 'sectarian codes' as not only infecting space but making it 'an animated entity', Debord argues that the capitalist spectacle makes commodification 'not only visible' but impossible to see beyond: 'we no longer see anything else; the world we see is the world of the commodity'.[40] In both cases a clear sense of restriction is at work: where sectarian codes predetermine our relationship with certain places, the capitalist spectacle preconditions our perspectives on the world. 'Following its logical development toward total domination', writes Debord, 'capitalism now can and must refashion the totality of space into *its own particular decor*'.[41] Capitalism advances through society creating what Karl Marx has termed 'a world after its own image',[42] just as sectarianism becomes – in R. Murray and F.W. Boal's phrase – 'a means of ensuring social homogeneity'.[43]

These points of convergence have significant implications. While Marx and Debord are well aware of the violence that underwrites capitalism's spatial domination – a phenomenon both call its 'homogenizing heavy artillery' – this violence often materialises in unwritten forms.[44] In fact capitalism's endurance is pervasive precisely because it is able to erase the debilitation it breeds. 'Capital can never openly admit that it is a system based on inhuman rapacity', writes Mark Fisher in *Ghosts of My Life* (2014).[45] Instead, it constantly masks its brute tenacity through an ever-expanding proliferation of images in which the camera is all-pervasive. With the formation of sectarian space mimicking the capitalist spectacle, however, this disavowed rapacity can become both visible and contemptible. There is, of course, a large gap between the sectarian violence Feldman describes and the aggressive 'commodity pricing' Marx and Debord depict. Indeed, as this chapter will go on to illustrate, the capitalist and sectarian spectacle are often in direct opposition – in conflict over a system of spatial control which the capitalist state ultimately dictates. But viewed in terms of their debilitating impact – the spectacle's 'motionless monotony' as Debord puts it – a set of cogent correspondences can be traced.[46]

As this book has been insisting, the experience of boredom is integral to this convergence. Boredom is a phenomenon that typifies the charged interface between capitalist imperatives and ethnic–national divisions. But boredom is also a phenomenon which tries to pass undetected. 'The banal does not even register on the cultural scale', notes Eugénie Shinkle. 'It is embedded in material culture, but its proper domain is that of the unconsidered.'[47] As Shinkle develops her argument, she suggests that it might even be possible to apprehend boredom as 'a photographic aesthetic or style'. That is to say, as an artistic practice which is concerned with 'the nature of the viewer's encounter with the image' and the 'resistance to engagement' that lies therein.[48] Hovering over this discussion is Azoulay's implicit wariness that the commercial language of photography could restrict her foundational 'principle' that anyone can 'renegotiate' the meaning of a photograph. To put this another way, the banal aesthetic – as Shinkle theorises it – appears particularly adept at achieving 'the stabilization' of meaning for which Azoulay criticises advertising photography.[49] Through an attention to photography's banal aesthetic, therefore, it might also be possible to apprehend the monotony of the Debordian spectacle or, as Shinkle puts it, to understand 'the totalitarian quality and sense of oppression that characterise late capitalist culture'.[50] In the context of Northern Ireland, it is around these terms that an earlier visualisation of sectarian space might also be held to reify the constrictive logic of the consumer capital unleashed following sectarianism's putative, post-conflict demise.

By way of his 1988 photographic series *Sectarian Murder*, Seawright makes a valuable contribution to this visual logic. Depicting a range of sites in which ethnic–national killings had taken place ten to fifteen years earlier, Seawright foregrounds not only the spatial effects of sectarianism but also the violence that so often underpins our experience of banality. Each photograph is supplemented with a press cutting which describes the sectarian murders with precision. Yet the photographs which accompany them contain absolutely no traces of the crimes themselves. Instead, Seawright portrays bruised terrains; unkempt spaces littered with rust and wreckage, often photographed from characteristically low viewpoints (Plates 12 and 13). These oblique angles throw the landscapes into further disarray, causing elements within them to fracture and blur, unsettling the viewer's gaze. The photographs are almost entirely devoid of people: at most a silhouette or an indiscriminate figure can be discerned in the distance. Abandoned, ruined and skewed, Seawright's landscapes are – perhaps to an even greater extent than his New Topographic antecedents – alienating and disconcerting in themselves. Yet crucially, as Liam Kelly notes, while 'a general feeling of tension is engendered by the image', it is through the accompanying text that such discomfort is explained: 'the text ties them down irrevocably to a place, a sub-culture and a value system of violence'.[51]

As this interdependency suggests, Seawright is aware that a sectarian land-scape can be formed only through a violent act – in this case those described by the newspaper extracts. However, by allowing the spatial repercussions of this activity to dominate his composition, Seawright also conveys something of the power that these sectarian landscapes have now come to possess. The images' point of view (POV) is integral to this sensation. Often shot at odd angles, the photographs of each scene could represent either the victim's or the assassin's viewpoint – dying at the wayside or lurking, ready to commit the crime. As such, when viewing these images, we are obliged to adopt this unsettled sense of place while also being made painfully aware that, although time has now passed, these spaces can still be considered only in the light of the murders they once contained. Whatever fresh perspectives we might read into these landscapes is categorically denied by the complete convergence between text and image. The permanence of Seawright's POV forces us to submit to the space's stifling power, just as the textual descriptions predetermine how these ominous land-scapes are to be understood.

Unable to obtain another perspective on this landscape, Seawright makes us experience something akin to the 'motionless monotony' Debord has described. In this we are aligned, once again, with Azoulay's frustration that capitalism's proliferation of images has 'concentrated' the viewer's gaze, diminishing the spectator's inherent ability to 'reopen the image and renegotiate what it shows'.[52] This is a classic case of the banal aesthetic as that which suppresses, in Shinkle's phrase, 'the affective – and potentially political – dimensions of the viewer's encounter with the image'.[53] Where the conflation of Seawright's POV and the newspaper descriptions constrain our interpretation of the image, Shinkle's banal aesthetic is likewise determined by 'the refusal of the image to acknowledge the mobility of the viewer's gaze'.[54]

Comparing *Sectarian Murder* with Michael Clarke's 1988 film *Elephant* helps to further illustrate what is at stake in such a petrified viewing arrangement. Famed for its lack of dialogue while depicting a string of sectarian murders in Belfast, *Elephant* can be understood as a porous text. As Richard Kirkland observes:

> Rather than a narrative, the film presents us with a series of seemingly random assassinations taking place across the suburbs and waste hinterlands of Belfast ... The assassins and victims are all male, all without uniform, and all without the obvious trappings of paramilitary iconography. No motives are indicated for their violence.[55]

Acting almost as an empty signifier, *Elephant* suggests that we should be the sole arbiters of its meaning. In this sense, remarks Kirkland, 'the film offers itself to the viewer, in Roland Barthes' terms, as classically "scriptable"', an effect that *Elephant*'s producer, Danny Boyle, has suggested was vital to the film's inception.[56] The 'inspiration', recalls Boyle, 'was to present material and leave it up to the viewer to make up his or her own mind'.[57] 'It wasn't trying to be some sort of moody thriller', Boyle states elsewhere, 'it was trying to speak to an ignorant mainland, really'.[58] Indeed, the moments in which the film's taciturnity breaks into such pedagogical utterances can be accurately located. Aside from the final scene, each of the film's murders closes with a static shot of the resultant corpse, lasting between 20 and 35 seconds. As such, these shots jar with the film's otherwise restless momentum, jolting our attention into a sharper relief and encouraging us to conduct what Michael Walsh describes as a 'merciless inspection of the unmoving body'.[59] Faced with death, but unclear as to why it has occurred or even what it represents, Clarke persuades his viewer to dwell on its futility.

In these static shots, Clarke shifts into the domain of the photograph. Here, the inertia of his footage gives over to the 'stillness' that Susie Linfield argues is definitive of photography.[60] Yet it is at these points that Clarke also gives us access to that profounder understanding of photography which Azoulay has advanced. Watching *Elephant*'s unmoving bodies, we become not only the film's 'addressee but also its addresser, one who can produce meaning for it and disseminate this meaning further'.[61] The affinities with Azoulay at this particular juncture are perhaps unsurprising given that we are looking at bodies, not landscapes. However, like the terrains in Seawright's *Sectarian Murder*, *Elephant* also thrusts its audience into the midst of Northern Irish violence so that they might experience and digest its implications. The power of Seawright's *Sectarian Murder*, derives from its ability to present its viewer with only a singular interpretation: no alternative readings or divergent perspectives. For *Elephant*, in contrast, the affective force stems from the multiplicity of meanings on display. Murders are undoubtedly happening, but the film's silent refusal to provide its audience with any referent by which these killings might be comprehended means that there is little restraint upon how such action can then be interpreted. It is perhaps for this reason that responses to *Elephant* vacillate so dramatically. For the film's British cameraman, John Ward, '*Elephant* is the best thing that's ever been done on Northern Ireland';[62] conversely, the Nationalist Northern Irish theatre director Pam Brighton argues that the film is 'absolute bollocks': it provides 'no analysis' and presents the Troubles 'as a hopeless sectarian problem with too many guns'.[63]

David Bate perceives within boredom a question of vision. 'It is not that there is not anything to see', Bate argues, 'rather that the subject cannot see it. Vision is colonized, inhabited by boredom.'[64] For Shinkle, such an assessment reiterates the banality that can underpin the photographic gaze, namely that 'rather than opening up the space of the image as a field of potential action, it becomes an enclosure, a trap for the eye, a perceptual void'.[65] As much is evident in Seawright's strict alignment between text and image – freezing both in a static, uncompromising gaze. Yet there are deeper resonances to Bate's analysis. For one thing, Bate's argument about boredom echoes Debord's depiction of consumer capitalism: 'it is not that there is not anything to see, rather the subject cannot see it';[66] 'commodification is not only visible, we no longer see anything else'.[67] In both these statements, moreover, we are given access to what has subsequently become late-capitalism's mantra, the misguided belief that – as Margaret Thatcher so famously put it – 'there is no alternative'.[68] But in suggesting that vision is *colonised* by boredom, Bate is also returning us to that loaded term deployed in both Feldman's definition of sectarian space and Debord's conception of the capitalist spectacle: 'Crowd violence colonized and inscribed anomalous social space with sectarian codes';[69] the spectacle succeeds in 'colonizing social life'.[70] Across these theorisations, space is seen to be invaded and transformed; it is disturbed and recoded in ways that restrict and realign the uncertainties that constitute our spatial understanding. In many ways these incursions are, to invoke Gilles Deleuze and Félix Guattari's terminology, a moment of deterritorialisation that facilitates the constrictions of reterritorialisation. Like the capitalist relations Deleuze and Guattari describe, sectarian expressions haunt their landscapes – controlling them through fear and agitation, as if they were part of some 'terrifying nightmare'.[71]

In Seawright's images, the convergence between the capitalist and sectarian spectacle is exposed through what Val Williams terms his 'personal schema': the intimate displeasure we are forced to feel as we are implicated in the only perspective on offer.[72] This effect begins with the artist himself, and nowhere is this more apparent than in the working methods Seawright employed when photographing those scenes of sectarian murder. As Liam Kelly writes of Seawright's methodology:

> Using an old diary from his youth, which noted significant political events among the fairly quotidian entries, Seawright spent protracted periods of time at these sites, considering the meanings associated with their location. In some cases, he re-enacted the route taken from the place from which a victim was snatched to the eventual spot of the murder or dumping of the body. Such reconstructions of reality built up tensions within the artist, as well as eliciting the lingering presence of gross transgressive acts from the location.[73]

As this practice implies, one way of visualising a space's repressive power is through a process that builds up 'tensions' within oneself. Through this, 'the lingering presence of gross transgressive acts' within that landscape may be elicited. Part of the effect of this technique, Williams has suggested, is to transform Seawright's photographs into acts of 'testimony' – an attempt to register the emotional effects of a sectarian space and to convey them to his viewer.[74] Indeed, for Declan Long, such 'photographic cartography' causes these images to emit a 'psychological' intensity.[75] And it is, perhaps, through the very intensity of this vision that sectarianism helps to expose the 'repression and terror' which can – to use Henri Lefebvre's terminology – underwrite the capitalist mirage 'of contentment, amusement or delight'.[76]

It is because of this psychological intensity that the banality of the image starts to subside. Having moved from the photographic plain to our personal psychology, we are transported from the monocular immediacy of this aesthetic towards the more mobile motives behind its production. 'Banal images ask the viewer to redirect their focus', writes Shinkle, 'to think of the photographic process as well as the product'.[77] As such, it is through this question of production –

Seawright's physical journey to these desolate terrains – that the convergence between capitalism and sectarianism begins to fracture. Indeed, to return to Kelly's account of Seawright's method, it is possible to trace the outlines of a psychogeographic practice in his approach. Just as Seawright seeks to record the personal 'tensions' induced by sites of sectarian murder, so psychogeography aims to 'study' the 'effects of the geographical environment on the emotions and behaviour of individuals'.[78] To achieve this, psychogeographers perform a *dérive* whereby they abandon themselves to 'the attractions of the terrain and the encounters they find there'.[79] In a likeminded fashion, Seawright spent 'protracted periods' 'considering the meanings associated with [his] location'.

Comparing Seawright's methodology with a psychogeographic approach is salutary, not least because this concept was initially designed to comprehend and ultimately displace the preponderance of the capitalist spectacle and the geographical ennui that it produces. Spawned against a background of capitalist planning in 1950s Paris, psychogeography sought to push the impressive walking activities of the late nineteenth-century flâneur towards more disruptive and transformative ends. As Keith Bassett comments:

> The *dérive* was thus to be more than just strolling; it was a combination of chance and planning, an 'organized spontaneity', designed to reveal some deeper reality to the city and urban life. The *dérive* was also distinguished from *flânerie* or mere voyeurism by its more critical attitude towards the hegemonic scope of modernity.[80]

In this sense, psychogeography became a mode of walking that aimed to 'overcome the processes of "banalisation"' – the process by which the every-day experience of an environment had become 'one of drab monotony', as Merlin Coverley explains.[81] It actively resisted the society of the spectacle, but crucially did so in an attempt to, in David Pinder's phrase, 'uncover hidden geographies and histories and subvert dominant representations of the city'.[82] Psychogeogrpahy was a consciously urban form. Yet, in its desire to consider the alterities held in marginal spaces, it was a practice that also resonates with a key strand in Northern Irish gallery photography – one advanced by practitioners who, as Graham has written, 'sought out such apparently empty non-places in Northern cities and realized that to look at these was to see something more than the obvious news story'.[83]

Here some care needs to be exercised. As Coverley observes, to fashion this internal disturbance the Situationists employed psychogeography as a tool that would outline how spaces could be 'rebuilt upon new principles that replace[d] mundane and sterile experiences with a magical awareness of the wonders that surround us'.[84] In this sense, psychogeography's spatial transformations were aimed at establishing a plurality of 'wonders' which would counter the monolithic boredom that Seawright's photography otherwise suggests. Seawright's psycho-geographical explorations are tacit certainly, and yet, if psychogeography possesses the transformative power that Coverley describes, then the multiplicity for which psychogeography strives should ensure that sectarianism's rigid spatial effects are distorted, no matter how loosely these psychogeographic techniques are applied.

A productive way of approaching this contradiction is to consider the contextual contingencies involved. While sectarianism and capitalism create a form of geographical stasis by suppressing any meanings that do not attest to their respective ideologies, it is important to realise that they do so from very different perspectives. Capitalism, in Debord's analysis, operates from an elevated position, whereby its effects are 'not only visible' but pervasive: it 'has succeeded in *totally* colonizing social life'.[85] The sectarian violence of the Troubles, in contrast, lacked such supremacy – its spatial dominance was continually contested – and consequently it constructed a space that was wary and defensive. This is something *Elephant* suggested. As a film directed towards a predominantly mainland audience, one way of interpreting its muted narrative is that it is a means of highlighting a major paradox of the Northern Irish Troubles: 'the fact that', as Kirkland writes, 'acts of violence, which are massively over determined within the North itself, hardly signify at all in other parts of the United Kingdom'.[86] The film's silence, then, possibly reflects the stifled impact acts of sectarianism tend to have in a wider UK context. From a British perspective, the repressive effects of sectarian actions have not 'succeeded in *totally* colonizing social life', a point which gains added traction when we remember that during the Troubles it was through a British viewpoint that the jurisdiction of Northern Ireland was ultimately decided. Operating beneath the larger guise of the British state, Northern Ireland's sectarian codes ultimately lacked the complete omnipotence of capitalism's social control.

The point here, then, is not that Northern Irish sectarianism was, or is, in any way inspired by a psychogeographic method. Instead I want to suggest that buried deep within sectarianism's destructive pattern of relating is perhaps a more enabling potential – something which might be understood to inhabit the same conceptual territory as a psychogeographic practice. As the image from Duncan's *Bonfires* series indicated, couched within the construction of a sectarian space is a complex relationship between people and place that might stymie capitalism's alienating and constrictive imperatives. Just as psychogeography aimed to overthrow the new concentrations of capital that were transforming the suburbs of Paris into 'temples of frenetic consumption',[87] so we should remember how the sectarianisms embedded in Craigavon's designated area also served to fracture the new city's fixed capital investments. Indeed, where a psychogeographer like Debord isolated those spaces yet to be corrupted by consumer culture through the production of 'The Naked City' map of Paris, Craigavon's residual 'sense of belonging' achieved much of this disruption in and of itself.[88] It would, for instance, be otiose to create 'The Naked City' map of Craigavon because – as Chapter 1 demonstrated – the North's complex spatial relationships had already helped to create something of a psychogeographic cartography. Looked at in one way, Craigavon's 'skeletal framework' can be seen to replicate the palpable topographic fractures Debord's map so artfully produced.[89]

Viewed from this perspective, sectarianism's spatial consequences generate something of a double negative. On the one side, they ape the spectacle's oppressive mode of spatial control but, on the other side, they deconstruct those spatial fixities that are imposed entirely from above. It is through this second aspect that sectarianism's destructive pattern of relating gives way to something else, something potentially less prescriptive and more productive – a means of counterbalancing those forces of change which are often invisible and incomprehensible. Indeed, one way of looking at the legacy of Seawright's *Sectarian Murder* series is in terms of its call to remembrance – its belligerent insistence that we should not forget the victims of these attacks. In the North's post-conflict landscape this becomes a particularly enabling encounter, one that gives voice to those traumatised people and places marginalised by the Peace Process and its insistence that we should forget the 'tragedies of the past'.

Azoulay's idea of 'watching' the photograph so as to 'renegotiate' its meaning looms large here. Just as Seawright's photographs might now challenge the amnesia of the Peace Process, so Azoulay's insistence on perpetually reopening the photograph serves to distort its temporal fixity. 'When the assumption is that not only were the photographed people there, but that, in addition, they are still present there at the time I'm watching them', Azoulay explains, 'my viewing of these photographs is less susceptible to becoming immoral'.[90] Alongside this, when Shinkle's sense of the banal aesthetic is conflated with psychogeography, it becomes a style that does not merely replicate capitalism's constriction of meaning, but actually pushes through the 'stabilisation of what is seen' so as to – in Azoulay's terms – 'completely overturn what was seen in it before'.[91] Placing these points in a Northern Irish context, there is, then, an opportunity to distinguish between sectarianism's two strands: its restrictions and its possibilities, its constrictions and its comforts. The question of boredom is integral to such distillations. After all, boredom not only describes the experience of life under the capitalist spectacle; it also helps to separate out those experiences which, in Lars Svendsen's phrase, 'come to us fully coded' from those that depend upon our own, personal, perceptions.[92] As my discussion of

Seawright's *Sectarian Murder* series has suggested, photography – and specifically its banal aesthetic – is an effective means by which boredom's often intangible discrepancies can be given a more material form. In its ability to shift a monocular species of spectatorship towards the more unstable terrain of photographic production, the banal aesthetic can help to relay a more personal and meaningful mode of representation.

It is with an awareness of sectarianism's shifting terrains that so much of Willie Doherty's visual art tends to operate. Beginning with phototexts before then moving into the realm of textless photographs and later film, Doherty's artistic oeuvre 'has always been very much concerned with the business of being in a place and living there all the time'.[93] These places are invariably desolate segments of Northern Ireland, and of Derry specifically – sites of deprivation and banality that echo the New Topographic aesthetic. Doherty's landscapes are, as Declan Long notes, 'ambiguous spaces, unpopulated *terrain vague* on the fringes of the city'.[94] In keeping with Seawright's *Sectarian Murder* series, however, Doherty is also alive to the ways in which these spaces – and our sense of photography – can be recalibrated by linguistic codes and ideologies. Such impressions are most clearly displayed in the phototexts Doherty produced between 1985 and 1992 where bold, authoritative texts are superimposed on to otherwise ambiguous images. The text endows these spaces with definition, enabling Doherty to communicate the portentous energies they might contain. As such, the phototexts seem to suggest a system of cartography: they become, as Doherty has stated, a means of 'mapping those spaces' to which his lens is instinctively drawn.[95] Alongside this idea of 'mapping', there is also a question of control. Once inscribed, any interpretation of the underlying landscape must account for the phrases with which it is overwritten. In this sense, the text becomes a means of manipulation: a tactic through which a space can be reconfigured or, as Maite Lorés expresses it, a 'process by which innocent situations are criminalised'.[96]

Take a phototext such as 'God Has Not Failed Us (The Fountain, Derry)' (1990) (Plate 14). This photograph depicts the decrepit fringe of a Protestant housing estate: flats are flanked by distended fencing, window meshes hang limply from their frames – the only path through this desultory landscape leads to a dank, dark, dead-end. The dictum that overwrites this landscape, however, pushes in another direction. The text tells us that 'GOD HAS NOT FAILED' these residents, that they are still valued and protected by a higher power. This scene of socio-economic decline is, then, aggressively recast by an overlying text which, in Raphael Samuel's terminology, now 'doubles in the role of a signifier'.[97] Considered in its composition, Doherty's phototext creates a sharp irony between word and image. Here the text becomes a mode of constraint – an abstract blessing by which the landscape's very real degradation can be reformed.

To watch this image is, in many ways, to return to that banal aesthetic Seawright foregrounded. Like Seawright, Doherty's text overrides the photograph – even 'discreetly obliterat[ing] part of the image from sight'.[98] As such, it moves towards the banal aesthetic by 'arresting', in Shinkle's phrase, the spectator's gaze: 'rather than opening up the space of the image as a field of potential action, it becomes an enclosure, a trap for the eye'.[99] Unlike Seawright's *Sectarian Murder* series, however, there is no absolute parallel between Doherty's word and image. Instead these phototexts create a gulf between text and photograph, emphasising a sense of constriction which raises broader questions about the consequences of misrecognition. Encountering a phototext like 'God Has Not Failed Us', we cannot help but recognise the gap between lived experience and imposed ideology. Yet, in so doing, moreover, we are also forced to acknowledge the corollaries of this distortion. Charles Taylor's discussion of 'the politics of recognition' highlights the consequences of this effect – what he calls the 'real damage' that 'a person or group of people can suffer' when the society 'around them mirror[s] back a confining or demeaning or contemptible picture of themselves'. Such misrecognition 'can be a form of oppression, imprisoning someone in a false, distorted, and reduced mode of being', Taylor explains.[100] Aware of these contingencies, our understanding of Doherty's image begins to change – emphasising the plight of that community which persists 'imprisoned' beneath the 'confining' rhetoric he deploys.

Read in these terms, Doherty's phototext shows sectarianism as aping – once again – the capitalist spectacle. Indeed, taken as a whole, the phototext demonstrates how the community – the 'US' God has not failed – operates through a narrowly defined ideology which does not match their lived reality. This is a landscape structured around an architecture of containment, 'environmental barriers' which, as Feldman has noted, translate 'an expression of community identity' into the 'regulat[ion] of community experience'.[101] Splicing expressions of community with the rigidities of ideology, we are watching an updated version of that New Topographic concern with cultures 'defined more by corporate commerce than community'.[102] In the context of Northern Ireland, however, this critique can also project forward: vividly manifesting the confined sense of selfhood that the consociational logic of 'two traditions' creates. As Adrian Little has written, the North's dependence upon 'two traditions' as *the* model for government creates 'static and unchanging forms of political agency' that underestimate the 'shifting political priorities and dynamics' within those very traditions.[103] The value of Doherty's early visualisations of these political divisions, however, lies not just in their emphasis upon their constrictions but also in their contingencies. After all, despite the delimiting effects of Doherty's self-imposed text, his underlying photograph suggests that a regulating architecture can become beaten and battered; dented and deformed like those window meshes that still somehow cling on.

There is undoubtedly a scripto-visual inheritance at work in Doherty's aesthetic. As many critics have noted, Doherty's phototexts consciously echo a male landscape art practice developed by figures like Richard Long and Hamish Fulton. But it is, I would argue, also possible to trace a line of influence from the feminist 'scripto-visual discourse' that has evolved since the late 1960s. Here, artists like Jenny Holzer and Barbara Kruger have similarly deployed a dialectic of text and image as a means of accentuating and materialising linguistic constrictions, specifically in relation to the identity politics formulated within capitalist societies.[104] Doherty's scripto-visual statements are conditioned, of course, by the sectarian characteristics of Northern Irish space. None the less, there are still instructive synergies between Doherty's phototexts and Kruger's socio-linguistic deconstructions.

Writing about Kruger's 1980s 'picture-texts', Alexander Alberro cites Roland Barthes's discussion of image and text and the 'second[ary] signifieds' their conjunction creates.[105] As Barthes puts it: 'the text produces (invents) an entirely new signified which is retroactively projected into the image'.[106] Through this merger it is possible to see how, in Barthes's phrase, 'the text loads the image, burdening it with a culture, a moral, an imagination'.[107] Yet there is also potential, as Alberro suggests in relation to Kruger, for the 'second signified' to create a different atmosphere – one that 'capture[s] the viewer's attention and troubles her preconceived notions'.[108] In many ways, this shift from constriction to ambiguity reiterates Azoulay's expanded ontology of photography, her belief that the photograph has 'no single individual author' and that its spectator can therefore engage in 'civic negotiations about the subject they designate'.[109] More importantly, perhaps, the movement from stable to contested meaning also returns us to Shinkle's suggestion that the rigidities of a banal aesthetic implicitly raise the more uncertain question of 'the photographic process'.[110] Certainly it is with an awareness of Doherty's 'processes' that his socio-linguistic deconstructions can be more fully understood.

As with Seawright, an analysis of Doherty's methodology allows us to comprehend how his phototexts can mark, to borrow Graham's phrase, 'an intervention on a psychogeographic scale'.[111] Like Seawright, Doherty's decision to traverse and photograph desolate domains suggests a concerted physical journey. The influence of Richard Long is unavoidable here. Like Doherty, Long is an artist whose walks through the landscape are as integral to the photographs that finally capture and preserve them. We can see this most obviously in a piece like *Throwing a Stone Around MacGillycuddy's Reeks, Ireland* (1977). In this piece, Long textually itemises his journey on to the image that marks its culmination. But where Long lists his methods to demonstrate a continuity between text and image, Doherty's textual additions serves to disconnect them. For Doherty, the physical journey is not suggested by the continuity between word and image but rather by the linguistic excursion necessary to break them. Taken from sermons and graffiti that preach discord and division, Doherty's textual inscriptions suggest a photographer actively scouring Northern Ireland's divisive terrain for phrases that contradict its geography. In a likeminded manner, those most committed of urban explorers, the Situationists, developed a tactic called détournement – a strategy which involved, as David Pinder has written, 'redirecting or hijacking materials such as texts … and setting them in other contexts to create different meanings and effects'.[112] Psychogeographers such as the Situationists were, in this sense, some of the earliest 'scripto-visual' practitioners, transforming capitalism's unyielding vocabulary in ways that could destroy the spectacle's crippling ennui.[113] While Doherty's inscriptions are not drawn from the language of capital, they do derive from an equally belligerent discourse. Like those psychogeographers before him, Doherty is equally deliberative when working these phrases into an incongruous landscape.

Doherty's methodology does not have the makings of a radical manifesto, but his détournements do unsettle oppressive discourses. As Long notes, Doherty's intention is not to work 'towards the revelation of an alternative political "truth"', but rather to illustrate what is at stake in the '*unfixing* of meaning' from a landscape.[114] Looking towards those inert landscapes made famous by the New Topographics, Doherty's textual additions serve to destabilise his seemingly listless geographies. In this he foregrounds the need to negotiate the subject of his images in ways that align with Azoulay's desire that we perpetually 'reopen' the photograph, that we actively 'watch' – rather than passively observe – the image. This is a valuable situation, not least because it encourages us to rethink the critical potential of photography's *terrain vague*. While Stallabrass has admonished contemporary photographers for their preoccupation with geographical ennui, the reading of Doherty's banal topographics that I'm advancing pushes this style towards the more enabling set of photographic encounters Azoulay has helped to theorise. By renegotiating the meaning of Doherty's phototexts, it is possible to understand how sectarianism's domineering façade might give way to something far less constrictive. Indeed, if we watch hard enough, Doherty's phototexts could even nudge us towards the more enabling experiences Liechty and Clegg perceive beneath sectarianism's destructive exterior: namely, sectarianism as an 'expression of positive, human needs especially for belonging, identity, and free expression'.[115] This is not to say that the ambivalences generated by Doherty's phototexts are particularly subversive. But it is to suggest that, with a knowledge of these nuances, any complexities within sectarianism's spatial transformation can be both revealed and reframed.

In Doherty's earliest phototexts – produced between 1985 and 1988 – détoured phrases are carefully calligraphed. Works like 'The Blue Skies of Ulster' (1986), 'Mesh' (1986), 'Stone Upon Stone' (1986), and 'The Walls' (1987) all utilise a typescript that is quite literally tainted with a sectarian flair (Plate 15). In these pieces, the texts are employed to determine Protestant and Catholic territories, so that one section of the landscape might be labelled via the green of nationalism, while another could be impressed with the royal blue of loyalism. The text's colour contrasts with the black and white photograph, deepening the phototext's ambiguity. In 'The Blue Skies of Ulster', for instance, the blue text assures the viewer that Ulster's 'BLUE SKIES' will never be forsaken, but this statement is ironically offset by the grey mists that actually constitute the photograph's subject matter. Additionally, these early phototexts also disclose a direct reference to location – the texts tell us that these photographs are portraits of: 'THE EAST/WEST BANK OF THE RIVER FOYLE', 'THE BLUE SKIES OF ULSTER', 'THE OAKS OF DERRY'. Through these directions the sectarian codes within the landscape gain an intense specificity; the divisions they impose can only be viewed as a product of the Northern Irish Troubles, while the locus of such geographical sundering is clearly, if not brazenly, defined. Indeed, the intensity with which these sectarian ideologies seek to comprehend these landscapes is lucidly evinced by the sheer expanse of the overlying text. The phototext 'The Blue Skies of Ulster', for example, is layered with words which extend almost entirely across the landscape. In these works from the 1980s, the text dominates the picture with a nervous energy, requiring as much as seventeen words to reshape the underlying terrain. The scale of this linguistic manipulation suggests not only that a plethora of sectarian codes subtend these spaces but, more crucially, that sectarian expressions are themselves unsettled and unstable. In this way Doherty suggests that such formations are, to use Stuart Hall's terminology, best thought of as 'a "production", which is never complete, always in process, and always constituted within, not outside, representation'.[116]

Such impressions accord with the status of sectarianism when these phototexts where produced. Between 1985 and 1987, the slow decline of sectarian violence, which had peaked in August 1971, was alarmingly reversed. Fuelled by the fierce Unionist backlash following the signing of the Anglo-Irish Agreement in 1985, ethnic–national divisions were hardened as a fresh spate of sectarian killings, intimidation and violence resurfaced in the North. The Anglo-Irish

Agreement had sought to solve the Troubles by promoting, amongst other things, cross-border co-operation between the North and South of Ireland. This aim was to be achieved, most contentiously, through the Agreement's second article and its proposal that an Intergovernmental Conference should give the Irish government, for the first time in history, a consultative role in the affairs of Northern Ireland.[117] In implementing such a policy, the political schisms within the North supplanted the broader question of the Northern Irish border. Rather than acknowledging and addressing the North's sectarian divisions, the Anglo-Irish Agreement moved them into an interior position and, consequently, the Troubles were reconceived as a question of North–South relations and not as a matter of two divided communities within the North itself. Jonathan Bardon's *History of Ulster* (2001) captures something of the sectarian turmoil that ensued:

> On 31 March 1986 loyalist gangs petrol-bombed eleven Catholic homes in Lisburn; further attacks followed, particularly in Belfast on 6 and 8 April; and the RUC reported seventy-nine sectarian attacks by loyalists on Catholic homes and dozens of petrol-bombings of Catholic schools, shops, churches and businesses in less than a month, between 1 and 26 April 1986. The marching season brought a new wave of violence and on 14 July a loyalist gang, numbering around fifty and armed with hatchets and cudgels, attacked twenty Catholic houses in Rasharkin, a village between Ballymena and Ballymoney; the secretary of state described these attacks as some of the nastiest and most vicious throughout 'the emergency' … The number of violent deaths was rising again: 54 in 1985; 61 in 1986; and 93 in 1987.[118]

This escalation is reflected in the overt insistence with which Doherty prints sectarian dialogues across his phototexts from this period. Indeed, if the Anglo-Irish Agreement is understood as a stark reminder of the interiority of sectarianism's subversive effects – its ability to be displaced by a higher power – then one way of reading the fierce reaction the Agreement sparked is as a frantic and renewed attempt to place the North's sectarian codes in a more prominent position. With this in mind, the nature of sectarianism in Northern Ireland becomes more complex and contingent. While sectarian ideologies can undoubtedly be seen to inspire deplorable acts of physical violence, they can also be seen to betray a far more understandable anxiety about the North's uncertain political outlook. The textually laden and colourfully divisive tones in Doherty's early phototexts gesture towards this possibility. By working layers of détoured rhetoric into his images, Doherty illustrates how sectarianism is not only manifested through acts of violence but also located in fretful, communal, assertions that attempt to clarify the North's equivocal political climate. As a phototext like 'The Blue Skies of Ulster' suggests, at this particular time voluminous sectarian statements can provide a clear and comforting foothold within a landscape that is otherwise misted over in political confusion.

Contrast this with some of the final phototexts Doherty produced before changing his artistic medium in 1992. The triptych 'Native Disorders' (1991) concludes a genre of phototexts which, since 1987, had become more clinical and controlled in their application of text on to image (Plate 16). With 'Native Disorders', however, Doherty marks another change in this aesthetic. Most profoundly, as Graham has observed, these phototexts 'dispense with the gaze across the landscape and stare down'.[119] As such, Graham continues:

> the writing is less imposed on the image than in the work from the late 1980s – it is more as if the words have come from the elements photographed, as if a layer has been peeled off and these words found 'traced' on the land.[120]

The relationship between text and image in these later phototexts is less ambiguous and more intertwined. There is, now, almost an organic unity to the palimpsests Doherty creates, with the layers of text and image naturally bleeding into one another. At the same time, however, the sectarian energies Doherty had fastidiously recorded seem to disappear. Doherty's lens now 'stare[s] down', peering into an anonymous landscape upon which no divisive language is imposed. Rather than sectarianism, it is as if Doherty is now concerned with the raw, ectoplasmic language ('BARBARIC MIRE', 'WEEPING') which helped to make that language of difference so prominent in his early work.

Such aesthetic changes chime, once again, with a wider understanding of sectarianism at this historical juncture. In the early 1990s sectarian violence was still profound. By November 1991 the Ulster Volunteer Force and the Ulster Freedom Fighters had killed 39 people while, concomitantly, the IRA appeared more prepared than before to become involved in tit-for-tat killing.[121] Yet this was also a period marked by what Bardon terms 'a perceptible shift in attitude'.[122] Talks about talks were being condensed into actual dialogue, first between John Hume and Gerry Adams and then, more covertly, between the British government and the IRA.[123] Even the terms on which these discussions were conducted also changed. As Bardon notes, these talks now centred upon a 'growing recognition' that 'the relationship between the two communities within Northern Ireland must be addressed before the North–South relationship can be resolved'.[124] In contrast to the Anglo-Irish Agreement, then, the search for the elusive formula that might halt the Troubles was now based upon a 'growing recognition' of the ethnic dimensions within the North itself. At this time, an organisation such as the Cultural Traditions Group could seek to emphasise the ways in which communal identities might produce a sense of personal stability and security. As their chairman put it:

the Group's philosophy involves a general acceptance of the validity of all cultural traditions, the importance of tradition in the creation of a sense of identity, the importance of group identity as a means of self-fulfilment and to give a sense of security to the individual, that difference is not necessarily destructive or damaging, and can be positively enervating in society.[125]

Far from being superseded, the North's ethnic divisions were becoming a sustained source of attention. Doherty supplies a sense of these new parameters in the downward gaze and introspective title of 'Native Disorders'. Yet in the foundational language of these images ('PRIMITIVE LINES', 'UNTAMED FORMS') Doherty also captures something of that desire to interrogate the divisive energies which continued to flood these spaces.

In the post-conflict period, the perception of sectarianism again has altered. The Good Friday Agreement's paradoxical insistence that a divisive voting structure is maintained, while sectarian symbols are curtailed, has contributed to a political discourse in which, to return to Hadaway, the North's 'two diametrically opposed' traditions are drained of meaning, with only 'their outer shells' left intact.[126] Indeed, as if complicit with this new dispensation, a major aesthetic shift in Doherty's career – his decision to produce photographs devoid of text – can be seen to pivot around this issue. By shifting from phototexts to photographs, Doherty removes the specificities of language from the surface of his work. In these later pieces, Doherty steers his attention away from the complexities of the North's sectarian cleavages, and focuses, instead, upon the apparent incomprehensibility that marks their formation. Doherty's landscapes are now littered with incongruous objects that reduce the Northern Irish Troubles – its legacies and its after-effects – to a series of 'incidents': road blocks, charred vehicles, scraps of clothing (Plate 17). No longer acknowledging the nuances that underpin these ruins, Doherty standardises the North's sectarian conflict into a more general and generalised set of hazards. What had been a critical and constructive engagement with sectarian division hereby morphs into a more nebulous and abstract portraiture of dissidence and discontent.

It is not too fanciful to see the cultural logic of capitalism's late (or postmodern) formation at play in this transition. After all, by translating the fluid complexities of ethnic–national difference into a non-specific threat, Doherty goes some way to achieving what Jameson has described as capitalism's ability to create an 'equivalence' between 'change' and 'standardization' – a mobile fixity that flows homogeneously.[127] Unlike his early phototexts or even Seawright's *Sectarian Murder* series, Doherty's later works lack the raw specificity that helps us understand the psychogeography of sectarianism. At this point in his career,

fetishised objects come to mask the unique dynamics of the Troubles, rendering Northern Ireland a divided society equivalent to any other in this now
'peace-processed world'.[128] In certain respects, the Good Friday Agreement has
served to enshrine this standardisation through its insistence on a two-traditions
model which 'cordons off the people who constitute those communities', as
Graham writes, 'trapping them in arenas where they are no better understood,
though they may exist more quietly and more peacefully'.[129] However, the value
of 'watching' Doherty's and Seawright's earlier engagement with Northern
Ireland's sectarian space lies precisely in our ability to redirect the ennui of these
images towards Northern Ireland's more contemporary political constrictions.
After all, as Azoulay reminds us, 'the verb "to watch" entails dimensions of
time and movement that need to be reinscribed in the interpretation of the still
photographic image'.[130]

The temporal flexibility Azoulay offers our understanding of Seawright's
and Doherty's photography should not be underestimated. Aside from their
indebtedness to the New Topographics, the other traditional way in which their
work has been viewed is via what David Campany has famously called 'late
photography'. Images in this mode typically 'contain no people, but a lot of
remnants of activity', Campany writes. As his terminology suggests, it is a strand
of landscape photography characterised by the photographer's arrival after an
event takes place. The parallels with Doherty's and Seawright's aesthetic are
immediate, indeed Campany cites them both as two of 'the more interesting'
practitioners in this mode.[131] But to align Doherty and Seawright with this
aesthetic is also limiting. Campany's schema assumes a temporal sequence,
one in which the 'late' is determined by its relationship to an event that has
preceded. His insistence upon a timeline ensures that the photograph's meaning
cannot detach from the moment of its making: the point at which the camera
shutter falls. What is missed, therefore, is Azoualy's expanded ontology of the
photograph. While she advocates an unfixing of the image, Campany treats
the image as a foreclosed entity: a document whose meaning cannot transcend
the point of its production. Azoulay's desire to extend the camera's semantics
has considerable implications. Just as it is possible to detach the photograph
temporally, so we can also unfix the very content of the image. In the case of
Seawright and Doherty, this means a refiguring of the sectarianism they depict
in ways that help us apprehend rigidities within the post-Agreement context.
As I have been insisting throughout this book, the Troubles need not be viewed
as a set of discrete and self-enclosed events. Instead there is much to be gained
from viewing the Troubles as a conflict in which past and present are fused, as a
conflict in which we might, to evoke Walter Benjamin's arresting phrase, 'brush
history against the grain'.[132]

Faced with the political disenfranchisement induced by the Agreement, we would do well to remember the instabilities that underpin sectarianism's now sclerotised surface. Duncan's image of a Loyalist bonfire on Belfast's Shore Road had already gestured towards such a reassessment and, in the 'King George V Playing Fields' image from the same *Bonfires* series, Duncan reignites this potential (Plate 18). Once again this marker of Protestant identity is delicately wrought. Stripped of its obvious sectarian trappings, the bonfire's only identifiable features are carried by the paramilitary graffiti on the wall that guides us towards the centre of his image. These graffiti fade as they progress, but in their anxious presence they remind us of the ways in which expressions of identity are – to return to Hall – 'never complete' and 'always in process'.[133] Like the text in Doherty's 'The Blue Skies of Ulster', the graffiti in Duncan's image try nervously to delineate the North's anomalous spaces.

In opposition to this, the relative fixity of the bonfire suggests that these fluid and contingent undercurrents may no longer be accessible in this derelict terrain. The bonfire's tyres are static and deflated, and they collapse the complexity of community formation into a syntax of repetition – one that is redolent of that 'motionless monotony' Debord has theorised. Here, the bonfire's constituent parts converge around their inherent emptiness, the individual element and the collective structure becoming synonymous through their shared vacuity. Looking at this image 'we no longer find ourselves dealing with a mass/individual pair', as Deleuze would write in relation to his conception of 'control societies'.[134] In Duncan's photograph the terms are visually equated, echoing what Debord has called the 'collective isolation' of the capitalist spectacle.[135]

That Duncan's image should centre upon a communications tower is telling in this respect. As the next chapter will demonstrate, it is through the augmenting of these mobile technologies that Deleuze's conception of a control society is remorselessly realised within the North. Imposed from above, the structures of state surveillance have further helped capitalism in its desire to '*totally* coloniz[e] social life'. And yet, caught in the freeze frame of Duncan's photograph, the capitalist technology also appears to be vulnerable: posed almost as an effigy ready to be ignited by the sectarian structure that lies beneath. It is through such images that we are perhaps reminded of the deeper, psychogeographic potential hidden within these divisive structures. The bonfire's anonymity certainly embodies the paucity of Northern Ireland's current political climate. But in its appropriation of the tyres and pallets of industrial production, this sectarian assemblage also goes some way to reconfiguring the weapons by which the capitalist spectacle maintains its unceasing flows of construction and consumption. Buried within these symbols of hate and destruction, Duncan's image seems to say, there is a radical politics and a popular poetics that speak of capitalism's undoing. The shape such resistance must take in light of capitalism's expanding technologies and debilitating temporalities is a question I will now explore.

Notes and references

1   Joseph Liechty and Cecelia Clegg, *Moving Beyond Sectarianism: Religion, Conflict, and Reconciliation in Northern Ireland* (Dublin: The Columba Press, 2001), p. 103.

2   'Economic, Social and Cultural Issues', *The Agreement: Agreement Reached in the Multi-Party Negotiations* (Good Friday Agreement, 1998), Paras 4–5, www.gov.uk/government/uploads/system/uploads/attachment_data/file/13665 2/agreement.pdf.

3   Peter Geoghegan, *A Difficult Difference: Race, Religion and the New Northern Ireland* (Dublin: Irish Academic Press, 2010), pp. 12–13. Geoghegan is building upon John D. Brewer's classic 'working definition of sectarianism' as a 'boundary marker to represent social stratification and conflict' (John D. Brewer, 'Sectarianism and Racism, and Their Parallels and Differences', *Ethnic and Racial Studies*, 15.3 (3 July 1992), 358–359).

4   Liechty and Clegg, *Moving Beyond Sectarianism*, p. 102.

5   Pauline Hadaway, 'Introduction', in *Where Are the People? Contemporary Photographs of Belfast 2002–2010* ed. by Karen Downey (Belfast: Belfast Exposed Photography, 2010), p. 8.

6   Colin Graham, 'Archetypes of an Uncertain Future', in *Bonfires*, by John Duncan, with essays by Colin Graham and Mary Warner Marien (Belfast: Belfast Exposed Photography, 2008), n.p.

7   Colin Graham, *Northern Ireland: 30 Years of Photography* (Belfast: Belfast Exposed, 2013), p. 173.

8   *Ibid*, p. 173.

9   Guy Debord, *The Society of the Spectacle*, foreword by Martin Jenkins, trans. by Ken Knabb, 2nd edn (Eastbourne: Soul Bay Press, 2012), p. 32.

10   David Harvey, *Rebel Cities: From the Right to the City to the Urban Revolution* (London: Verso, 2012), p. 16.

11   Karen Downey and David Chandler, 'Preface', in *Bonfires*, n.p.

12   Conor McCabe, *The Double Transition: The Economic and Political Transition of Peace* (Belfast: Irish Congress of Trade Unions and Labour After Conflict, 2013), p. 18.

13   Graham, *30 Years of Photography*, p. 173.

14   *Ibid.*, pp. 17–18.

15   *Ibid.*, p. 43.

16   *Ibid.*, p. 47.

17   John Tagg, 'The Currency of the Photograph', in *Thinking Photography* ed. by Victor Burgin (London: Macmillan, 1982), p. 114.

18   Roland Barthes, *Image Music Text*, trans. by Stephen Heath (New York: The Noonday Press, 1977), p. 20.

1. Martin Parr, 'Titanic Belfast'. From the series *Welcome to Belfast* (2017). © Martin Parr/ Magnum Photos.

2. 'City Centre Approach, Road/Rail Link', *Craigavon New City: Second Report on the Plan* (Craigavon: Craigavon Development Commission, 1967). © Craigavon Museum Services.

3. 'Craigavon: Local Centre', *Craigavon New City: Second Report on the Plan* (Craigavon: Craigavon Development Commission, 1967). © Craigavon Museum Services.

4. 'Craigavon: City Centre Station', *Craigavon New City: Second Report on the Plan* (Craigavon: Craigavon Development Commission, 1967). © Craigavon Museum Services.

5. 'Craigavon: Main Path Circuit', *Craigavon New City: Second Report on the Plan* (Craigavon: Craigavon Development Commission, 1967). © Craigavon Museum Services.

6. Victor Sloan, 'City Centre (with Pony)'. Black-and-white photograph (1982). © Victor Sloan.

7. Victor Sloan, 'Craigavon Centre'. From the series *Moving Windows* (1985). Silver gelatin print, toner and gouache. 23.5cm × 23.5cm. © Victor Sloan.

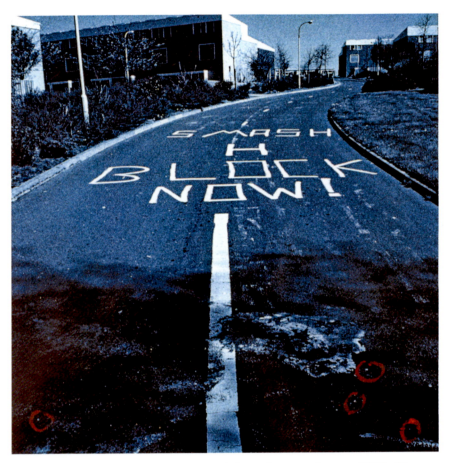

8. Victor Sloan, 'Road, Rathmore, Craigavon'. From the series *Craigavon* (1985). Silver gelatin print and toners. 26cm × 26cm. © Victor Sloan.

9. Victor Sloan, 'Moyraverty Community Centre, Craigavon II'. From the series *Vietnamese Boat People* (1984). Silver gelatin print, toner and watercolour. 24cm × 37.5cm. © Victor Sloan.

10. Victor Sloan, 'Vietnamese Boat People, Burnside, Craigavon'. From the series *Vietnamese Boat People* (1984). Silver gelatin print. © Victor Sloan.

11. John Duncan, 'Shore Road'. From the series *Bonfires* (2008). Framed C-type print. 100cm × 120cm. © Victor Sloan.

Friday 25th May 1973

'The murdered mans body was found lying at the Giants Ring
beauty spot, once used for pagan rituals. It has now become a
regular location for sectarian murder.'

12. Paul Seawright, 'Friday 25th May 1973'. From the series *Sectarian Murder* (1988). Framed C-type print with text. 75cm × 100cm. © Paul Seawright.

Friday 22nd September 1972

'The man left home to go to a bar for a drink, and never returned.
He was found the following morning dumped on waste ground behind
the Glencairn estate. He had been stabbed in the back and chest, and
his body showed signs of torture.'

13. Paul Seawright, 'Friday 22nd September 1972'. From the series *Sectarian Murder* (1988). Framed C-type print with text. 75cm × 100cm. © Paul Seawright.

14. Willie Doherty, 'God Has Not Failed Us (The Fountain, Derry)'. From the series *The Fountain Derry* (1990). Black-and-white photograph with text mounted on aluminium. 122cm × 183cm. © Willie Doherty.

WE SHALL NEVER FORSAKE THE BLUE SKIES OF ULSTER
FOR THE GREY MISTS OF AN IRISH REPUBLIC

15. Willie Doherty, 'The Blue Skies of Ulster' (1986). Black-and-white photograph with text. 152cm × 46cm. © Willie Doherty.

16. Willie Doherty, 'Native Disorders I' (1991). C-type photograph with text mounted on masonite. 114cm × 152cm. © Willie Doherty.

17. Willie Doherty, 'Border Incident' (1994). Cibachrome photograph. 122cm × 183cm. © Willie Doherty.

18. John Duncan, 'King George V Playing Fields'. From the series *Bonfires* (2008). Framed C-type print. 100cm × 120cm. © John Duncan.

19 Susan Sontag, *On Photography* (Harmondsworth: Allen Lane, 1978), p. 178.
20 Julian Stallabrass, 'Sebastiao Salgado and Fine Art Photojournalism', *New Left Review*, 223 (May–June 1997), 135.
21 Jessica Evans, 'Introduction', in *The Camerawork Essays: Context and Meaning in Photography* ed. by Jessica Evans (London: Rivers Oram, 1997), p. 16.
22 *Ibid.*, p. 30.
23 *Ibid.*, p. 32.
24 Ariella Azoulay, *The Civil Contract of Photography* (New York: Zone Books, 2008), pp. 12–14.
25 *Ibid.*, pp. 13–14.
26 Graham, *30 Years of Photography*, p. 16.
27 Graham, 'Archetypes of an Uncertain Future', n.p.
28 Azoulay, *The Civil Contract of Photography*, pp. 11–14.
29 *Ibid.*, p. 14.
30 Stallabrass, 'Sebastiao Salgado and Fine Art Photojournalism', 143.
31 Cited in Britt Salvesen, 'New Topographics', in *New Topographics* ed. by Britt Salvesen and Alison Nordström (New York: Eastman House, 2010), p. 9.
32 A notable exception is Sarah Tuck, *After the Agreement: Contemporary Photography in Northern Ireland* (London: Black Dog Publishing, 2015).
33 John Rohrbach, 'Introduction', in *Reframing the New Topographics* ed. by Greg Foster-Rice and John Rohrbach (Chicago: University of Chicago Press, 2010), p. xiv.
34 Wendy Cheng, '"New Topographics": Locating Epistemological Concerns in the American Landscape', *American Quarterly*, 63.1 (March 2011), 151.
35 'Declaration of Support', in *The Agreement*, Para. 2.
36 Allen Feldman, *Formations of Violence: The Narrative of the Body and Political Terror in Northern Ireland* (London: University of Chicago Press, 1991), p. 28.
37 Liechty and Clegg, *Moving Beyond Sectarianism*, p. 103.
38 Debord, *Society of the Spectacle*, pp. 29–30.
39 *Ibid.*, p. 38.
40 *Ibid.*, p. 38.
41 *Ibid.*, p. 115.
42 Karl Marx and Frederick Engels, *Manifesto of the Communist Party*, trans. by Samuel Moore (Moscow: Progress Publisher, 1967), p. 47.
43 R. Murray and F.W. Boal, 'The Social Ecology of Urban Violence', in *Social Problems and the City: Geographical Perspectives on the Northern Problem* ed. by D.T. Herbert and D.M. Smith (Oxford: Oxford University Press, 1979), p. 154.
44 Marx and Engels, *Manifesto of the Communist Party*, p. 47; Debord, *The Society of the Spectacle*, p. 114.
45 Mark Fisher, *Ghosts of My Life: Writings on Depression, Hauntology and Lost Futures* (Winchester: Zero Books, 2014), p. 31.
46 Debord, *Society of the Spectacle*, p. 114.
47 Eugénie Shinkle, 'Boredom, Repetition, Inertia: Contemporary Photography and the Aesthetics of the Banal', *Mosaic*, 37.4 (December 2004), 169.

48   *Ibid.*, 169.
49   Azoulay, *The Civil Contract of Society*, p. 14.
50   Shinkle, 'Boredom, Repetition, Inertia', 172.
51   Liam Kelly, *Thinking Long: Contemporary Art in the North of Ireland* (Kinsale: Gandon Editions, 1996), p. 28.
52   Azoulay, *The Civil Contract of Photography*, pp. 13–14.
53   Shinkle, 'Boredom, Repetition, Inertia', 168.
54   *Ibid.*, 168.
55   Richard Kirkland, 'The Spectacle of Terrorism in Northern Irish Culture', *Critical Survey*, 15.1 (2003), 81.
56   *Ibid.*, 85.
57   Brian McIlroy, *Shooting to Kill: Filmmaking and the 'Troubles' in Northern Ireland* (Richmond: Steveston Press, 2001), p. 129, quoting Danny Boyle on the BBC *Open Air* programme after *Elephant*'s broadcast.
58   Quoted in *Alan Clarke* ed. by Richard Kelly (London: Faber, 1998), p. 198.
59   Michael Walsh, 'Thinking the Unthinkable: Coming to Terms with Northern Ireland in the 1980s and 1990s', in *British Cinema, Past and Present* ed. by Justine Ashby and Andrew Higson (London: Routledge, 2000), p. 295.
60   Susie Linfield, *Cruel Radiance: Photography and Political Violence* (Chicago: University of Chicago Press, 2010), p. 164.
61   Azoulay, *The Civil Contract of Photography*, p. 14.
62   Quoted in Kelly, *Alan Clarke*, p. 197.
63   *Ibid.*, p. 199.
64   Quoted in Shinkle, 'Boredom, Repetition, Inertia', 176.
65   Shinkle, 'Boredom, Repetition, Inertia', 179.
66   Quoted in Shinkle, 'Boredom, Repetition, Inertia', 176.
67   Debord, *Society of the Spectacle*, p. 38.
68   For the late capitalist ideologies carried by this statement see Mark Fisher, *Capitalist Realism: Is There No Alternative* (Winchester: Zero Books, 2009).
69   Feldman, *Formations of Violence*, p. 28.
70   Debord, *Society of the Spectacle*, p. 38.
71   Gilles Deleuze and Félix Guattari, *Anti-Oedipus: Capitalism and Schizophrenia*, trans. by Robert Hurley et al. (Minneapolis: University of Minnesota Press, 2000), p. 140.
72   Val Williams, 'Circumstantial Evidence', in *Inside Information: Paul Seawright Photographs 1988–1995* by Paul Seawright (London: The Photographers' Gallery, 1995), n.p.
73   Kelly, *Thinking Long*, p. 28.
74   Williams, 'Circumstantial Evidence', n.p.
75   Declan Long reiterates this point when he describes Seawright as 'favouring self-consciously personal modes of response' (Declan Long, *Visual Art and the Conflict in Northern Ireland: Troubles Archive Essays* (Belfast: Arts Council of Northern Ireland, 2009), p. 21).
76   Henri Lefebvre, *The Production of Space*, trans. by Donald Nicholson-Smith (Oxford: Blackwell, 1991), p. 144.

77 Shinkle, 'Boredom, Repetition, Inertia', 81.

78 Guy Debord, 'Introduction to a Critique of Urban Geography', in *Situationist International Anthology* ed. by Ken Knabb (Berkeley: Bureau of Public Secrets, 1981), p. 5.

79 Guy Debord, 'Theory of the dérive', *Internationale Situationniste*, 2 www.bopsecrets.org/SI/2.derive.htm [accessed 24 July 2017].

80 Keith Bassett, 'Walking as an Aesthetic Practice and a Critical Tool: Some Psychogeographic Experiments', *Journal of Geography in Higher Education*, 28.3 (2004), 401.

81 Merlin Coverley, *Psychogeography* (Harpenden: Pocket Essentials, 2007), p. 13.

82 David Pinder, 'Old Paris Is No More: Geographies of Spectacle and Anti-Spectacle', *Antipode*, 32.4 (2000), 380.

83 Graham, *30 Years of Photography*, p. 87.

84 Coverley, *Psychogeography*, p. 84.

85 Debord, *Society of the Spectacle*, p. 38.

86 Kirkland, 'The Spectacle of Terrorism', 83. Danny Boyle recalls how it was intended that *Elephant* 'would only go out in England, Scotland and Wales' (Kelly, *Alan Clarke*, p. 195).

87 Debord, *Society of the Spectacle*, p. 117.

88 'More than planning is required', *Portadown Times*, 9 June 1967, p. 23.

89 Liam O'Dowd, 'Craigavon: Locality, Economy and the State in a Failed "New City"', in *Irish Urban Cultures* ed. by Chris Curtain, Hastings Donnan, and Thomas Wilson (Belfast: Institute of Irish Studies, 1993), p. 56.

90 Azoulay, *The Civil Contract of Photography*, p. 16.

91 *Ibid.*, pp. 13–14.

92 Lars Svendsen, *A Philosophy of Boredom*, trans. by John Irons (London: Reaktion Books, 2008), p. 31.

93 Fionna Barber, 'Ghost Stories: An Interview with Willie Doherty', *Visual Culture in Britain*, 10.2 (2004), 194.

94 Declan Long, 'Invisible Matter', in *Ghost Story: Willie Doherty* by Willie Doherty (Belfast: British Arts Council, 2007), p. 17.

95 Barber, 'Interview with Willie Doherty', p. 190.

96 Maite Lorés, 'The Streets Were Dark with Something More than Night: Film Noir Elements in the Work of Willie Doherty', in *Willie Doherty: Dark Stains* by Willie Doherty (San Sebastián: Kulturunea, 1999), p. 112.

97 Raphael Samuel, *Theatres of Memory: Past and Present in Contemporary Culture* (London: Verso, 2012), p. 365.

98 Declan Long, 'One Place Twice', in *Willie Doherty: Photo/Text/85/92* by Willie Doherty (London: Matt's Gallery, 2012), p. 6.

99 Shinkle, 'Boredom, Repetition, Inertia', 179.

100 Charles Taylor, 'The Politics of Recognition', in *Multiculturalism: Examining the Politics of Recognition* ed. by Amy Gutmann (Princeton: Princeton University Press, 1994), p. 25.

101   Feldman, *Formations of Violence*, p. 31.

102   Rohrbach, 'Introduction', p. xiv.

103   Adrian Little, *Democracy and Northern Ireland: Beyond the Liberal Paradigm?* (Basingstoke: Palgrave Macmillan, 2004), p. 28.

104   Annette Iggulden, 'Women's Silence: In the Space of Words and Images' (unpublished doctoral thesis, Deakin University, 2002), p. 5.

105   Alexander Alberro, 'Picturing Relations: Images, Text, and Social Engagement', in *Barbara Kruger* ed. by Alexander Alberro, Martha Gever, Miwon Kwon and Carol Squires (New York: Rizzoli, 2010), p. 196, quoting Barthes, *Image Music Text*, p. 26.

106   Barthes, *Image Music Text*, p. 27.

107   *Ibid.*, p. 26.

108   Alberro, 'Picturing Relations: Images, Text, and Social Engagement', p. 196.

109   Azoulay, *The Civil Contract of Photography*, p. 13.

110   Shinkle, 'Boredom, Repetition, Inertia', 181.

111   Graham, 'Motionless Monotony: New Nowheres in Irish Photography', *In/Print*, 1 (2012), 14.

112   Pinder, 'Geographies of Spectacle and Anti-Spectacle', p. 368.

113   Neil Charles Mulholland, 'Why Is There Only One Monopolies Commission? British Art and Its Critics in the Late 1970s' (unpublished doctoral thesis, University of Glasgow, 1998), p. 76.

114   Long, 'One Place Twice', p. 6.

115   Liechty and Clegg, *Moving Beyond Sectarianism*, p. 103.

116   Stuart Hall, 'Cultural Identity and Diaspora', in *Identity: Community, Culture, Difference* ed. by Jonathan Rutherford (London: Lawrence and Wishart, 1990), p. 222.

117   Alan Morton, 'Anglo-Irish Agreement – Description of Contents' http://cain.ulst.ac.uk/events/aia/describe.htm [accessed 24 July 2017].

118   Jonathan Bardon, *A History of Ulster* (Belfast: Blackstaff Press, 2001), p. 770.

119   Graham, 'Inscription / Trace', in *Willie Doherty: Disturbance* by Willie Doherty (Dublin: The Hugh Lane Gallery, 2011), p. 12.

120   *Ibid.*, pp. 12–13.

121   Bardon, *A History of Ulster*, p. 812.

122   *Ibid.*, p. 830.

123   G.K. Peatling, *The Failure of the Northern Ireland Peace Process* (Dublin: Irish Academic Press, 2004), p. 57.

124   Bardon, *A History of Ulster*, p. 828, quoting Padraig O'Malley, *Northern Ireland: Questions of Nuance* (Belfast: Blackstaff Press, 1990), p. 100.

125   Maurice Hayes, *Whither Cultural Diversity?* (Belfast: Community Relations Council, 1993), p. 9.

126   Hadaway, 'Introduction', p. 8.

127   Fredric Jameson, *The Seeds of Time* (New York: Columbia University Press, 1994), p. 15.

128   Malachi O'Doherty, 'Peace process piffle makes me want to hit out', *Belfast Telegraph*,

1 August 2012 www.belfasttelegraph.co.uk/opinion/news-analysis/peace-process-piffle-makes-me-want-to-hit-out-16191837.html [accessed 24 July 2017].

129   Colin Graham, '"Let's Get Killed": Culture and Peace in Northern Ireland', in *Irish Postmodernisms and Popular Culture* ed. by Wanda Balzano, Anne Mulhall and Moynagh Sullivan (Basingstoke: Palgrave Macmillan, 2007), p. 173.

130   Azoulay, *The Civil Contract of Photography*, p. 14.

131   David Campany, 'Saftey in Numbness: Some Remarks on the Problems of "Late Photography"' (2003) http://davidcampany.com/safety-in-numbness/ [accessed 24 July 2017].

132   Walter Benjamin, 'Theses on the Philosophy of History', in *Illuminations* ed. by Hannah Arendt, trans. by Harry Zohn (London: Fontana Press, 1992), p. 248.

133   Hall, 'Cultural Identity and Diaspora', p. 222.

134   Gilles Deleuze, 'Postscript on the Societies of Control', *October*, 59 (Winter 1992), 5.

135   Debord, *Society of the Spectacle*, p. 115.

4

Monotony and control: rereading internment

We glint like metal fish
Trapped beneath a sieve of light
Scales and fins moulded in one die.
Custodians of silver and gold,
Believe the noble lie:

When you made my hands, you shaped
Them with barbed wire. The flesh
Congealed beneath the twisted net –
Head-line, heart-line, fate-line,
The eradicable scars.

(Ciaran Carson, 'The Maze')[1]

The introduction of internment during the Northern Irish Troubles can provide a unique insight into the evolution of capitalist control. A security measure which aimed to detain – without trial – established figures and new recruits within the North's militant Republican communities, internment proved both tragic and misguided in its effects. For Jonathan Bardon internment was nothing more than 'a major blunder',[2] for Paul Bew and Gordon Gillespie it was a 'gamble' which 'visibly failed'.[3] Its introduction on 9 August 1971 created widespread rioting and a renewed campaign of violence that would prove to be as bad as anything since the outbreak of the Troubles. 'Army like ants, bombs thudded all night', as Medbh McGuckian remembers it.[4] By October there had been over a hundred explosions in Belfast, with 2,100 families forced to move.[5] For many, internment had been expected to 'get on top of the gunmen', yet, as these results suggest, it struggled to contain even a minority of the Provisional IRA. Ultimately, as J.B. Bell has noted with some precision, 'internment did not crush the Provos but unleashed them'.[6]

Inside the internment camps, conditions were equally chaotic. Initially containing more Republican sympathisers than actual 'gunmen', these compounds not only failed to secure the long-term detention of wanted paramilitaries, they also created what Mary Corcoran has termed a 'revolving door of arrest, interrogation and release'.[7] Indeed, it was the brutality of this process – the mal-treatment of internees during arrest and the experiments in sensory deprivation during interrogation – for which internment is best remembered and was most vehemently opposed. The detention centres became a symbol of British brutality and, more than that, they were tinged with the spectre of genocidal persecution. Internment had been unilateral in its targeting of Catholics, and Long Kesh, the largest of the compounds, was frequently recast as a 'concentration camp' by anti-internment literature. These wartime resonances – 'machine-gun posts define a real stockade' as Heaney so memorably described Long Kesh – were an embarrassment for the British government.[8] The very existence of internment camps appeared to confirm that the Troubles was, indeed, a war. As if acknowl-edging the need for a penal – rather than military – architecture, Long Kesh was renamed HM Prison Maze in 1972.

There are other ways of looking at internment, however. In Ciaran Carson's 1974 poem 'The Maze', labyrinthine imagery is yoked to internment's material reality. Through this, he conjures, in turn, a more fluid and permeable sense of the detainment that forms his poetic subject. Carson engages with the military architecture of Long Kesh and, in so doing, presents this form of incarceration as plastic and malleable. The camp's 'barbed wire' perimeters become expansive in their ability to ensnare different generations, while the general experience of entrapment becomes a 'fate-line' 'we' all seem to share. In this way, Carson's poem presents internment as an intentionally porous project. It is a system of detainment best symbolised through the image of a 'sieve' – a structure of enclosure that looks out as much as in. The 'noble lie' of wartime valour is still present in this poem, but Carson is keen to illustrate how this context has been 'twisted' out of shape. Like the material symbols of internment, its social consequences have also been altered, becoming part of that larger 'maze' or 'net' from which it is seemingly impossible to escape.

The value of Carson's poem, then, stems from its ability to position intern-ment as being on the cusp of change: an operation caught between an archi-tecture of detention and a system of coercion. In fact, in its image of a 'sieve', 'The Maze' anticipates – in strikingly similar terms – the ways in which Gilles Deleuze would come to read society's transition away from sites of discipline and towards systems of control. For Deleuze, techniques of social control could supersede the self-contained particularity of disciplinary enclosures so as to create a structure that was 'like a self-deforming cast that will continuously change from one moment to the other, or like a *sieve* whose mesh will transmute from point to point'.[9] As with Carson's poem, in a society of control, sites of detention can come to lose all sense of their temporal and spatial specificity. Disciplinary logics now combine so as to modulate continuously across society, leaving little opportunity for us to hide. Just as, in Carson's poem, 'we' are 'trapped' and 'moulded in one die', so, for Deleuze, we are permanently ensnared in an overarching circuit of control. For Deleuze this change is comparable to the fact that in late capitalist societies 'the corporation has replaced the factory', and because, in Deleuze's terms, 'the corporation is a spirit, a gas' – an entity that is able to expand continuously, without impediment.[10] This is not to say that disciplinary structures are no longer present. Rather it is to acknowledge that their social functions have now come to transcend their physical limits. As Michael Hardt and Antonio Negri have written in relation to Deleuze's work, in the society of control one can be a 'factory worker outside the factory, student outside school, inmate outside prison'.[11]

This context is important because it suggests that the standard narrative surrounding internment's introduction needs questioning. To develop the implications of Carson's aquatic imagery, internment was an operation that had been expected 'to separate the IRA "fish" from the "water" of the Catholic community'.[12] However, to reach this conclusion is to consider internment as a project striving solely for containment and not one also working towards control. Considered as a form of control – an omniscient 'sieve of light' as Carson puts it – the introduction of internment begins to cast a very different shadow. The operation's 'revolving door' of arrests and releases hints, for example, at the 'short term and rapid rates of turnover' that Deleuze will come to identify as an integral part of a control society's capitalist foundations.[13] But it also speaks to the porous nature of internment during the Troubles: its status as a mode of confinement that operated synchronically with events beyond its parameters. Such a view chimes with internment's historical origins, where the camps were never actually considered self-contained sites. Conceived in colonial Cuba in 1896, internment was designed to 'concentrate' civilians while Spanish troops escalated their military manoeuvres against rebel forces elsewhere.[14] Internment began, in other words, as a crude means by which violence could be intensified rather than subdued; its existence within an increasingly violent landscape being evidence of its very purpose rather than its failure.

Understood in these terms, the violence that followed the introduction of internment in 1971 did indeed connote an older system of concentration, but its significance derives from more than historical repetition. Rather, as Carson's poem has suggested, it is because of the way in which this older system of discipline was adapted during the Troubles that the policy of internment is worth revisiting. In its appetite for data and its dependency on new capitalist temporalities, internment transformed Northern Irish society and, as David Lloyd has suggested, helped to 'create a new apparatus of biopolitical power'.[15] Viewed as animating new technologies of control, it is possible to reorientate internment so that it no longer speaks solely of failure, but can also teach us about the complex ways in which capitalism has intersected with the Northern Irish Troubles. The monotony I refer to is a specific by-product of this exchange. By paying attention to its various manifestations, it is possible to trace the emergence of new forms of control as well as alternative modes of community and resistance.

Internment was a symbol of crude brutality, Catholic oppression and mis-guided security. But it also spoke of the successful extension of control, a widespread attempt at surveillance and the stupefaction that could be induced by distorted temporalities. It was an operation which transformed the appearance of traditional temporal co-ordinates, creating something close to what Jonathan Crary has termed '24/7 homogeneity' – a timescape in which all significance and legibility is effaced by 'monotonous indistinction'.[16] The security forces in Northern Ireland were quite conscious of imposing this monotony upon Nationalist communities, but they were also encouraged to do so by resistance from below: the introduction of internment also triggered concerted com-munal opposition. As women were not initially arrested they often organised themselves in opposition to internment's systems. Yet, the more they rebelled against these structures, the more vulnerable they became to the forces of control. By 1973 they were also being lifted.

The monotony of internment was one that gained its strength through the constant denial of variety. It robbed individuals of the opportunity to create their own temporal rhythms and so induced, as Crary has said of 24/7 societies, a state 'of neutralisation and inactivation, in which one is dispossessed'.[17] Through its experiments in sensory deprivation, internment became the product of an unbounded appetite – one that extended beyond the visible and penetrated the dark recesses of an internal conscience. In this, internment revealed something of the way in which its models of control would follow the dominant logic of capitalism. Just as Marx has compared capitalism's insatiable thirst for twenty-four-hour production to that of a vampire which 'lives the more, the more labour it sucks', so during internment the boredom created was one which was strengthened, parasitically, the more temporality it could efface.[18] In both cases the conclusions could be fatal. For Marx the point of completion would be 'the premature exhaustion and death of this labour-power',[19] while for Deleuze it was the construction of 'dividuals': an impersonal identity compiled from 'masses, samples, data, markets, or "banks"'.[20] Internment would be phased out in 1975, but the impetus it gave to this digitisation of society has seen its effects extend well beyond that date.

An act of cultural and historical retrieval that takes monotony as its point of departure is complicated, however, by the fact that in addition to its figuration in the discourses of control, boredom has also played a different role in the narratives of those who were actually interned. The absence of a prison term has made internment notorious for its expanding sensations of vacuity, empty-time or *langeweile* (longer whiles) to draw on Martin Heidegger's conception of ennui.[21] In 1919 this became the source of a neurasthenic condition known as 'barbed-wire disease' and, as a result, it has often encouraged a mode of life-writing that tries to circumvent such afflictions.[22] As S.A. Kinnier Wilson has noted, much of the writing about life behind the wire tends to prioritise 'the amusing trifles of camp life and their power to detract materially from the searing and depressing monotony of camp existence'.[23] The example of internment in Northern Ireland differs little in this respect. 'Prison is meant to depress, to demoralise, to drain you of stamina and confidence and conviction' wrote Danny Morrison of his time in Long Kesh and, in a bid to avoid such 'defeatism',[24] the journals of those interned during the Troubles are frequently driven by a sense of what Gerry Adams calls the 'happy, funny, enjoyable people who made the best of their predicament'.[25] In such cases, the monotony of internment either undergoes a deliberate act of distortion or is consciously erased from the material history of the prisoners' account.

Any new attempt to reread the effects of internment has to negotiate the narratives of these long-term internees. Their writing has proved integral to the biography of the Republican movement and has helped to illustrate how those detained were able to undermine, in Lachlan Whalen's phrase, 'the success of Long Kesh as a disciplinary machine'.[26] For those detained, camps like Long Kesh came to function as a 'university of revolution' – a space within which paramilitary structures were rethought and radical politics emerged – and it is in these accounts that the disruptive agency of the prisoners can best be perceived. Yet, in documenting their subversive behaviour, these narratives have also added to the aura of internment's failure without accounting for the newer mechanics it sought to achieve. Emphasis needs to be shifted towards the military imperatives behind the operation: its new models of counter-insurgency and their impact upon future military initiatives in the North. Rather than in the classic texts of internment – Adams's *Cage Eleven* (1990) or Morrison's *West Belfast* (1989) – it is through more marginal accounts – John McGuffin's *The Guineapigs* (1974), Seamus Deane's *Gradual Wars* (1972) and Mary Beckett's *Give Them Stones* (1987) – that internment can be effectively reread.

The role of literature should not be underestimated in this respect. Indeed, Deleuze's essay places literature, in the form of Franz Kafka's *The Trial*, at 'the pivotal point' in his explanation of society's transition from disciplinary to control.[27] As Carson's poem has also demonstrated, when it comes to rereading internment we must take seriously literature's ability to elucidate Deleuze's thinking. To put this another way, the emergence of control societies 'must be examined', to use Seb Franklin's terms, 'through both the development of computation and the tracing of this logic within non-computational [literary] culture'.[28] Carson's compressed lexical and metrical form suggested that literature would be particularly alive to this task. But in the ambiguities of his poem, he indicated that this writing would also be both elusive and obscure. In what follows, then, it is often through compact literary qualities – through compressed syntax, allegories and metaphor – that we ascertain a clearer picture of how internment operated with a digital logic, how it was a regime of monotony and control.

Arguably, before internment was introduced in 1971, there was no such thing as a society of control in Northern Ireland. Since 1922 there had always been a Special Powers Act, which enabled internment to be introduced on three previous occasions (1922–1924, 1938–1945 and 1956–1961).[29] But these operations were introverted and consciously detached from the rest of Northern Irish society. Certainly they were far from the revolving door of arrest and release instigated by internment in the 1970s, and they were nothing compared to what we might understand a society of control to mean today. Now, it is possible to consider Northern Ireland as controlled in diverse ways – through the layered analysis of governmental data; through qualitative research into family expenditure and lifestyle statistics; through the mass surveillance programmes of Britain's GCHQ – yet, before internment was introduced in 1971, such a variegated network of social control was difficult to countenance, whether considered physically or imaginatively. Instead, at the start of the Troubles the model for controlling Northern Ireland depended upon what Brigadier Frank Kitson called 'the handling of information'.[30]

Writing of social control from the perspective of counter-insurgency, Kitson was conscious of the fact that militant populations could be contained only through good intelligence, and that such information currently came in ineffective forms, if, in fact, it came at all. The reasons for such paucity were complex but, as Kitson acknowledged, they were

inherent in the way in which intelligence organizations work, collecting information as they do by operating informers and agents, or by interrogating prisoners to mention only a few of their methods. Information collected in this way is immensely valuable for providing data on which policy can be worked out, and it forms the background to operational planning. But only occasionally can it be used to put troops directly into contact with the enemy because material about enemy locations and intention is usually out of date before it can be acted upon by the soldiers.[31]

While the intelligence services were not always able to churn raw data into a profitable shape, Kitson's study argues that this could, and should, be possible were the Army to adapt devices and techniques that had been 'designed for industry or commerce'.[32] The point is not that there were no mechanisms through which Northern Irish society could be controlled. Rather the issue is that these devices were not currently in use and that – up to 1971 at least – there was no real sense as to how such a broad spectrum of 'contact information' could be extracted at speed.

The prospect of social control was, then, not without its structural difficulties. Even if this system of mass surveillance could be created, there was always a danger that it might create more confusion than control. As Guy Debord would comment, just prior to Deleuze's discussion of control:

> Surveillance would be much more dangerous had it not been pushed along the path of absolute control of everyone, to the point where it encounters difficulties created by its own progress. There is a contradiction between the mass of information collected on a growing number of individuals, and the time and intelligence available to analyse it.[33]

It is partly for this reason that Deleuze emphasises how the society of control connects to broader changes within the capitalist world system, specifically the shift from an industrial to a service-based economy. Where the factory requires fixed sites and prolonged periods for production, Deleuze's corporation has the pace and energy to congeal around disparate locations and varying amounts of information. Hence, for Deleuze, 'control is short term and of rapid rates of turnover, but also continuous and without limit, while discipline was of long duration, infinite and discontinuous'.[34]

In the context of Northern Ireland, this model of capitalist control gains further definition through the spectre of ethnic–national violence. Internment was introduced in response to a rising tide of violence and so – instead of creating what Debord terms 'an absolute control of everybody' – it was an operation that focused on an exclusive facet of society, those individuals Kitson would call 'the enemy'. In practice this meant that internment repressed, almost exclusively, the North's Nationalist population. It was not, for instance, until 1973 that the first Loyalists were lifted and, by the time internment was finally phased out in 1975, a total of 107 Protestants had been interned as compared to 1,874 Catholics.[35] The state may not desire such overt discrimination – the RUC warned that 'unilateral action against republicans would be indefensible' – but its presence did allow the coercive dynamics of social control to become more concentrated and thus more effectively deployed.[36]

It is with an awareness of these conditions that the story of internment's turbulent introduction can be reconstructed. Since 1969 the RUC had been withdrawn

from Nationalist areas, restricting the supply of fresh information about organisations like the IRA. The Army, meanwhile, 'had found it hard to set up an intelligence network' and, on middle-grade issues – operational personnel, bombing
targets – they were virtually 'poverty-stricken'.[37] At the start of the 1970s, recalls
Colonel Robin Evelegh, 'the security forces were not permitted access to the
population census or to such aids to surveillance as driving licences, or to security
records'.[38] The need for this 'contact information' became clear when 1,800
troops raided Nationalist houses in the early hours of 23 July 1971. Before internment could be properly enacted, a list of possible detainees was needed, and
through these raids it was hoped the internment working party could gather
enough material to, in the words of one officer, 'put flesh on the skeleton'.[39]

This was to be internment's dry-run, but, rather than internees, the targets
were documents. As the *Sunday Times* reported:

> Provisionals and Officials were wary of keeping documents about their own activities;
> but each kept excellent files on the other. These, according to military sources, the
> dawn raids picked up. By the beginning of August, after more raids, the working party
> reckoned its list was complete.[40]

What is striking about this list, however, is the degree to which it was aug-
mented. It had over four hundred names on it and, as the *Sunday Times* calculated:

> No more than 120–130 were 'gunmen' … The other 300–350 were 'sympathizers'
> … But, in turn, this blanket term 'sympathizer' concealed enormous variation. At
> one extreme were those who had actively helped the 'gunmen' group: sheltered
> them, stole cars for them, and the like. In the middle were a group who were
> 'too close for comfort': the speechmakers, the propagandists, the radical grassroots
> activists … And then there was the police contribution: a motley group, 150 or
> more, whose interest was solely that they had been interned before – and thus were
> of 'proven' Republican sympathies.[41]

Sympathiser was indeed a broad category, but its inclusion betrayed a deeper
desire for fresh data. Alongside IRA members, those in contact with them
might also possess that live information which could otherwise go, in Kitson's
phrase, 'out of date before it can be acted upon'. According to Kitson's study,
in increasingly subversive campaigns, 'a lot of low grade information is more use
tactically than a small amount of high grade material'.[42] Deploying internment
on such a wide scale was, then, an obvious way of garnering a large number of
these 'low grade' sources, and, when the operation was introduced on 9 August
1971, listed amongst the arrests were 'retired republicans, trade unionists, civil
rights campaigners, a drunken man picked up at a bus stop and several people
held on mistaken identity'.[43]

This was Kitson's desire for rapid 'contact information' writ large and, although he opposed internment, the Brigadier was soon connected with the operation. In Republican propaganda internment was deemed another Kitsonesque experiment, conjuring his background in colonial counter-insurgency campaigns. 'Round the world the truth will echo / Cromwell's men are here again', states Paddy McGuigan in his 1971 song about the operation.[44] Yet, as McGuigan's image of a globalised transmission of truth suggests, if this was an older form of colonial control, it was one studded with the trappings of modernity. The lifting was haphazard at best and it required new technologies to impose a degree of order. Rubber bullets – created specifically for the Northern Irish conflict – were used on a large scale during the violence that followed the swoops.[45] Hand-held civilian Pye Pocketphones were also deployed which, unlike the military's conventional Larkspur A41 radios, operated on an Ultra High Frequency that was not restricted in built-up, urban areas.[46] The introduction of internment proved so chaotic that, less than a day into the operation, the RUC set up a 24-hour counter-rumour phone-line – a service that carried with it all the banalities of an emergent post-industrial economy.[47]

If internment before the Troubles was best measured in years, then this late-capitalist manifestation was one that tended to operate in hours. It is in this guise that the boredom of Deleuzian control appears at its most pronounced. Part of the project's speed can be gleaned from the number of initial arrests and releases in themselves. 'Of the 342 [first] arrested', notes the British government's 1972 Diplock Report, '116 were released within 48 hours'.[48] By 10 November, 1971, '508 had been released' from a total of 980 arrests.[49] This was not an exercise in detainment so much as an operation run with rapid rates of turnover. And, as the November figures testify, it functioned on a scale that could be extended and made continuous. To return to Deleuze's formulation, it was a case of control being, 'short term … and without limit'.

In some of the holding centres, those arrested were tasked with exercises that replicated this model on a micro scale. As Brian Turley, one of those first lifted, recalls in McGuffin's *The Guineapigs*:

> We arrived at between 8 a.m. and 9 a.m. in the camp. We were forced to sit with our feet against the wall, our hands behind our heads, and look at the ceiling for approximately fifteen minutes at a time. This and various other 'exercises' went well into Tuesday morning, approximately 3 a.m. we were allowed to lie on the floor for two hours without any covering of any kind.[50]

Temporal vectors were distorted through a series of 'exercises' which, in addition to those Turley describes, included press-ups, running on the spot and walking in circles while micturating. These continued 'at half-hour intervals all during the night', notes Turley, and if they were refused, the 'exercises' were forcefully imposed.[51] Officially, these drills 'were devised to counteract the cold' but, as even the British government conceded, what was conceived as 'a system of voluntary changes of position at set times' became 'a form of physical drill compulsorily performed' and 'thoughtlessly prolonged'.[52] In this totality, time became a repressive agent, its rhythms effaced by a recurrent, oppressive, monotony from which there was seemingly no release. The exercises created brief repeatable chunks of intense 24/7 control and, although their effect varied, they left those detained confused and constrained. 'Tuesday brought the same routine. Every position was a torture to me', wrote Sean McKenna in his account for *The Guineapigs*, 'time is hard to remember'.[53] When Crary describes 24/7 control as having the power to induce a state 'of neutralisation and inactivation, in which one is dispossessed', it is in situations like these that his argument is of particular relevance.

For twelve of those first detained this experience was taken to new extremes. As Paddy Hillyard notes, 'internment provided the first opportunity for interrogation in depth to be used by the army' and, across a period of eight days, this small group of internees were subjected to 'a selection of techniques based upon the psychology of sensory deprivation'.[54] According to the British government's Parker Report, this consisted of 'wall standing, hooding, noise, bread and water diet and deprivation of sleep'.[55] While these were, in Alfred McCoy's phrase, 'simple, even banal procedures', they were simultaneously enacted and viciously maintained.[56] Subjected to all five of these techniques for periods of up to sixteen hours at a time, the internees would be beaten if they decided to resist and repositioned if they happened to collapse from exhaustion. 'On numerous occasions I fell flat', Micky Donnelly tells us, 'when this occurred I was lifted and feeling was beaten back into my arms and hands and I was put back into my original position'.[57] The casual violence behind these techniques reveals something of their roots in the interrogational practices of earlier colonial campaigns.[58] But their manifestation in 1971 was also indebted to developments in psychology. Research into the 'monotonous conditions [that] exist in civilian occupations' had provided an insight into possible models for sensory deprivation and, in another example of the military's co-option of civilian expertise, the techniques used during internment's deep interrogations actively drew upon their findings.[59] As Tim Shallice has recognised, 'the Ulster methods are those produced by the conscious use of available scientific knowledge, for an attempt was clearly being made to reduce the change in sensory input – a scientific abstraction – to its practical limit'.[60]

The effect of this form of sensory deprivation was as intricate as it was depraved; suffice it to say it created what psychological research has termed a state of 'emotional exhaustion', with subjects becoming 'dull and listless' and clouded by a feeling of 'indifference and apathy'.[61] This was an intense, concentrated form of control in which time was distorted in the most debilitating of ways. As Patrick Shivers states in his staccato account of the procedure, the wall standing

> must have gone on for two or three days; I lost track of time. No sleep. No food. Knew I had gone unconscious several times, but did not know for how long. One time I thought or imagined I had died.[62]

In its extreme and imposed linearity, time enveloped the detainees with an inescapable and exhausting sense of monotony. The form of Shivers's account is telling – the stunted syntax reduces his experience into a binary algebra: an on/off, yes/no, processing of what occurred. 'I lay there for a long while. Can't recall. Then taken out.'[63] There is a tentative alignment between computational and non-computational systems in such writing, with the fluid experience of reality compressed into an almost static signal. Indeed, as the French collective Tiqqun have argued, under the auspices of capitalist control 'each person [is] to become *a fleshless envelope*, the best possible conductor of social communication, the locus of an infinite feedback loop which is made to have no nodes'.[64]

This was the society of control at its most oppressive, the point at which capitalism's 'dividualising' – vampire thirst – for monotony attained a degree of satisfaction. In fact, it was precisely because of its play with capitalist modalities that sensory deprivation can be understood as such a powerful mode of torture. In the critical and creative work of Seamus Deane, for example, the parallels between sensory deprivation and consumer capitalism are striking and entrenched. Both are shown to nullify individuality and suppress temporal variety, and through this comparison Deane illustrates something of the forceful logic with which sensory deprivation could operate. In an article from 1975, Deane states the case accordingly:

> Nothing disorientates a culture more than the loss of its self-awareness, which has to in the nature of things be its relationship to time. Just as an individual can be stupefied by having his sense of time destroyed by techniques of torture (like those practiced in Northern Ireland by the British Army), so too can a whole culture. And modern America demonstrates how seductively time can be replaced by pleasure. Technology increased the forms of pleasure almost to infinity, and the citizen becomes merely a consumer.[65]

The twin concepts of citizen and consumer – self-awareness and stupefaction – are crucial here, and not just for Deane. In their pairing they illustrate how boredom can be the result of an imposition upon a site of difference, a clash between above and below which, as I have previously suggested, is so often muffled in philosophical discussions of ennui.

The politics of this boredom stems, then, from its collective formation – the fact that it impacts an entire population or, as Deane puts it, 'a whole culture'. Such a view is in keeping with Deane's more recent pronouncements about capitalism where, like Crary, he is conscious of its desire for monotony. As Deane writes in his 1997 study of nationhood and modernity, 'it is Capital that presides over the world of boredom' and capital that ensures 'all exceptionalism, all variety, is replaced by sameness'.[66] That sensory deprivation replicates this suppressive force not only illustrates the strength of these techniques but also conveys the extent to which these psychological effects are also indebted more generally to the experience of late capitalism. Both strive towards similar ends – the flattening of difference and the repression of resistance – and both achieve this via similar means: through an experience of monotony and control.

In Deane's first poetry collection, *Gradual Wars*, he emphasises how this intricate, sometimes tense relationship between capitalism and sensory deprivation was integral to internment's success as a data-gathering operation. Published a year after internment was introduced, *Gradual Wars* is riven with anxieties about how the conflict has started to impinge upon personal freedoms. The result, as Robert Tracy has commented, is a collection that suggests 'the impossibility of keeping private life inviolate'.[67] Tellingly, however, Deane communicates much of this violation through details synonymous with the operation, namely temporal distortion, spatial entrapment and the technologies of surveillance. While there is a certain obscurity to much of the poetry in *Gradual Wars* – a sense that 'Deane was struggling with his reactions to the conflict' as Seán Lucy expresses it – in the poems that deal with internment, Deane's verse finds a degree of coherence, particularly as it tries to communicate the disturbances created by this search for data.

The opening of elegy 'Twelve' at the start of *Gradual Wars* is a good example of this process:

The light gibbets the mirrors,
The moon watches the moulded
Clouds like an eye.
The mouth of the phone gazes,
The door handle is not moving,
The crypts of water sigh.

Cancel the light, hood the mirrors,
Let the birds of fright fly,

Minervae of the gloom
Before the unilateral moon
Nightingales the listening rooms
Where unhooked phones lie.[68]

This is a space cast in a chiaroscuro of observation and entrapment. A panoptic moon 'watches' a fixed domain of 'moulded clouds' and static 'door / handles', while the spectre of internment is suggested by both the 'hood' and 'gibbets'. These terms are connotative of both the gallows' bodily constraint and the hooded men who underwent deep interrogation. Twelve internees were subjected to this treatment, making the elegy's title ('Twelve') weigh heavy with significance. But the elegiac status is also important because it couples the experience of sensory deprivation with that of death ('crypts'): the ultimate site of lost agency and absolute submission. Running against this, though, are images of release. The 'phones' in this poem lie 'unhooked' and 'gaze' through a 'mouth' that conceals ideas of interrogation – of making a subject speak – with the penetrative possibilities of this technology. This poem might depict a 'room' of desolation, but it does so at the behest of a surveillance that seeks to transcend spatial restraint. In this, Deane neatly anticipates Lloyd's assertion that during internment 'the subject's speech, extracted by the infliction of corporal pain, was the path to the psychic and physical control of the population'.[69]

In *Gradual Wars* the flattening of temporal difference through torture – envisaged in one poem as a process in which 'the hours opened and closed / like a lock' – is a topic that pushes Deane's verse into chaotic, dreamlike imaginings of a stupefied subconscious.[70] The poem 'Overdose', for example, equates an experience of sensory deprivation with that of a hallucination. Here, the descent into nightmarish vision provides a surreal opportunity for release, similar to what the victims of sensory deprivation have described:

The bulb is swinging and dummy waves
Go up and down on the wall.
He leans back like an oarsman
To sing himself down
The long stream of nightfall
To the darkness he craves.

His voice is as blond as a cry
From a potholer choired alone
In a cathedral under the ground
Where the windows are wet rocks.
He calls out for help but the stone
Scatters his voice in flocks.

The bulb is slowing. He waits
For the cloaking shadows to stop;
In a clutch of sleep he watches
The clock face drizzle and drown,
Until his head opens salt and clean,
And silence flourishes sea-green.

Then he sings again, and his hands,
His hands are gathering crops.[71]

This submersion into a watery, insubstantial landscape is registered as a submission into an immaterial world unbounded by the clock. It is a vacuous space of release and restoration, but it is also an ephemeral experience that serves a very different purpose. The closing admission into empty-time – the ultimate site of boredom – also 'opens' the subject out, establishing a mode of communication ('he sings again') redolent of talking or squealing under torture. With singing no longer purely a restorative act, the 'gathering' it enables also lends itself to a more allegorical reading – the harvesting of data becoming a 'crop' by which society can be controlled.

The allegorical form that undergirds this reading is significant. Where Shivers's staccato account of sensory deprivation hinted at the convergence of computational and non-computational structures, Deane's poetic recourse to allegory presents an almost active threat to the efficacy of social control itself. This is no longer writing as command and response, but rather reading as a process of demystification – what Alexander Galloway would term a 'digging through manifest meaning to get at latent meaning'.[72] In its opening sections, 'Overdose' is particularly arrested by the idea of plumbing depths – like 'a potholer' trying to ascertain what lies 'under the ground'. Galloway contrasts such deep reading with what he calls, after Deleuze, 'control allegory': a 'computerised' mode of reading that 'scans the surface of the text looking for new interpretive patterns'.[73] Deane's work is not immune from this process either. 'Overdose' opens with metaphors that convert an analogue signal ('swinging ... waves') into digital scanning ('up and down'). Yet in the poem's ambiguous and bodily ('hands') conclusion, Deane encourages an intuitive reading practice that struggles to be predicted. In this important sense his poetry offers itself (either consciously or unconsciously) as a mode of resistance, a non-computational form – that is able to evade the 'dividualising' impulses of control.

One of the most striking things about internment's introduction in 1971 was its porosity, its ability to extend its influence beyond the confines of its camps and holding centres. Initiating a strategy of rapid arrest and release, the details of the operation were renowned, even if its interrogative techniques remained officially repressed. While this expansion was a complex and intricate procedure, it is important to realise the extent to which it depended upon a distinct facet of society: the female relatives of those interned. The gender politics created by internment is one of its most remarkable features, and a crucial way in which the project was able to create that larger web, or sieve, of social control.

The internment swoops brought the operation into a domestic sphere, often causing significant psychological damage to the women left behind. As Sharon Pickering notes:

> house raids had the effect of cutting directly into the cores of women's lives as individuals, as mothers, as partners and as part of communities, largely because of the highly invasive and personal nature of the raids. Security forces have the legislated power to search and destroy an entire house – in effect search and expose someone's life in the process of harassment.[74]

There was an implicit but clear link between the female body and the house during these raids. The search for male suspects ensured, as Lynda Edgerton states, that 'the traditional maternal role as guardian of the family was being confronted by external alien elements'.[75] Threatened in this way, 'women invariably reported a sense of fear during house raids', states Pickering, and this 'fear often had a physical impact'.[76]

A 1972 *Survey of Internees' Families*, conducted by the Northern Ireland Civil Rights Association (NICRA), captured some of the ways in which the wives and mothers carried the scars of this operation. Of the fourteen women interviewed:

> All but one said they felt acutely depressed at times – and one added that her brother had said she 'acted nervous'. Six of them were on tablets for their nerves and appeared to have had them prescribed fairly soon after their men were lifted. Two of them also suffered from chronic illnesses. Three reported difficulty in eating and a loss of weight which they measured from the way their clothes fitted.[77]

Like the men detained, the women left behind underwent considerable mental and physical damage from which there was seemingly little release. 'Many years after they were last raided', notes Pickering, 'women would lie awake waiting for the early morning raid'.[78] Nine of the houses surveyed by the NICRA 'had been searched at least once since the father had been interned',[79] while elsewhere the sister of two internees recalls that their house was searched 'nineteen times in one week'.[80] These raids combined with the indiscriminate nature of the arrests to suggest that the operation was perpetually unfinished, that with internment anyone could be lifted next. In this, internment reiterated the continuous nature of its constraint, but it also became a potent example of how, as Deleuze puts it, 'in the societies of control one is never finished with anything'.[81] Akin to the men who were lifted, the women who remained were also deprived of sleep, temporally confused and placed under constant psychological strain.

Through such gendered alignments, interment can be read as having extended the military dimensions of the Troubles. While women have regularly experienced violent confrontation during times of war, their sex has also meant they are, as Cynthia Enloe argues, 'denied access to "the front", to "combat"'. For Enloe, men need to 'claim a uniqueness and superiority that will justify their dominant position in the social order', and this means that 'the military has to constantly redefine "the front" and "combat" as wherever "women are not"'.[82] The split between male internees and female dependants corroborates this definition, and in much of the literature written against internment the barbed wire was often envisaged as a distinctly masculine front line. When women are represented, they tend to be placed upon internment's periphery, acting as marginal figures whose presence serve to demarcate the edges of the camp.

The parallels between male and female experiences of internment have often passed unnoticed, however. Gerry Adams's *Cage Eleven* is, as Mary Sullivan notes, 'one of the few prison narratives to mention women who have spent years visiting men' during the Troubles. Yet, as Sullivan goes on to observe, even this 'narrative does not discuss women in any detail; when women are mentioned, they are named as the girlfriend or wife of a prisoner'.[83] This is, perhaps, relatively unsurprising. Like so much of the life-writing about internment, Adams's account was composed from within the camps and thus physically unable to countenance how male and female experiences might overlap. Paradoxically, then, it is in the realms of fiction, in novels like Mary Beckett's *Give Them Stones*, that some of the clearest comparisons have been made. That this novel is indebted to genre of life-writing – described by one early reviewer as 'more autobiography than creative fiction' – is a telling formal attribute.[84] If nothing else, it acknowledges the need for internment's gendered entanglements to be given a factual, authentic voice.

Spanning a period of over sixty years, *Give Them Stones* weaves a personal narrative of growth and maturation into the political and social history of Northern Ireland since the late 1920s. During this time Beckett's protagonist, a West Belfast Catholic called Martha, experiences two distinct phases of internment: its introduction during the Second World War and its manifestation during the Troubles. For Beckett, internment has had a significant impact upon the familial structure in Northern Ireland and, as such, it is an event whose influence has persisted. As she states in an interview from 1995: 'It was a tremendous problem; it happened in every generation. When you speak of peace, you have to remember this: since 1972 generations have lived with internment. It made people who were only nationalists into Republicans'.[85] But while Beckett is keen to emphasise the genealogy of this 'problem', she isolates the introduction of internment during the Troubles as a particular point of concern.

In *Give Them Stones*, this issue is highlighted by the distinct shift Beckett draws between the internment of the 1950s and its implementation in the 1970s. In this novel interment before the Troubles is a marginal event; one that is easily forgotten, and steeped in a sense of silence and isolation. It is an experience of exile and rejection, and this is realised in both metaphorical and literal ways when, for example, Martha reflects on her father's internment from her own position as a returned wartime evacuee. Uncertain whether she 'was sad or happy to be home', Martha recalls how

> I was tired of looking after myself all alone. I remembered the way my father used to have the place warm and welcoming when I'd come home from school and I began to be horrified at myself that for five and a half years I had not seen him or spoken to him or written to him. I was ashamed that just because he was powerless and useless to me I had nearly forgotten all about him.[86]

The internment of Martha's father has rendered him not only 'powerless' but also largely invisible. Over the course of 'five and a half years' he has become a forgotten figure, a man whose plight has been unable to transcend the site of his incarceration. In this context the longevity and confinement associated with internment's pre-Troubles manifestation is particularly pronounced, but Beckett frames it so as to also emphasise the divergence between male and female experiences of incarceration at this time. Martha has undergone her own form of exile yet, in direct opposition to her father, she has also grown through her absence – returning to Belfast with 'a wee bit of satisfaction in independence'.[87] Her father, in contrast, will only come to attain his release having contracted TB – a disease that will leave him as 'limp and thin' as Martha's faded memory of his time as an internee.[88]

Set against this, Martha's experience of internment during the Troubles is direct and intimate. Her growth into marriage and motherhood allows Beckett to develop her interest in internment's domestic repercussions, and it is on these terms that the unique facets of the 1971 operation appear at their most distinct:

> I worked myself into a right state over the boys' safety. Boys and men had been lifted all over the parish and more in the next where I had been reared, and every day there was word in the papers from the IRA men to say, 'They didn't get me!' There were rumours too of men having been tortured. They were made to stand for hours and

hours against a wall with bags over their heads, not allowed to eat or drink or go to
the lavatory and when they fell they were kicked up again …

I didn't sleep at night. I'd drop off and then waken up shaking. I'd get up in the
morning with a terrible dragging feeling that there was another day to be got through.
One night when we were both lying awake because the soldiers' lorries were even
noisier than usual tearing around, Dermot said, 'Martha, you'd need to see the
doctor. He'll give you tablets or something. You're beginning to be very wrecked
looking'.[89]

While one of the purposes of this account is to document the Army's brutality,
it also provides an important indication of internment's fluidity. Unlike its wartime incarnation, 'word' of the internees was no longer contained and 'rumour'
of their plight spread fear throughout the communities that had been raided. As
McGuffin has noted, one of the effects of sensory deprivation was an exaggerated reportage that allowed the security forces to 'hold it over many suspects
as a threat'.[90] But in Beckett's imagining these rumours also serve as a means
of highlighting the links between male and female experiences. Just as the men
were 'tortured' during their time inside, so Martha's maternal worries cause her
to be physically and psychologically 'wrecked' at home. Like the internees, she
becomes sleep-deprived and, so aligned, discovers that her perception of time
has been reduced – transformed into 'a terrible dragging feeling', a monotonous
need to survive 'another day'.

Beckett's account reveals the distinct dimensions of internment during the
Troubles, but her attention to familial responsibility also illustrates the manner
in which this version of internment expanded its punitive procedures away from
the camps – in this instance, extending its late capitalist temporalities into the
heart of domestic and maternal life. Martha is caught in a patriarchal battle – a
war between the British Army and the IRA – but she also engages in her own
'small and unexpected acts of defiance', most notably through the process of
baking and providing her community with the metaphoric 'stones' of the novel's
title.[91] As Gerry Smyth notes, it 'is the one thing that she can call her own, the
one means she has to express herself as well as to assert her independence'.[92]
When the internment raids begin, for example, Beckett's protagonist presses
on with this autonomous enterprise, kneading out the strain of the operation by
making bread: 'my hands were trembling but I kept on baking'.[93]

The gesture may be small but it is still significant. Continuing with her
domestic and communal duties, Martha poses an active threat to Northern
Ireland's nascent control society by downplaying the military raids as an effective form of intimidation and coercion. The novel's autobiographical style adds
to this dissident strain. Suggesting that such behaviour was not simply the work

of fiction, Beckett cuts through the ideological ambiguities of the novel form to suggest that the conflict's expansion into private and domestic realms had a material basis during internment. As Pickering has noted in her study of policing and resistance in Northern Ireland, 'women often reported using aspects of the home to defy the security forces as they raided'.[94] In similar terms, Martha carefully deploys her private identity to disrupt interrogations by the military: '"Are you a Republican?" he asked and I shrugged. I was going to be a heroine but instead I said, "I am a home baker"'.[95]

Alongside these more or less spontaneous actions, the introduction of intern-ment also 'brought with it a new layer of women activists who were the friends, relatives and partners of those interned'.[96] The nature of this female activism was diverse – in 1971 women both replaced men in local branches of the NICRA and helped to organise a major rent and rate strike against internment – but one of their earliest and most iconic responses to internment came in the form of bin lid bashing: a system devised to warn against Army raids. Lynda Edgerton explains how the procedure operated:

> When troops entered an area, local women would begin banging their bin lids on the pavement; the noise would carry through the area and alert others to follow suit. On the Derrbeg estate in Newry, the women were labelled 'the petticoat brigade'. This warning system had its origins in an earlier period when women in working-class communities heralded the presence of Housing Trust inspectors, who had the power to inspect homes for cleanliness before families would be considered suitable applicants for Housing Trust accommodation.[97]

Central to the effectiveness of this warning system was a notion of porosity and modulation. The sound was designed to 'carry through' areas while, as Begoña Aretxaga notes, those reacting to this warning would use 'open house doors, alleys, and backyards' to escape.[98] In this respect, we are returned again to Deleuze's conception of control, the modulating 'sieve' whose mesh transmutes 'from point to point'. Crucially, however, this was an act of subversion. It was a form of counter-control, activated from below and weighed against the author-ity of the state – as in Derek Mahon's powerful coupling of 'sirens, bin-lids' in 'The Last Fire of Kings'.[99]

Where the impact of 'sabotage' once represented a threat to the machines of earlier disciplinary societies, these bin-lids modulated against the emergent logic of social control – 'jamming' the system like a 'virus', to use Deleuze's terminology.[100] Nevertheless, the success of this particular strategy remains unclear. According to Aretxaga it 'constituted as much a parody of military power as a system of warning', yet its status as a mode of feminine resistance did have important repercussions.[101] For one thing, it propelled women into the militarised and public landscape of the Troubles, changing the contours of Republican society and shifting its margins into new terrains. The labelling of these female activists 'the petticoat brigade' gestured towards this possibility. Despite its derogatory overtones, the term illustrated how a normally concealed facet of feminine identity was a far more visible force: a 'brigade' that could come together, not only as victims of harassment but as agents of resistance.

Two impulses coalesced through this positioning. On the one hand, this exteriority made women an obvious and immediate conduit for the dispersion of internment's repressive monotony. As Beckett has suggested, the intimidation of women at home could have equivalences to the torture of the men interned. On the other hand, however, the exclusion of women from the camps also made them an effective site for opposition and subversion. Aside from bin-lid bashing and anti-internment protests, this period also witnessed women engaged in more militant activity through auxiliary sections of the IRA. Although often performing 'domesticated and subordinated' functions, some female volunteers also became active combatants, involved in 'robberies, the planting and detona-tion of roadside mines and car-bombs, kidnappings and assassinations'. In this respect, notes Corcoran, elements of the IRA's leadership 'had broken with previous Republican orthodoxies on women's roles on the basis that British military strategists had "failed to appreciate" the contribution of women in other colonial struggles'.[102]

It did not take long for the security forces to respond to such tactics. By the time internment was phased out in 1975, a total of 33 women had been interned, the first of whom was Liz McKee on 1 January 1973. Women had been interned in Northern Ireland under earlier Unionist governments – eighteen during the 1940s and one during the 1950s – but the insular nature of these operations, and the persistence of wartime censorship, meant that, as McGuffin tells us, these earlier cases 'aroused no public outcry whatsoever'.[103] Things were different during the visible and porous operation of the 1970s, however. Interned against a backdrop of military brutality, wrongful arrests and the horrors of 'in depth' interrogation, female internees became a subject for sharp condemnation. As the NICRA's 1973 *Information Sheet on Women Internees* stated, with vehemence:

Nowhere else in Western Europe would this situation be permitted. Nowhere else in Western Europe are there young girls incarcerated for their political beliefs. The hypocritical Tories in the British Government would have the rest of the world believe that England is still the Mother of Democracy – yet they are guilty of a crime that even in the heyday of Orange-Unionism was never committed – the internment of women and girls.[104]

Clearly, women were a special case. The prospect of a female internee threatened masculine interpretations of the conflict – 'the assumption that women were passive victims of war' as Aretxaga expresses it – and thus their incarceration appeared not only anomalous but somewhat depraved. [105]

Despite its controversies interment was fast becoming a profitable tool. By 1974 the Army had managed to amass detailed information on over 40 per cent of the North's population; a telling figure given that the Catholic population totalled 31 per cent in the 1971 census. [106] Such advances were not entirely surprising. As Allen Feldman has noted, by the mid-1970s the Northern Irish security forces could collect data through video scanners, phone taps, covert photography and close-circuit television – that matrix of rapid contact information Kiston had envisaged and with which we are so familiar today. [107] In that classic blend of military capitalism, all these data were to be indexed and enumerated by an 'infinitely expandable' computer programme considered, by 1974 standards at least, 'the most advanced to be adopted by the security forces in Northern Europe'. [108] While these developments hinted at internment's irrelevance as a means of 'screening' potentially dissident populations, they were also deeply indebted to the systems of control this operation had initiated. If nothing else, the possibility that any adult could be detained without trial served to establish and naturalise the totalitarian and repressive remit necessary for these newer systems of control. By the mid-1970s internment would become an unnecessary component of the security force's information economy but, as Lloyd has noted, it had been the 'means to the normalization of state violence and of the intrusive practices of surveillance that it required'. [109]

Perhaps predictably, the phasing out of internment was a slow and laborious procedure. The British government frequently pronounced its desire to end the project but, because of its eristic status, the rate of release was often erratic. In keeping with internment's porous nature, the numbers detained were always said to depend upon the wider levels of violence within Northern Ireland. The releases also needed to balance Unionist demands for reprisals with Nationalist calls for concessions. At times this relationship could become a crude process of give and take – 'you play the orange card one week and the green card the next week', recalls William Whitelaw. [110] Even so, when Merlyn Rees took office as Secretary of State for Northern Ireland, he was able to fix Christmas 1975 as the date for internment's final dissolution. By August 1975, 339 long-term internees had been released in under a year, but the political wrangling continued. Many Nationalist responses to this final phase of internment argued that the nature of these releases was not only too slow but intentionally insensitive. Internment was ending, yet the British government still refused to acknowledge the damage the operation had caused. As Fathers Brian Brady, Denis Faul and

Raymond Murray stated in relation to what they felt was Rees's 'banal' recipe for release:

> This particular formula tends to make the human tragedy of the internees as impersonal as the daily bulletin about the fall in the Financial Times Industrial Share Index and the devaluation of the pound sterling since it was floated.
>
> The internees are reduced to a numbers game played by the gnomes of the N.I. Office, the RUC Special Branch and the Governor of Long Kesh.[111]

In many respects, this depersonalisation marked the culmination of internment as an exercise in control. Far from their initial value to a growing information economy, the internees had now become commodities in an ongoing publicity war. Yet the nature of this transition also registered the fact that internment had now successfully managed to drain the detainees of almost all their original identity. By this stage of the operation, they had become mere 'numbers' – data to be indexed like Tiqqun's *'fleshless envelope'* or the *'dividuals'* of Deleuze.

Part of the effect of this depreciation was the production of a boredom that also served to mask the very mechanics of such control. Like the humanity of the internees, the scars of their internment were also suppressed as the project's military dimensions dovetailed with the capitalist dynamics that had given it so much momentum. Internment bestowed more power on the Army, allowing them to develop 'an entirely independent security policy' which, in turn, enabled Northern Ireland's indigenous security forces to reintroduce a structure of 'normal policing'.[112] Thus, in stark contrast to its colonial roots, by 1975 internment had become the origin of a counter-insurgency policy that aimed to 'normalise' the Troubles under a revitalised rubric of law and order. Indeed, Northern Ireland's position within the United Kingdom has meant that the normalisation of what was once a colonial practice has had far-reaching consequences. As Lloyd has noted, because of these changes Northern Ireland has become 'the cusp through which colonial practices – internment, coercive interrogation, suspension of habeas corpus, imprisonment without trial or term – could be "domesticated" into the so-called "mainland"'.[113] The transition from internment to the UK's counter-terrorism legislation did not happen overnight, but it was certainly a logical next step.

As these arguments suggest, the legacy of internment during the Troubles is still unfolding. Carson's poem 'The Maze' had positioned internment as being on the cusp of a broader social change, and in a poem from 1989, titled 'Ambition', he returns to this idea, presenting internment as a starting point – the first step on a difficult journey to an elusive and unknown destination:

Now I've climbed this far it's time to look back. But smoke obscures
The panorama from the Mountain Loney spring. The city and the mountain are on
    fire.
My mouth's still stinging from the cold sharp shock of water – a winter taste
In summer – but my father's wandered off somewhere. I can't seem to find him.
We'd been smoking 'coffin nails', and he'd been talking of his time inside, how
Matches were that scarce you'd have to split them four ways with your thumbnail;
And seven cigarette ends made a cigarette. *Keep a thing for seven years,*
You'll always find a use for it, he follows in the same breath … it reminds me
Of the saint who, when he had his head cut off, picked up his head and walked
With it for seven miles. And the wise man said, *The distance doesn't matter,*
It's the first step that was difficult.[114]

In this section temporal images – of looking back, of 'time inside', of winter during summer – point to a disorientated timescape that represents both the experience of his father's internment in 1938 and the changing condition of Belfast following the introduction of internment in 1971. As Neal Alexander notes, the poem views 'the crisis period of Internment … self-consciously from the perspective of a contemporary situation following the contentious Anglo-Irish Agreement of November 1985'.[115] For Carson, the '*distance*' between these events '*doesn't matter*'. Instead, he is concerned with origins, with the fact that internment might somehow form the basis for Belfast's current predicament – that its obscuration under the 'smoke' of conflict can be traced back to the 'cigarette ends' which act as a synecdoche for the seven weeks his father spent as an internee.

Despite the energy required to undertake this journey, Carson is also aware of the widespread paralysis internment hoped to induce. It is a vision we have seen in his earlier poem 'The Maze', in which that modulating sieve ensured 'we' were all ensnared. As 'Ambition' proceeds, Carson develops this idea through the image of a road – a chronotope that marks the shifting temporalities and fissures of modern surveillance:

And if time is a road, then you're checked again and again
By a mobile checkpoint. One soldier holds a gun to your head. Another soldier
Asks you questions, and another checks the information on the head computer.
Your name. Your brothers' names. Your father's name. His occupation. As if
The one they're looking for is not you, but it might be you. Looks like you
Or smells like you. And suddenly, the posthumous aroma of an empty canvas
Postman's sack – twine, ink, dead letters – wafts out from the soldiers'
Sodden khaki. It's obvious they're bored: one of them is watching Wimbledon
On one of those postage-stamp-sized TV screens. *Of course, the proper shot,*
An unseen talking head intones, *should have been the lob*. He's using words like
Angled, volley, smash and *strategy*. Someone is *fighting a losing battle*.[116]

This stanza provides us with another glimpse of the dissipated '*dividuals*' Deleuze described. This is a landscape in which 'your name' is stripped of its personal value as it is encoded through the lives of others and their attendant statistics. Alongside this deindividualisation, however, Carson is also keen to stress the ways in which internment can be placed at the origin of a landscape that is both invisible and uncanny in its control. Like the 'posthumous aroma' of his father's 'Postman's sack', this section of the poem presents the 'TV screens' and 'head computers' as an 'unseen' commentator – a Deleuzian spirit or gas – that can monitor human activity and decide what the '*proper shot*' should be. In many important ways, Carson's work is one that strives to tease out the provisional nature of such ubiquitous and axiomatic systems of control. Yet, in this particular part of 'Ambition', Carson seems to be '*fighting a losing battle*' – unable to escape the boredom of a landscape in which the predictive technologies of social control are continually kept in play.

Deleuze's recourse to Kafka had suggested that literary analysis is necessary if we were to trace the abstract disciplinary shifts that undergird social control. The writers I have considered likewise describe Northern Ireland's complex transition towards the control society's unending and invasive modulations. At times, the form of this writing has been infected by the cybernetic logic necessary for such computation. At other points, however, the writing's literary qualities, its use of allegory or life-writing, serves to disrupt the smooth functioning of this system – 'jamming' its socio-technological mechanisms with a non-computational language of its own. The legacy of internment must be read through these complex responses if it is ever to be fully understood, and much of its significance is lost if it is considered only as a failed attempt at incarceration. This was undoubtedly one of its aims, but it was also an attempt to monitor a specific segment of Northern Irish society. McGuffin, Deane, Beckett and Carson foreground this alternative perspective and, in so doing, help to process the historical experiences and struggles of colonial and postcolonial peoples that are, to use Neferti X.M. Tadiar's terms, often 'remaindered by a theoretical and political genealogy of present-day global capitalism'. As Tadiar goes on to observe, by attending to these experiences it is possible to comprehend 'the very conditions for the emergence of new biopolitical forms of control and value extraction as well as of new forms of resistance and insurgency'.[117]

It is because of these competing perspectives that we can realise how, in its play with monotony and control, internment represented another fraught attempt to redress the divisions of Northern Ireland through a politics of boredom. In its flattened temporalities and construction of '*dividuals*', internment was a product of a late capitalist logic that sought to efface difference and repress division. Yet, it was also because of the brutality with which this capitalist monotony was imposed that internment was so fiercely resisted. Its introduction extended the conflict to new arenas and, as such, created new layers of communal activism and anti-state violence along what had previously been the margins of the Troubles. Capitalism, in this sense, was a means of escalating conflict as much as containing it. But, as the evolution of its surveillance technologies has demonstrated, the systems of control that internment instigated also became flexible enough to accommodate such disruption. As such, these structures of capitalist repression are still in place, and in increasingly domesticated forms. A rereading of internment as initiating systems of monotony and control can help to remind us of this fact. But the importance of such a reassessment goes further than this. In illustrating how this system has evolved as a means of controlling conflict, it also highlights how the intersection of capitalism and the North's ethnic–national division has created – once again – an uneasy means of containing difference, not a coherent system through which conflict can be resolved. The persistence of this process in post-conflict '"imaginings' of the Troubles is the subject of the next chapter.

Notes and references

1   Ciaran Carson, 'The maze', in *The Wearing of the Black: An Anthology of Contemporary Ulster Poetry* ed. by Padraic Fiacc (Belfast: Blackstaff Press, 1974), p. 36. Reproduced by kind permission of the author c/o The Gallery Press (www.gallerypress.com).

2   Jonathan Bardon, *A History of Ulster* (Belfast: Blackstaff Press 2001), p. 682.

3   Paul Bew and Gordon Gillespie, *Northern Ireland: A Chronology of the Troubles 1968–1993* (Dublin: Gill and Macmillan, 1993), p. 37.

4   Medbh McGuckian, 'Women Are Trousers', in *Border Crossings: Irish Women Writers and National Identities* ed. by Kathryn Kirkpatrick (Tuscaloosa: University of Alabama Press, 2000), p. 171.

5   Community Relations Commission Research Unit, *Flight: A Report on Population Movement in Belfast during August 1971* (Belfast: Northern Ireland Community Relations Commission, 1971), p. 1.

6   J.B. Bell, *The Secret Army: The IRA*, 3rd edn (New Brunswick, NJ: Transaction, 2003), p. 382.

7   Mary Corcoran, *Out of Order: The Political Imprisonment of Women in Northern Ireland, 1972–1998* (Cullompton: Willan Publishing, 2006), p. 2.

8   Seamus Heaney, *Wintering Out* (London: Faber, 1972), p. v.

9   Gilles Deleuze, 'Postscript on the Societies of Control', *October*, 59 (Winter 1992), 4. My emphasis.

10 *Ibid.*, p. 4.

11 Michael Hardt and Antonio Negri, *Empire* (Cambridge, MA: Harvard University Press, 2001), pp. 231–232.

12   Carol Ackroyd, Karen Margolis, Jonathan Rosenhead and Tim Shallice, *The Technology of Political Control*, 2nd edn (London: Pluto Press, 1980), p. 36.

13   Deleuze, 'Postscript', p. 6.

14   Reviel Netz, *Barbed Wire: An Ecology of Modernity* (Middletown, CT: Wesleyan University Press, 2004), p. 132.

15   David Lloyd, *Irish Culture and Colonial Modernity 1800–1900: The Transformation of Oral Space* (Cambridge: Cambridge University Press, 2011), p. 180.

16   Jonathan Crary, *24/7: Late Capitalism and the Ends of Sleep* (London: Verso, 2013), p. 30.

17   *Ibid.*, p. 88.

18   Karl Marx, *Capital: Vol. I*, trans. by Ben Fowkes (London: Penguin 1990), p. 342.

19   *Ibid*, p. 376.

20   Deleuze, 'Postscript', 5.

21   Martin Heidegger, *The Fundamental Concepts of Metaphysics: World, Finitude, Solitude*, trans. by William McNeill and Nicholas Walker (Bloomington: Indiana University Press, 1995), pp. 96, 98.

22   A.L. Vischer, *Barbed Wire Disease: A Psychological Study of the Prisoner of War* (London: John Bale, Sons & Danielsson, 1919), p. 31.

23   S.A. Kinnier Wilson, 'Introduction', in *Barbed Wire Disease*, p. 9.

24   Danny Morrison, *Then the Walls Came Down: A Prison Journal* (Dublin: Mercier Press, 1999), p. 119.

25   Gerry Adams, *Cage Eleven* (Kerry: Brandon, 2002), p. 11.

26   Lachlan Whalen, '"Our Barbed Wire Ivory Tower": The Prison Writings of Gerry Adams', *New Hibernia Review*, 10.2 (Summer 2006), 124.

27   Deleuze, 'Postscript', 5.

28   Seb Franklin, 'Humans and/as Machines: Beckett and Cultural Cybernetics', *Textual Practice*, 27.2 (2013), 251.

29   Tom Hadden, Kevin Boyle and Colm Campbell, 'Emergency Law in Northern Ireland: The Context', in *Justice under Fire: The Abuse of Civil Liberties in Northern Ireland* ed. by Anthony Jennings (London: Pluto Press, 1990), p. 2.

30   Frank Kitson, *Low Intensity Operations: Subversion, Insurgency, Peace-Keeping* (London: Faber and Faber, 1971), p. 95.

31   *Ibid*, pp. 95–96.

32   *Ibid*, p. 142.

33   Guy Debord, *Comments on the Society of the Spectacle* (1988) www.notbored.org/commentaires.html [accessed 24 July 2017].

34   Deleuze, 'Postcript', 6.

35   CAIN, 'Internment – A Chronology of the Main Events', http://cain.ulst.ac.uk/events/intern/chron.htm [accessed 24 July 2017].

36   Martin J. McCleery, 'Debunking the Myths of Operation Demetrius: The Introduction of Internment in Northern Ireland in 1971', *Irish Political Studies*, 27.3 (2012), 424.

37   Sunday Times Insight Team, *Ulster* (Harmondsworth: Penguin, 1972), p. 262.

38   Robin Evelegh, *Peace Keeping in a Democratic Society: The Lessons of Northern Ireland* (London: C. Hurst & Company, 1978), p. 66.
39   Sunday Times, *Ulster*, p. 263.
40   *Ibid.*, p. 263.
41   *Ibid.*, pp. 263–264.
42   Kitson, *Low Intensity Operations*, p. 73.
43   McCleery, 'Debunking the Myths', 416.
44   Séamas Ó Tuathail alleges that while Kitson 'served in Aden and Cyprus … he perfected the methods of torture now perpetrated on innocent suspects in the North of Ireland' (Séamas Ó Tuathail, *They Came in the Morning* (Dublin: Sinn Féin (Official), 1972), p. 22). In fact, 'Kitson criticised the timing of internment, arguing that had it been implemented simultaneously with direct rule from London, political gains could have been made' (H. Bennet and R. Cormac, 'Low Intensity Operations in Theory and Practice: General Sir Frank Kitson as warrior-scholar', in *The Theory and Practice of Irregular Warfare: Warrior-scholarship in counter-insurgency* ed. by Andrew Mumford and Bruno C. Reis (Abingdon: Routledge, 2014), p. 115).
45   John McGuffin, *The Guineapigs* (Hamondsworth: Penguin, 1974), p. 149. For a history of the rubber bullet see Ackroyd et al., *The Technology of Political Control*, p. 28.
46   Colonel Michael Dewar, *The British Army in Northern Ireland* (London: Arms and Armour, 1996), p. 197.
47   Richard Deutsch and Vivien Magowan, *Northern Ireland 1968–73: A Chronology of Events – Volume 1, 1968–71* (Belfast: Blackstaff, 1973), p. 118.
48   McCleery, 'Debunking the Myths', 416.
49   Sir Edmund Compton, *Report of the Enquiry into Allegations against the Security Forces of Physical Brutality in Northern Ireland Arising out of Events on the 9th August, 1971* (London: HMSO, 1971), para. 9.
50   McGuffin, *The Guineapigs*, p. 49.
51   *Ibid.*, p. 49.
52   Compton, *Report*, quoted in *The Guineapigs*, p. 51.
53   McGuffin, *The Guineapigs*, p. 48.
54   Paddy Hillyard, 'Law and Order', in *Northern Ireland: The Background to the Conflict* ed. by John Darby (Belfast: Appletree Press, 1983), p. 40.
55   Lord Parker, J.A. Gardiner and Lord Gardiner, *Report of the Committee of Privy Counsellors Appointed to Consider Authorised Procedures for the Interrogation of Persons Suspected of Terrorism* (London: HMSO, 1972), p. 3.
56   Alfred W. McCoy, *A Question of Torture: CIA Interrogation, from the Cold War to the War on Terror* (New York: Metropolitan Books, 2006), p. 8.
57   McGuffin, *The Guineapigs*, p. 69.
58   Lloyd, *Colonial Modernity*, p. 181.
59   W.H. Bexton, W. Heron and T.H. Scott, 'Effects of Decreased Variation in the Sensory Environment', *Canadian Journal of Psychology*, 8. 2 (1954), 70.
60   Tim Shallice, 'The Ulster Depth Interrogation Techniques and Their Relation to Sensory Deprivation Research', *Cognition*, 1.4 (1972), 387.

61   Ibid., 391.

62   McGuffin, The Guineapigs, p. 61.

63   Ibid., p. 63.

64   Tiqqun, 'The Cybernetic Hypothesis', Tiqqun 2 (Paris: Les Belles-Lettres, 2001), p. 49.

65   Seamus Deane, 'An Irish Intelligentsia: Reflections on Its Desirability', Honest Ulsterman, 46–47 (November 1974–February 1975), 30.

66   Seamus Deane, Strange Country: Modernity and Nationhood in Irish Writing since 1790 (Oxford: Oxford University Press, 1997), p. 168.

67   Robert Tracy, 'An Ireland / The Poets Have Imagined', The Crane Bag, 3. 2 (1979), 87.

68   Seamus Deane, 'Fourteen Elegies: Twelve', in Gradual Wars (Shannon: Irish Academic Press, 1972), p. 23. All references to this edition. Reproduced by kind permission of the author and Irish Academic Press.

69   Lloyd, Colonial Modernity, p. 185.

70   Deane, 'Fourteen Elegies: Eight', p. 18.

71   Deane, 'Overdose', p. 42.

72   Alexander R. Galloway, Gaming: Essays on Algorithmic Culture (Minneapolis: University of Minnesota Press, 2006), p. 86.

73   Ibid., p. 87.

74   Sharon Pickering, Women, Policing and Resistance in Northern Ireland (Belfast: Beyond the Pale, 2002), p. 182.

75   Lynda Edgerton, 'Public Protest, Domestic Acquiescence: Women in Northern Ireland', in Caught up in Conflict: Women's Responses to Political Strife ed. by Rosemary Ridd and Helen Callaway (Basingstoke: Macmillan Education, 1986), p. 67.

76   Pickering, Women, Policing and Resistance, p. 183.

77   Nicholas M. Ragg, Tracy Doherty, Joe O'Hara and Brian Buckley, Survey of Internees' Families (Belfast: NICRA, 1972), p. 4.

78   Pickering, Women, Policing and Resistance, pp. 187–188.

79   Ragg et al., Survey of Internees' Families, p. 4.

80   Siobhán, 'Raids 1', in 'Strong about it all ...': Rural and Urban Women's Experiences of the Security Forces in Northern Ireland ed. by Helen Harris and Eileen Healy (Derry: North West Women's / Human Rights Project Publications, 2001), p. 20.

81   Deleuze, 'Postscript', p. 5.

82   Cynthia Enloe, Does Khaki Become You? The Militarization of Women's Lives (London: Pandora Press, 1988), p. 15.

83   Megan Sullivan, Women in Northern Ireland: Cultural Studies and Material Conditions (Gainesville: University Press of Florida, 1999), p. 26.

84   Aubrey Dillon-Malone, 'Middle Third', Books Ireland, 116 (September 1987), 172.

85   Megan Sullivan, 'Mary Becket: An Interview by Megan Sullivan', Irish Literary Supplement (Fall 1995), 10.

86   Mary Beckett, Give Them Stones (London: Bloomsbury, 1988), p. 59.

87   *Ibid.*, p. 49.

88   *Ibid.*, p. 61.

89   *Ibid.*, p. 128.

90   McGuffin, *The Guineapigs*, p. 108.

91   Katie Donovan, *Irish Women Writers: Marginalised by Whom?* (Dublin: Raven Arts, 1988), p. 32.

92   Gerry Smyth, *The Novel and the Nation: Studies in the New Irish Fiction* (London: Pluto, 1997), p. 136.

93   Beckett, *Give Them Stones*, p. 125.

94   Pickering, *Women, Policing and Resistance*, p. 187.

95   Beckett, *Give Them Stones*, p. 123.

96   *Ibid.*, p. 84.

97   Edgerton, 'Public Protest, Domestic Acquiescence', p. 65.

98   Begoña Aretxaga, *Shattering Silence: Women, Nationalism and Political Subjectivity in Northern Ireland* (Princeton: Princeton University Press, 1997), p. 71.

99   Derek Mahon, 'The Last Fire of Kings', *New Collected Poems* (Oldcastle: The Gallery Press, 2012), p. 64.

100 Deleuze, 'Postscript', 6.

101 Aretxaga, *Shattering Silence*, p. 71.

102 Corcoran, *Out of Order*, pp. 6–7.

103 McGuffin, *Internment*, p. 82.

104 NICRA, *Information Sheet on Women Internees* (Belfast, 23 May 1973), p. 1.

105 Aretxaga, *Shattering Silence*, p. 66.

106 Paul Wilkinson, *Terrorism and the Liberal State*, 2nd edn (Basingstoke: Macmillan, 1986), p. 160.

107 Allen Feldman, *Formations of Violence: The Narrative of the Body and Political Terror in Northern Ireland* (Chicago: University of Chicago Press, 1991), p. 87.

108 Robert Frisk, 'Army's computer has data on half the population in Ulster', *The Times*, 5 December 1974, p. 1.

109 Lloyd, *Colonial Modernity*, p. 185.

110 R.J. Spjut, 'Internment and Detention without Trial in Northern Ireland 1971–1975: Ministerial Policy and Practice', *The Modern Law Review*, 49.6 (November 1986), 722.

111 Brian J. Brady, Denis Faul and Raymond Murray, *Internment 1971–1975* (Dungannon: St Patrick's Academy, 1975), p. 136.

112 See Kevin Boyle, Tom Hadden and Paddy Hillyard, *Law and State: The Case of Northern Ireland* (London: Martin Robertson & Company, 1975), p. 42; Caroline Kennedy-Pipe, *The Origins of the Present Troubles in Northern Ireland* (London: Longman, 1997), p. 75.

113 Lloyd, *Colonial Modernity*, p. 186.

114 Ciaran Carson, 'Ambition', in *Collected Poems* (Oldcastle: The Gallery Press, 2013), p. 138. Reproduced by kind permission of the author and The Gallery Press, Loughcrew, Oldcastle, County Meath, Ireland.

115 Neal Alexander, *Ciaran Carson: Space, Place, Writing* (Liverpool: Liverpool University Press, 2010), pp. 112–113.
116 Carson, 'Ambition', p. 139.
117 Neferti X.M. Tadiar, 'Life-Times in Fate Playing', *South Atlantic Quarterly*, 111.4 (2012), 800.

5

'The brightest spot in Ulster': total history and the H-Blocks in film

> When you pass it on the motorway after dark, it is squared off in neon, bright as an airport. An inflammation on the black countryside. Another of our military decorations.
>
> (Seamus Heaney, 'Christmas 1971')[1]

In May 2013, the Maze Long Kesh Development Corporation (MLKDC) produced a short film that expressed its vision for the future development of Northern Ireland's most infamous prison site. Aside from the lavish nature of its plans, the video also captured something of the MLKDC's ambition to conceal the complexity of the prison's history through a language of commercial regeneration and redevelopment. The upbeat but generic music of Bangor's indie band Kowalski, and their song 'Outdoors', is heard over a montage of construction, where quickly cut footage creates a stage on which corporate meetings, cappuccinoed conversations and artistic activities unfold. This action takes place amidst a freshly laid turf, foregrounding a new beginning, but also signifying a covering over – a burial of this space's disruptive history in which so many were interminably locked inside.[2]

Some markers of the site's former uses do punctuate this footage, however. A 1960s sports car circles the new stage, reminding us of the place's brief tenure as a racing track; a light aircraft flips acrobatically overhead in tribute to the area's Second World War airfields; and cattle are unloaded on to new pastures, a gesture that seemingly returns us to the space's origins as farmland. But the site's most controversial contribution to the history of Northern Ireland – its function as a high-security (H-Block) prison during the Troubles – is almost consciously forgotten. At several moments during the video, the prison's now redundant façade looms momentarily in the background; the perimeter walls which surrounded the H-Blocks providing a fleeting backdrop that jars against the mundane activities which dominate the film. This historical referent is a major reason why the site has become, in the words of the MLKDC, 'an unprecedented development opportunity' and yet, despite its importance, the prison appears to have a relatively minor role in its regenerative vision.[3] Instead, scenes of vacuous consumption and placeless construction push the history of the H-Blocks towards the margins of what it is possible to represent.

Despite continued claims that the H-Blocks 'were a focal point of the Troubles', marginalisation was, in fact, a defining feature of this site.[4] For all their resonance, the protests and the hunger strikes held in this prison do not sit easily in a broader narrative of the conflict. 'The outside was scared to make the logical extension of the struggle we were in', remembers one veteran of the H-Blocks. 'They felt fairly in control of the military campaign, but not of the Hunger Strike.'[5] During the dirty protests, perhaps the most unknowable and extraordinary incident of the Troubles, life within and without the prison was disconnected, and in a radical way. The modes of resistance deployed by as many as four hundred nonconforming prisoners created a non-modern social forma-tion that was fiercely different from anything envisaged by dissident subjects operating beyond the prison walls. Through the hunger strike, those within the prison would attempt to disseminate their vision – their deaths inspiring, it was hoped, a widespread revolution. This moment of rupture never arose, however, and, in subsequent imaginings of the H-Block struggles, its presence has been dramatically exfoliated. The tragedies of the H-Blocks have been best honoured, to invoke the paradoxes of the Good Friday Agreement, 'through a fresh start'.[6] As the former Republican prisoner Thomas 'Dixie' Elliott reminds us, 'the hunger strikers didn't die for a peace process'. But, in spite of this, it is still the rhetoric of 'peace and reconciliation' that governs the memory of this site.[7]

Describing Northern Ireland's 'headlong rush towards the global market place', Colin Graham notes that one ineluctable effect of a profit-hungry, post-conflict politics is the relentless 'erasure of the ideological mess of history by the cleansing power of entrepreneurialism's fetish for progress'.[8] In many ways, the Maze/Long Kesh development marks an extension of this process. Here the prison's richly layered history has not only been eroded, it has subsequently been restructured so that it might, in the words of the MLKDC, 'demonstrate how economic development can consolidate and build upon our peace'.[9] Where once there was a fluid history pregnant with possibility, there is now – to use Slavoj Žižek's phrase – 'a closed continuity of "progression" leading to the reign of those who rule today'.[10] In the late 1970s and early 1980s, the H-Blocks represented many things: a potential endpoint for capitalism, a volatile inter-face between modern and non-modern social formations, a paradoxical site of unthinkable squalor and ecstatic conviviality, a place of incomprehensible detri-tus on the margins of the Troubles. Today, what remains of the prison is history at its most banal: a blank space for multinational investment, a misunderstood location for touristic pleasure, a myopic shrine to terror.

This chapter will interrogate those aspects of the Maze/Long Kesh development that have reduced the history of the H-Blocks to such mundane coordinates. It also seeks to construct an archaeology of the spaces and histories that have been occluded as a result of this post-conflict reimagining. To do so, I will investigate the oral testimonies that expose these alternatives, as well as exploring how three films about the H-Blocks have tried to present its history in more enabling ways. Terry George's *Some Mother's Son* (1996), Les Blair's *H3* (2001) and Steve McQueen's *Hunger* (2008) have all attempted to give the prison's frequently abstracted events a material form. Unlike the often depopulated terrains of photographic engagements with the prison, these cinematic responses are able to capture the prison's principal actors, as well as the disordered temporalities they served to initiate. That said, the two earliest H-Block films do display some pitfalls in their genre, inasmuch as they allow the conventions of what might loosely be termed 'mainstream cinema' to mask the intricacies of their subject matter. It is arguably, therefore, in McQueen's account that we get a fuller sense of the historical shifts animated by the H-Blocks. In its experimental form, *Hunger* captures something of the fragmented and non-modern dialectics personified by the nonconforming prisoners. That this film eventually reverts to a more familiar and mythic projection of the hunger strike also serves to demarcate the limits of what it is currently possible to say in relation to this historically unstable episode. As such, although these films demonstrate a willingness to explore other ways of comprehending the prison's past, they ultimately endorse the reductive terms through which the site's redevelopment has been framed.

An important overarching context for this discussion comes from David Harvey's work on what he terms 'monopoly rents'. Contemplating how globalisation has managed to displace the so-called 'natural monopolies' of space, place and political protectionism, Harvey is drawn to what he sees as capitalism's co-option of 'heritage' and 'culture' in an attempt to re-create these waning, exclusory powers. As he writes: 'the idea of "culture" is more and more entangled in attempts to reassert such monopoly powers precisely because claims to uniqueness and authenticity can best be articulated as distinctive and non-replicable cultural claims'.[11] Arguably, it is this search for distinction that has made cultural heritage such a powerful industry in what is otherwise an overcrowded marketplace. 'Capitalism cannot do without monopoly powers', Harvey continues, and so the spatial specificity indexed by notions of heritage comes to exert 'a significant drawing power upon the flows of capital more generally'.[12]

Since their closure in 2000, the prison's post-functional buildings have been constantly recognised (if in a misguided way) as providing a unique sense of place – a distinct 'hook' upon which international investment can be hung.[13] As stated in an early proposal for the prison to be retained as a museum: 'museums put places, which often offer completely indistinguishable services (the same retail outlets and similar small business), "on the map" and so contribute to local economies'.[14] Subsequent plans for the site's redevelopment have followed a similar logic. The remaindered (now grade one listed) prison buildings have frequently been heralded as creating a 'unique', 'historically significant' environment upon which multinational capital is free to speculate.[15] In 2013 Terence Brannigan, Chair of the MLKDC, anticipated that global investors would plough £100 million into the site's redevelopment by 2016.[16] Bolder still was the Northern Irish Assembly which, in 2012, saw the prison's 'significant location' as providing 'scope for £250 million of private sector investment'.[17]

Yet as profitable as this sounds, there are a marked set of tensions that underlie the pursuit of monopoly rents. For one thing, the confluence of capitalism and distinction creates something of an aporia – a deep contradiction between that which standardises (namely capitalism's desire to reproduce its own image) and that which strives to be different (i.e. sites of authenticity and exception). Harvey will counter the obvious outcome of this conflict – that is, the steady creep of 'banal cosmopolitanism' – by asserting that, through its search for authenticity, capitalism must support 'local cultural developments that can be antagonistic to its own smooth functioning'.[18] With the Maze/Long Kesh development still unrealised, Harvey's perception of capitalism's uneasy compliance with local cultural development does seem to hold true. Nevertheless, as this chapter will illustrate, the prospect of capital accumulation has still served to transform the cultural perception of this site, allowing its fragile history to disappear under the weight of those market-driven imperatives that besiege our present. Rather than extrapolating a dynamic sense of history, the H-Block redevelopment hands us a tamer – often static – version of its past.

History may not be delimiting in and of itself, but it can become so under certain circumstances – for example, when its intricacy is denuded by a heritage industry operating under capitalism's insatiable thirst for progress. To be entangled in this process is to touch upon the sense of boredom that Thomas Dumm has described as arising 'when people find experience infiltrated by a process of ordering that diminishes the uniqueness of their lives'.[19] Such a view is, in turn, close to Michel Foucault's famous conception of history as a twofold 'questioning of the *document*'.[20] For what is being described here is not only the construction of a seamless sense of history – the continuum of past into present that Foucault associates with a 'total history' – but also the destruction of historical instability: the preclusion of a 'general history' which speaks of 'divisions, limits, differences of level, shifts'.[21] The history ordered by the dictates of continuity is a history that has no space for those disturbing moments

that otherwise punctuate the past. It is, to evoke Walter Benjamin's arresting image, 'a process of empathy whose origin is the indolence of the heart,
acedia, which despairs of grasping and holding the genuine historical image as it
flares up briefly'.[22] Benjamin's evocation of acedia is entirely appropriate in this
context. Instead of trying 'to blast a specific era out of the homogeneous course
of history', the total view of history is listless and inert.[23] It is a 'sad' condition
in which history is unable to tolerate anything other than 'the boring repetition
of plagiarized plots and unoriginal personalities', to use Elizabeth Goodstein's
terminology.[24]

Much of the Maze/Long Kesh has now been demolished to make way for its
redevelopment, but a 'representative sample' of buildings has also been preserved. Almost all these retained structures relate to the site's status as a prison
and include, in particular, an H-Block (H6) and the prison hospital, both of
which were constructed around the site's former Second World War airfields.
This arena of military infrastructure – 'literally the brightest spot in Ulster',
as Seamus Heaney once described it – had a strong visual impact during the
Troubles: it was brooding, brutal, and unmistakably British.[25] As several commentators on the development have noted, the preservation of these buildings
is thus a politically loaded gesture – one capable of supporting 'an iconic representation of the ideology of resistance against the state'.[26] Yet the specific terms
under which these buildings have been preserved locate these structures in an
even narrower historicism, in which the legends of Republicanism and a desire
to monetise the site have gradually coalesced. On the one hand the H-Blocks
were the site of a discordant conflict between the state and nonconforming
prisoners; on the other hand, the ongoing attempt to transform the prison needs
to be seen in the context of the Northern Irish Assembly's desire to create an
economic peace dividend through the cultivation of monopoly rents. In both
cases, the result has been the construction of a mythically motivated memory
of the site, and it is on these terms that the cultural logic of capitalism and the
hystericised symbols of Republicanism have started to converge.

The H-Block at the heart of the Maze/Long Kesh development has a particularly potent history that allows us to see the historical insufficiencies at
work in the prison's subsequent imaginings. The complex of buildings that once
constituted this site include both the Nissen huts in which Republicans forged a
political (Prisoner of War) identity during the years of internment, and also the
more modern H-Blocks, which were constructed in an attempt to undermine
these claims to special category status. Based around a pioneering cell-unit
arrangement known as a 'clover leaf', the site's eight H-Blocks were notable for
their emphasis upon strict forms of regulation: they were made almost entirely

from prefabricated concrete, allowing for a highly repetitive design, and each block was divided into three segments which could effectively seal inmates in various parts of the prison at any time.[27] This standardised structure of 'phases' and 'wings' – separating each block's 96 cells from their central administration areas and washhouses – sought to strip the prisoners of their communal affinities: dividualising them, as internment had so many others, in accordance with the social dictates of a capitalist state.

Internment's rapid churn of arrest and release enabled it to become an intentionally widespread operation, penetrating almost all aspects of Nationalist society. With the construction of the H-Blocks, however, these optics were thoroughly internalised. In the H-Blocks, inmates were constructed as separate entities; they were deprived of paramilitary associations through their habitation of an individual prison cell, their donning of a prison uniform, and their codification within the prison's filing system – a 'black book' that contained their prison number, photographs and thumb prints.[28] The emphasis of this disciplinary arrangement was thereby placed upon reforming the prison population. Indeed, as David Lloyd has noted, in its stress upon the prisoner's profound isolation, the H-Block regime was one that can be traced back to the nineteenth century and, specifically, to Mary Carpenter's belief that prisons should be designed to move inmates away from modes of 'anarchic association' and towards conceptions of the 'economic individual'.[29] The Republican prisoners were intensely aware of this strategy. Bobby Sands, leader of the 1981 hunger strike, famously dubbed the H-Blocks 'the Breaker's Yard': a prison whose principal aim was 'to turn out apathetic people who'll be doing nothing but watching the gate for their day of release'.[30] It was against this brutal imposition of apathy that Sands and his comrades rebelled. In what amounted to a five-year set of blanket and no-wash (dirty) protests, these non-conforming prisoners, now known as the Blanketmen, sought to counteract the H-Block strategy – undermining the prison's architecture and its alienating regime.

The protest began on 14 September 1976 when the first IRA man sent to the H-Blocks refused to wear the prison uniform. During the years of internment political prisoners had worn their own clothing and so donning a uniform was held not only as succumbing to a criminal identity but also as acquiescing to the prison's dividualising practice. 'The uniform as lever inserts the prisoner into the machinery of incarceration as an identical and interchangeable component', notes Allen Feldman. It creates 'an undifferentiated mass in order to isolate, individualize and segment the prisoner as a divisible penal unit'.[31] Rejecting a uniform that was commonly dubbed 'the monkey suit', these nonconforming prisoners were forced naked into their cells with only a blanket to keep them warm.

Prison rules required inmates to wear clothes when leaving their cells and so, persisting in a denuded state, these prisoners were confined for 24 hours a day. Isolated and constricted, the Blanketmen developed some innovative channels for communication. The H-Blocks' prefabricated structure meant that the prisoners could perforate their cell walls by uncovering, with concerted effort, the shackle holes used by cranes to drop each pre-cast section into place.[32] Alongside this, crevices were also found around the heating pipes that ran the length of the blocks, while the cracks and fissures around window and door frames provided other openings. These gaps allowed messages (comms) to be passed between the cells and across the wings, often with the help of string threaded from their blankets. It was a system that became known as 'shooting the line', and it enabled inmates to stay in constant contact despite their physical separation.[33]

During those points when 'life in the cells settled down to the monotony of tombs', Irish classes would also take place.[34] Led by a minority of fluent speakers, the language was soon taken up by entire blocks. 'Within two years', remembers a former prisoner, 'everything said out the door was in Gaelic'.[35] Pejoratively dubbed 'Jail-talk', after Gaeltacht, the Irish spoken in the non-conforming wings was a further means of binding inmates together. But the presence of Irish in the H-Blocks had other consequences. In its foreign nature, this lexicon also obstructed the guards' ability to decode the prisoners' conversations, creating a collective space of difference – an oral community which the prison authorities found impossible to penetrate. As Melanie McMahon observes in her extraordinary analysis of the H-Blocks, 'the language itself may be said to contain alternative social logics and a culture store to which the Other has no point of entry'.[36]

Despite or perhaps because of such resistance, the H-Blocks entered a deeper state of disrepair. Two years into the protest, notes David Beresford, 'a dispute started over the circumstances in which the prisoners were allowed to wash and go to the toilet':

> Brawls ensued with prison officers over the emptying of their chamber pots and they started slopping out by throwing the contents through the spy-holes and windows, the warders sometimes throwing it back. The openings were then blocked, so the prisoners resorted to pouring the urine out through cracks and dispersing the excrement by smearing it on the walls. The 'dirty protest' was under way.[37]

Like spoken Irish, the prisoners' scatological smearings provided another axis around which they could cohere into an alternative communality – one which was equally inaccessible to the prison guards. While the prisoners were amazed at 'how you just got immune to the shit', for the guards the smell created a pungent barrier they were reluctant to cross.[38] 'You could actually see, as I saw and the inmates must have seen, the revulsion of the prison officers as they were coming onto their shifts', recounts an ex-prison Welfare Officer. The odour of excreta would stick to the prison officers, to their clothes and their skin, and it proved difficult to expunge. 'He would usually have to spend about four hours trying to get the smell off', continues the ex-Welfare Officer. 'That became a daily barrier he had to overcome.'[39]

In their strange, abnormal appearance, these protests produced what Foucault would term a historical 'discontinuity'.[40] That is to say, a rupture in which the historicist narrative of progress and development is called into question and comes under scrutiny. 'People to this day don't understand what was going on in the H-Blocks', recalls a veteran of the protest. 'This was our life-style for two, three, four, five years. It had become an alternative life-style for us.'[41] In Irish history, there was no clear precedent for the modes of resistance deployed during the blanket and no-wash years. Indeed, with the H-Blocks constantly refashioning the prisoner's bodies so as to denude their political status, it is tempting to read conditions within the prison as representing a 'limit zone' – a distorted, biopolitical realm in which, as Giorgio Agamben has written, sovereignty is imbued with 'the power to decide the point at which life ceases to be politically relevant'.[42] In their dirty, naked form, these nonconforming prisoners personified, almost too literally, the depoliticised *homo sacer* – or bare life – that Agamben sees as the essential outcome of this sovereign decision.

I have written elsewhere of biopolitics's relevance to the H-Blocks, but in the context of this chapter Agamben's arguments have a limited scope.[43] This is largely due to his inability to understand the colonial implications of the biopolitical infrastructures he invokes, namely that of the concentration camp. As the previous chapter demonstrated, we need to be careful when readings such structures – especially as they impinge upon the carceral history of Northern Ireland. While a postcolonial reading of the H-Blocks is possible, the prison is not comparable to the death camps that form Agamben's principal subject. The anger surrounding Sinn Féin's suggestion that the H-Blocks and Auschwitz shared a comparable cultural capital has emphasised this point clearly enough.[44] Consequently, I intend to put the work of Agamben to one side while I plumb the specific historical, political and cultural functions of the H-Blocks. This prison had been designed to produce economic individuals and so one, often neglected, way of reading the protests that followed is as a spontaneous and active response to that regime – a conscious attempt to subvert the alienating architectonics of the H-Blocks through acts of collective resistance within and between their cells. Through their no-wash and dirty protests, the Blanketmen managed to establish an alternative communal identity, and did so in ways that cannot be reconciled with a history of penal resistance.

It was arguably because of this discordance that the Blanketmen decided to expand their struggle. They had built a radical, alternative sociality amongst themselves, but this endeavour remained futile so long as it was unintelligible to those beyond the prison walls. 'At its core the protest was about legitimating the armed struggle *outside* of jail', notes Denis O'Hearn. 'They had to win their struggle *not* primarily for themselves but to validate the right of oppressed people to resist.'[45] The prisoners' reversion to the more familiar tactic of hunger striking was an attempt to realise this ambition. It was to be, in another break from historical precedent, a staged strategy of dying designed to inspire a revolutionary upheaval throughout Northern Ireland and beyond. 'They fully expected a coupling of this act of self-directed violence with mass insurrectionary violence outside the prison', notes Feldman, a point which the prisoners actively debated before embarking on their fast.[46] 'A lot of the debates were concentrated on that aftermath of the Hunger Strike, its consequences. We were very analytical', recalls one prisoner.[47] Sands, the first hunger striker to die, often placed the role of such violence in the context of the founding of a socialist state. As another prisoner remembers: 'he [Sands] said to some extent there was a need for the violence, because there was no way they could overthrow the capitalist system without the use of force. That America and the European community would never allow a left-wing socialist Ireland on their door-steps.'[48]

Since the onset of the Troubles, the IRA had constantly shirked its communist associations. The fear here was that members would foster a parliamentary agenda at the expense of the military campaign.[49] Indeed, when the Long Kesh internees started to dabble with socialism, remembers Eamonn McDermott, senior IRA prisoners became 'very resistant': 'there's the one story of the old Republican who says "if I ever get hold of that bastard Karl Marx I'll kill him"'.[50] In the H-Blocks, by contrast, 'there was no old IRA, Catholic Nationalists'. Here the majority of Republican prisoners went on the Blanket when they were just nineteen. 'We were the second generation of IRA people who had joined in '74 and '75', recalls a former prisoner. 'We had become socialists, and individuals had become Marxists.'[51] Like the being-in-common that emerged through an inversion of Craigavon's capitalist dynamics, the reworking of the prison's dividualising regime plunged the Blanketmen into communalism – a steadfast belief that people could 'be dedicated to one another rather than to themselves'.[52] Much to the trepidation of the IRA leadership, then, elements within the H-Blocks became intent on establishing not just a United Ireland but a socialist one. 'Only the greater mass of the Irish nation', wrote Sands during his hunger strike, 'will ensure the achievement of the socialist Republic'.[53] The turn to hunger striking was, at least in part, an attempt to realise this ambition – a cathartic gesture from which it was hoped a socialist uprising would ensue.

In 'terms of totalization', writes Foucault, 'revolutions are never more than moments of consciousness'.[54] When they fail to arise, though, they are effectively written out of history. Despite the death of ten hunger strikers, those outside the prison did not unite in a widespread insurrection. There was considerable rioting in Belfast the night Sands died but, as Seamus Deane has written, 'the point of crisis was passed without anyone seeming to know why the explosion did not come'.[55] The strike was envisaged as a means of projecting the prisoners' communality outward. Beyond the prison walls, however, these deaths were widely received with the conservatism of a historical acedia. For both their supporters and their opponents, the act of starvation resurrected a long history of Republican prison struggles, replete with a discourse of martyrdom which could be either heralded or decried. Padraig O'Malley's *Biting at the Grave* (1990) has widely been recognised as the representative example of such a reductive reading:

> And who were they, I wondered, who could harden themselves to abandon life with a casual disregard for the terminal consequences of their actions, eyes fixed on a star in a galaxy of patriot-ghosts imploding in their imaginations, their bodies sacrificial offerings to the glutinous [sic] gods of a degenerate nationalism, minds impervious to the importunings of those who did not inhabit their closed universe.[56]

Understood in these terms, the material conditions that produced the protests are eroded. The Blanketmen's being-in-common is replaced by 'a galaxy of patriot-ghosts', their unsettled history rewritten as a seamless story of perpetual martyrology – 'the boring repetition of plagiarized plots and unoriginal personalities'. When returned to 'the same mythic content', notes Lloyd, 'history becomes the eternal repetition of the same cycle of sacrifice and rebirth'.[57] In death, the hunger strikers succeeded in fulfilling this monotonous destiny, even though it was far from the socialist revolution for which many of them were fasting.

Cast in this bright, if boring light, the incomprehension of the dirty protest has been widely forgotten or, at least, radically reconfigured. In the shadow of this Republican lore, notes Lloyd, the no-wash protests were reconceived 'as an acting out of ritual defilement for which the hunger strikes became a mode of symbolic purification'.[58] Where once there was a prison hidden from society and filled with that which it could not recognise, there has now emerged a site steeped in an almost intractable sense of myth: a legend of heroic self-sacrifice or of foolish self-indulgence. Innocuous prison buildings, such as the hospital in which the strikers died, have been rendered impossibly resonant and contentious places. As the archaeologist Laura McAtackney came to realise during a tour of the prison, this particular space was clearly perceived as 'a cultural if not a sacred site'.[59] It is in terms of this sacralisation that the prison's redevelopment has been constantly framed – a misconceived sense of the site's distinction, in which a boring repetition of martyrdom has gained precedence. For the time being, then, other possibilities about what the prison might mean have been shuffled off into the margins of memory; what Foucault would term the 'discontinuity' of the H-Blocks' 'raw material' has hereby been effaced.[60]

The prison finally ceased institutional operations in September 2000 and, in the spirit of urban renewal that has gripped so much of post-conflict Northern Ireland, proposals for reconstruction invariably took hold. By May 2006, the newly formed 'Maze Consultation Panel' had produced a 123-page *Masterplan and Implementation Strategy*. Integral to its vision were two state-sponsored initiatives: one for a new Multi-Purpose Sports Zone, the other for an International Centre for Conflict Transformation. This Centre was to incorporate the retained prison buildings – including the hospital where the ten hunger strikers had died – but it was to be a facility directed towards the future, focusing on the site's contribution to the Peace Process and not on the turbulent events it once contained. In keeping with this trajectory, plans for the Sports Zone also attempted to move the site away from its murky past, creating a cross-community stadium (known as the 'Terrordrome' by its critics) in which Gaelic games, rugby and football could all be played. If these proposals were implemented, then the *Masterplan* argued that the prison, 'so long a symbol of conflict', could 'become a symbol of the ongoing transformation from conflict to peace'.[61] In many ways, this positioning has served to obfuscate the site's discontinuous history. In its attention to the language of 'symbol' and 'transformation', the plans have distorted the conflicts within the prison – professing to 'capitalise on the strategic location and unique assets of the site' in a way that will prioritise a discourse of myth and martyrology.[62]

What is striking about the Maze/Long Kesh development, then, is the rhetorical strategies through which it has been advanced. For instance, when it came to the retention of the prison buildings, the terminology that justified their preservation overlooked their historical dissonance, preferring instead a mythological perception of their past, presented as the triumph of progression and continuity. As Northern Ireland's Historic Buildings Council reported:

> When a building, or part of it, is listed, one of the criteria to be taken into consideration is its Historical Interest, which can be taken as its historical significance within Northern Ireland, and also its social importance to the community. The Maze buildings are not buildings of architectural beauty by any stretch of the imagination, but they may well be touched by that Terrible Beauty identified by WB Yeats. This prison, for its inmates and prison staff, and their families, played a significant part in the evolution of the late 20th century history of Ireland.[63]

Understood in these terms, preservation becomes little more than a means of securing a narrative of 'evolution', a mode of remembrance that can only visualise the prison in terms of what the Buildings Council goes on to term its contribution to 'the continuum of our history'.[64] Although the prison's listing makes reference to Yeats's emotive imagery, the revolutionary violence this describes is nullified by its inclusion in a narrative of progression and development. Foucault has warned against this process, and his search for a 'general' history sees him castigate these 'notions of development and evolution'.[65] This is because, as David Webb has commented, implicit in their usage is 'the unfolding of a single idea, which thereby confers unity on the process (as though the idea were a substance undergoing change, but remaining essentially itself)'.[66] Consequently, instead of acknowledging the widespread fracture the hunger strikers hoped to generate, the site's 'Terrible Beauty' is left lifeless and inert – part of a historical continuum rather than a means by which that singular account could be halted and restarted. The invocation of Yeats is, as such, nothing more than a static marker – a plagiarised symbol or brand through which it is hoped the site's putative distinction can be cultivated.

The H-Blocks – the largest, most oppressive, and most visually striking of the prison structures – were once home to an alternative sociality, one that defied the state's aggressive attempts to dividualise and control its inmates. By the twenty-first century, the one remaining H-Block has become a symbol of the North's tentative parlance with the language of peace dividends and monopoly rents – the retained prison buildings now incorporated into a 'unique Belfast-to-New York design collaboration, as a showcase to attract international developers and investors'.[67] Though these plans for redevelopment have so far failed, the project is still valuable because it allows us to comprehend some of the tensions implicit in what Harvey has termed capitalism's attempt to 'appropriate and extract surpluses from local differences'.[68] As I have been arguing throughout this book, the intersection of capitalism and the North's ethnic–national divisions has frequently given rise to a sense of boredom and inertia. The plans for the prison's redevelopment seem little different in this respect. Again, this is reflected most clearly in the architecture of the site, and the manner in which the decision to retain only 'a representative sample' of the former prison buildings has excised the prison's discordant raw material. As Brian Graham and Sara McDowell have observed, 'preservation in itself is a form of sacralising place through its reconstruction as material heritage'. Linking this sacralisation, and the mythopoeia it presupposes, to the construction of the Maze/Long Kesh as 'a zero-sum heritage site', Graham and McDowell argue that as it currently stands the redevelopment can only 'represent a singular claim within a republican narrative of resistance'.[69]

Conceived in these terms, the workings of the heritage industry and the rise of a Republican mythology combine so as to extirpate the prison's historical complexity, while also creating a singular identity upon which the site's distinctive qualities can be hung. Indeed, as J.E. Tunbridge and Gregory Ashworth go on to note, 'the production of a largely homogeneous heritage product greatly simplifies many marketing, and especially promotional, problems'; something they feel to be particularly valuable 'in the early stages of tourism development, most especially for foreign markets'.[70] Of course, what is lost in this attempt to capitalise on the prison's past is the incomprehensibility of life in the H-Blocks themselves. It is this historical acedia, what Deane has described as 'a sad history ... of touristic pleasure', which creates 'a combat with boredom at its centre'.[71] As this suggests, the terms on which this conflict tends to be fought are equally reductive. For example, the often invoked alternative to preservation – the belief that the prison should simply be 'erased from the map' – threatens not only the entirety of its history but also the prospect of monopoly rents that its redevelopment could yield.[72] As such the Northern Irish Assembly has been unable to respond to demands for the prison's demolition, leaving the Maze/Long Kesh development in a prolonged state of hiatus. When the MLKDC's promotional videos present a prison structure lost amongst scenes of ubiquitous construction and consumption, it is precisely this confluence of history and inertia that is unwittingly revealed.

While the Maze/Long Kesh developers have proved unwilling to countenance the unsettled histories the H-Blocks contain, the prison's reimagining in film has considered and contested its past in a much more productive fashion. This is largely because of the ways in which these productions have managed to engage with the modern/non-modern intersection the H-Blocks represent. Indeed, *Hunger*, the most unconventional of these engagements, derives much of its critical purchase from its desire to depict the boredom that emerges at this interface. As such, the film is one that opens itself to being read through an aesthetic of ennui and is, perhaps, best understood on these terms. For Deane, a productive representation of boredom always 'involves an intensification of the rhetorical strategies which are needed to create a text that is, simultaneously, driven towards completeness and dispersed amidst fragmentary incoherences'.[73] This compositional model seeks to 'make a virtue of monotony' since, in its attention to incoherence, it becomes 'one way in which the drive towards telling one story (say, the nationalist one) can be stalled'.[74] As such, Deane's perception of boredom provides a succinct template by which the directive to create a continuous and homogeneous history (say, a capitalist one) can be curtailed by the story of its own making. Rather than attaining a sense of progression, the attention to fracture and dispersion produces a historical narrative that is denied the sense of closure and completion it desires. Of the three films that have been made in relation to the H-Blocks, it is *Hunger* which has come closest to achieving this effect. However it, too, has proved unable to push such 'fragmentary incoherences' to any truly disruptive ends.

The depiction of history on screen has, of course, long been seen as a means for its reinvigoration. In 1983, R.J. Raack argued that, with its 'quick cuts to new sequences, dissolves, fades, speed-ups, [and] slow motion', film was well placed to 'recover all the past's liveliness'.[75] *Some Mother's Son*, *H3* and *Hunger* deploy these cinematic techniques to varying degrees, but they are certainly all concerned with using this medium to uncover some of the concealed facets of the H-Blocks. This is not to say that these films are necessarily subversive. While they were produced by different studios, their status as publicly funded – 'capital-intensive' – cultural products means that they are also concerned,[76] almost inevitably, with the dissemination and maintenance of what Harvey has called those 'special marks of distinction that attach to some place [and] which have a significant drawing power upon the flows of capital more generally'.[77] As much was evident in John Myerscough's 1988 recognition that the arts – including film – can 'raise the profile and business attractiveness of a region and stimulate tourism'.[78] Yet, while these factors have undoubtedly placed the critical potential of Northern Irish cinema under some strain, it is also important to remember the contradictory forces that can subtend the pursuit of monopoly rents. As Harvey writes, capitalism 'can even support (though cautiously and often nervously) all manner of "transgressive" cultural practices precisely because this is one way in which to be original, creative and authentic as well as unique'.[79] Such 'support' can, as in the case of the Maze/Long Kesh development, still promote a mundane account of the North's 'unique' history. But it can also make space for alternatives to these banal imperatives, and can do so in a manner that is often compelling.

It is on these terms that cinematic responses to the H-Blocks have been able to explore the prison's disordered history, testing the limits of what it is possible to represent and what it is acceptable to say. *Some Mother's Son*, for example, engages with the H-Block struggles from a predominantly female perspective, a pointedly gendered reading which reframes traditional perceptions of the prison protests as a chronicle of Irish male sacrifice. The film is structured around the experiences of a middle-class mother, Kathleen Quigley (Helen Mirren), whose bourgeois pacifism is steadily politicised following the imprisonment of her son, Gerard (Aidan Gillen), as an IRA volunteer. As the film's title suggests, Kathleen's political awakening will always be superseded by the primacy of the familial realm. But the film juxtaposes these competing demands to illustrate the friction between the lifestyles and ideals of those within and without the H-Blocks. In many ways, *Some Mother's Son* is a conventional piece of filmmaking, yet, in its attention to Kathleen's uncertain relationship with the H-Blocks, the film adds a degree of complexity to the rendering of its subject.

The film begins with Margaret Thatcher's arrival at Downing Street in 1979, before outlining how her Northern Irish policy would focus around a counter-insurgency of 'isolation', 'criminalisation' and 'demoralisation'. Although much of the H-Block crisis preceded Thatcher's premiership, starting the film in this way is significant because it emphasises how these disciplinary dynamics were focused exclusively within the prison. As the Conservative MP, Farnsworth (Tom Hollander), explains during this opening vignette: 'We want to make the prisons an asset, not a liability'. The narrative that results is an intimate account of how Kathleen and her son Gerard are steadily enmeshed within this governmental directive. Portraying Gerard's progression from an IRA combatant to a nonconforming prisoner and hunger striker, the film constantly balances the costs of his actions against the lives of his family, and his mother in particular. Although Kathleen will come to call off his hunger strike and is, thus, ultimately unable to countenance the prisoners' political vision, the focus upon their relationship allows the film to make an important assertion about the H-Blocks – emphasising how the prison community sought to awaken those often disengaged elements within the North's Catholic middle-class. 'You have this massive middle ground who don't know where they're going, who don't understand the implications', remarks a former Republican prisoner. 'For us, the Hunger Strike concentrated the whole Irish struggle into a small black-and-white understandable issue.'[80] *Some Mother's Son*, then, places no great emphasis on a saga of martyrdom or mythic self-valorisation. Instead, the film tries to locate the hunger strike within a wider attempt to decentre the state's desire to transform the prisoners into economic individuals. It shows the Blanketmen to be energised by communal attachments which actively defy Westminster's desire to 'isolate' and 'demoralise' their political affiliations through a dividualising regime.

However, for all its emphasis on the need to communicate and externalise this message, the dramatic logic of the film constantly stunts the effectiveness of this variegated view of history. As George has acknowledged, there was always some concern about how he paced the film: 'the subject matter was so maudlin that if you slowed down anywhere, the audience would start to get morose, so we started off going at the speed of a train, and we kept that pace up right through'.[81] Betraying the constraints and demands of a commercial cinema, the imperative for action both belies the complexity of George's intervention – relegating that which does not propel the narrative to the level of the 'morose' –

and, in so doing, justifies the erosion of nuance under the pretext of a relentless need for speed. The film therefore gains its momentum by constantly building to a series of climactic confrontations, initially between the IRA and the British state but, as the plot develops, increasingly between Kathleen and the strands of Republicanism with which she is tentatively aligned. According to Brian Neve, this fast editing style follows the 'Hollywood practice' of the film's financers and, in its 'rigorous cutting to the spine of the drama', it has the disadvantage of excluding 'the ironies of a different type of cinema'.[82] *Some Mother's Son* is thus susceptible to undermining the relative ingenuity of its interpretation – with its subscription to a high-tempo aesthetic inhibiting its ability to interrogate the fresh perspectives it has otherwise managed to accentuate.

Understood in this way, the film comes close to producing what Fredric Jameson has called an 'absolute present', a temporal logic which typifies the 'historical tendency of late-capitalism' and its popular cinema.[83] Thinking of action films in particular, Jameson notes how the demand for a succession of 'self-sufficient moments of violence ... gradually crowds out the development of narrative time and reduces plot to the merest pretext or thread on which to string a series of explosions (much like a trailer preview)'.[84] In *Some Mother's Son*, such a foreshortening is encapsulated in the prison visits between Gerard and Kathleen, a set of encounters which thematically and visually encapsulate the relationship between those within and without the H-Blocks throughout the film. In the first of these, listening to Gerard, we learn of the active and material means by which he has entered into the dirty protest, and the circumstances by which he continues to survive and to exist; watching Kathleen, we witness the verbal and visible incredulity of his situation, its grotesque outline and execrable contours: 'how can you live like this?' she asks. As we watch their exchange, we are nudged towards what veterans of the protests have described as the incomprehensibility that shrouds their experiences, and yet the film denies itself an opportunity to probe this disconnect. Rather than pausing at this intersection, the primacy of the drama dominates, with the scene lurching towards a sudden and fraught embrace between mother and son as Gerard tries to smuggle a 'comm' outside the prison. This act initiates Kathleen's uneasy participation in Republican politics, but it also moves the film away from a direct engagement with the disjunctions it has started to expose. With her now carrying a message for Sinn Féin, Kathleen's interaction with the H-Blocks' unknowable dynamics leads only to an 'explosive' confrontation with the Republican hierarchy, not a nuanced interrogation of that odious prison life she has just encountered.

From this point, the prisoners' voice is repeatedly denied any meaningful interaction with that middle ground it is hoping to inspire. While George is at pains to stress how the prisoners saw their acts of individual sacrifice in explicitly collective terms – 'they were all dying for each other', states George, 'I tried to get that across in the film' – the insistence on action will not allow this being-in-common to be articulated beyond the prison.[85] To do so could mean falling into the trap of what George has termed a 'morose' narrative, a diversion that would unsettle a film whose trajectory is now locked upon the dramatic – 'absolute present' – posed by the strikers' impending deaths. Thus, 'my son is dying, we have no time' becomes the film's closing refrain, while the motivation for this death remains perpetually unaddressed. Despite the fraught political negotiations that come to shroud Gerard's decaying frame, the hunger striker is effectively silenced in the closing scenes. As Peter Mahon has suggested, Gerard's status as a mere 'son' renders him a '"political infant" (from the Latin, *infans*, "unable to speak")'.[86] A mute presence – only able to make obscure demands that his family should 'respect my beliefs' and 'not let me down' – Gerard leaves the H-Block message indecipherable and unknown to precisely those individuals outside the prison he is desperate to convert.

With this in mind, a more direct and sustained engagement with the H-Blocks arguably comes from *Hunger* and *H3*. Both these films focus exclusively on the convulsions within the H-Blocks, as the protests transition towards the prospect of a hunger strike and the fatalities that lie therein. Unlike *Some Mother's Son*, however, the strength of these films derives from their intense concentration upon the material conditions of the H-Blocks themselves. Both directors remained faithful to the prison architecture, allowing it to dictate how they shot.[87] 'I'm longing to have a field to put a camera in', admits Blair, 'but it has given me a great empathy with the subject matter'.[88] The claustrophobic structure became a means of accessing the prison's shibboleths, and the films feed off these constrictions, unlocking the hidden histories of this building, although in quite different ways. *H3*, for example, engages with the site through the eyes of a young IRA volunteer, Declan McCann (Aidan Campbell). Declan's cellmate, Seamus Scullion (Brendan Mackey), is the Officer Commanding for H-Block 3, and the film weighs Seamus's seniority against Declan's naivety as a means of educating its audience in the customs and endurance of the dirty protest. 'How do you stick it?' asks Declan early in the drama – a question that becomes increasingly rhetorical as the film proceeds. As the film unpacks the modes of resistance the prisoners have adopted, attention is focused upon the sociability these practices and techniques can attain. Seamus thus secretes a sizeable transistor radio inside his rectum with a knowing series of winks; stashes of home-made cigarettes are 'shot' between cell doors with all the drama of a prison escape; and Declan is inculcated into the dirty protest through a didactic exchange that tries to mask his evident repulsion with a jocular, if strained, camaraderie:

DECLAN: (*hopping with discomfort*) How do you go to the toilet?
SEAMUS: Just go into the corner, and let nature take its course.
(*Declan defecates, uncomfortably*)
DECLAN: What do I do with it?
SEAMUS: Spread it on the wall. Gets rid of it permanently, kills the smell and gives them a bit of hassle … Use a bit of sponge from your mattress … Go on – get decorating.
(*Declan reluctantly spreads his faeces on the cell wall*)
DECLAN: I'm sorry.
SEAMUS: (*laughing*) Don't be. I'll get my revenge later on.

Although this manipulation of the H-Block architecture worked against the socio-economic reforms demanded by the prison regime, the film consciously refrains from explicating the productive alterities these methods also establish. Instead, *H3* directs its attention towards what it presents as the prisoners' implicit desire to return to some form of 'normality' – a desire made visible not only through the recurrent disbelief of the as yet unassimilated Declan but also through the evident demoralisation of established members within the H-Block community. For this reason, the dramatic logic of the film will go on to draw its impetus from the prisoner's turbulent experiment with compliance, as well · their successful immersion into electoral politics. These arcs help to ensure that the film has, in the words of its producer Juanita Wilson, 'all the elements of good drama', but they do so at the expense of the radical sociality the H-Blocks came to embody. As Wilson goes on to assert, the film is 'a political story certainly, but political with a small "p" because what we always liked about the project was the fact that it was about what carried them through this difficult situation'.[89] It is this attention to politics 'with a small "p"' that creates space for the H-Blocks' convivial culture and the active historical circumstances they have created. But the film's apolitical approach also produces kinks within the celluloid. There are notable silences and fissures about what the prison protests actually revealed and what they ultimately came to mean. At these points the substance of the prisoners' material circumstances can express little more than euphemistic phrases of 'giving them a bit of hassle' or of being 'carried through this difficult situation'. What is suppressed at such moments – and intentionally so – are the specific details of what made this situation 'difficult' and why.

In cinematic terms, *Hunger*'s visualisation of the H-Blocks is more unconventional and potentially more disturbing. In contrast to earlier films about the protests, McQueen introduces us to the prison through two competing perspectives – initially that of the prison officer Raymond Lohan (Stuart Graham), before then supplying the more traditional entrance of a newly sentenced and non-conforming prisoner, Davey Gillen (Brian Milligan). Constructed in this way, the film is able to disclose the incommensurable social logics at work within the H-Blocks, a feat it achieves through its relentless pairing of substances, situations and circumstances, all of which are captured in poignant, elongated shots. Thus the loneliness of Lohan's domestic routine rubs against the prisoners' claustrophobic, shit-filled intimacies; where Lohan changes into the Queen's uniform to enforce the law, Gillen will strip naked ready to defy the imperatives of the British state.

In contrast to a movie like *Some Mother's Son*, *Hunger* is a film where a slow editing of image and object suggests a multilayered narrative precisely because it stretches or over-extends its own possibilities. If the film depends upon conjoining competing elements, it also strives to create a series of object lessons. 'It's all about how you can make something which is a small object actually be an explosion', states McQueen, 'that one thing can then make you think of several other things'.[90] As life within the prison unfolds on screen, the alternative sociality of the Blanketmen can be sensed in these visual metaphorics. It can be detected in the disconnect between the prison's brutally mechanised appearance and the Blanketmen's naked vulnerability. It can be felt in the schism between Lohan's listless lunchbreak and Gillen's careful preparation for his visits. Where first we watch Lohan mindlessly fold the foil from his sandwiches, we then see Gillen meticulously prepare his comms using scraps of Clingfilm. 'In the H-Blocks', writes Feldman, 'there was no reality outside the various systems and counter-systems of representation and objectification that were violently hurled back and forth through the recesses of the prison'.[91] What *Hunger* captures is not only the extent to which this fraught intersection conditioned circumstances within the prison but also the degree to which it created a space that was incompatible with the social practices at work beyond its walls. When we do see Lohan outside the H-Blocks he appears, in Eugene McNamee's phrase, to have lost the 'capacity for authentic human interaction', as if his experience of prison life has made him a marginal figure, unable to integrate with wider society.[92]

As these observations suggest, *Hunger*'s effectiveness in visualising the H-Blocks resides at the level of structure: its contrasts, its juxtapositions, its entanglements. While *H3* is overtly conscious of the fact that, in Wilson's terms, 'it's a feature film, it's drama', *Hunger* seems to starve its audience of the traditional markers of modern cinema.[93] It gives us 'a different diet', states Jason Solomons, one that leaves us 'without the structures we normally depend on to understand film'.[94] In *H3*, the dramatic arcs are invariably tied to the prisoners' attempts to purify their bodies after years of exhausted defilement. For this reason, a defining image of the film becomes Seamus's luxuriant immersion in a bath of warm water – a symbolic baptism that *H3* will reinvent, and through which the 'perpetual rupture' of life on the Blanket will come to adopt a singular dimension.[95] Through their experiments in conforming, their absorption in electoral politics and, finally, through their hunger strike itself, *H3* presents the H-Block crisis as a steady progression towards an appropriate mode of redemption. For those who endured these transitions, however, a sense of biological contamination and historical dislocation invariably broke through:

> At the start of the Blanket Protest you'd think, 'My God! How am I going to stick with this!' Then you would look at the Blanket Protest from the position of the Dirty Protest. 'Well we had our wee bogs and showers. Then what were we complaining about?' Then when the Hunger Strike started we were thinking, 'For fuck's sake, the Dirty Protest was all-right. What were we complaining about?'[96]

H3's quest-like structure, which falls into the trap of creating that evolutionary synthesis critiqued by Foucault, is reconfigured in *Hunger*'s opening two-thirds. Here the dirty protests are presented as an intractable lived condition, counterpoised against the H-Block regime: a relentless battle of urine and detergent, a constant conflict of brutality and assassinations. As such, the defining image of this film – initially at least – is not one of restoration, but one of gyrations: a dialectic with no solution, a narrative with no visible end. In many respects, this is a compositional prerogative that replicates the subversive play with boredom Deane has identified; it is a story whose drive towards completion finds itself 'dispersed amidst fragmentary incoherences', and through this exaggerated depiction of ennui, as Lloyd has noted, 'the stretches of boredom and stillness' that constituted life on the Blanket can be 'interrupted by sudden and extreme violence'.[97] McQueen has likened his film to that of a journey downstream: 'you're given a sense of your surroundings – landscape and so forth – and all of a sudden there is a rapid, so your surroundings have been fractured, your surroundings have been disrupted'.[98] It is at these points of fracture that we glimpse the incomprehensible – the alternative sociality the H-Blocks embodied and the spirit of resistance they inspired.

There is, of course, another, final layer to the film's historic subject matter, and, although the journey downstream has so far lacked a destination, the prospect of a hunger strike brings one sharply into view. 'And then the last part I wanted to be the waterfall, the loss of gravity, descent, death', McQueen tells us.[99] *Hunger* moves towards this point of closure through a sustained dialogue between Bobby Sands (Michael Fassbender) and his local Parish Priest, Dom Moran (Liam Cunningham). This daringly extended debate written by McQueen and Enda Walsh, is virtually the only conversation in a film initially envisaged as silent, and it is through this discourse that the disjunctions *Hunger* has visualised are both tentatively verbalised and gradually effaced. The camera remains motionless for some twenty minutes as Sands's rigid revolutionary principles gradually grate against Dom's unwavering belief in humanity's moral mode. 'It shows the two sides', McQueen says, 'the Catholic Church wanted people for God, of course, and the Republicans wanted people for some kind of socialism'.[100]

For Deane, the ecclesiastical doctrine is merely a means of reinforcing the state's political idiom 'while appearing to be independent of it'.[101] As such, its presence at the threshold of the prison is one which can slowly extend the conflict within the H-Blocks back out into wider society. *Hunger* deploys this potential to dialogically unravel how the Blanketmen are alienated not just from normal social values but from the Republican movement as a whole:

> *SANDS:* We are on the frontline. We created the protest. It's our responsibility. Leadership have been very clear to me, Dom. Four and half years of the no wash protest, as much as it has highlighted republicanism to some extent, it has also distracted from the wider development of the organization.

This is a significant assertion, acknowledging the prisoners' dissociation where a film like *H3* – through its use of flashbacks to the prisoners' IRA operations – would suggest an inherent cohesion between the violent Republicanism espoused within and without the prison. As Feldman reminds us, 'the assumption of a seamless evolutionary continuity in the development of Republican ideology and tactics obscures the particular experiential basis of their resistance'.[102] *Hunger* has gone some way to acknowledge this 'experiential' mode of resistance. But the problem the film now highlights is the unpalatability of the Blanketmen's condition and how, moreover, their decision to advance their cause through a hunger strike is equally inscrutable:

> *DOM*: You say you're soldiers. It's all about the 'freedom'. But you've got no appreciation of a life, Bobby. You no longer know what a life is, you men. Four years living in these conditions, no one expects you to be normal. There is nothing normal about ye … And this situation here, the future of the Republican movement is in the hands of you men, who have lost all, all sense of reality. You think your head's on right? Locked up here 24 hours a day in piss and shit. And you are making decisions that could see so many men die? Build a statue to Bobby Sands! You're joking me.

Caught between reading Sands's actions in terms of a monotonous lineage of Republican martyrology – 'I've heard you eulogising Wolfe Tone, Connolly, MacSwiney' – while also recognising the perverse conditions that have shaped Sands's thinking, Dom's discourse snags at the hunger strikers' underlying predicament. The grotesque conditions the Blanketmen have endured are at once clearly visible to those outside their community and yet, in that stark difference, they are also thoroughly incomprehensible. The first part of the film hinted at this condition through its visual dialectics, and in so doing created something close to what Foucault would term a '*Heterotopia*': a confused state, in which 'things are "laid", "placed", "arranged" in sites so very different from one another that it is impossible to find a place of residence for them, to define a *common locus* beneath them'.[103] The turmoil that defines the heterotopia is, of course, also what makes it so disconcerting. In their discordance, notes Foucault, 'they secretly undermine language', destroying the syntax by which 'words and things … "hold together"'.[104]

Representing a violent interface between capitalist and non-capitalist social formations, as the H-Blocks invariably did, the history they emit expresses precisely such an instability: 'one in which the narratability of the event enters into crisis', as Lloyd expresses it.[105] Indeed, it is largely for this reason that the concept of historical continuity is so pervasive and 'indispensable', so comforting and restorative.[106] As Foucault writes, in its commitment to cohesion, a 'total' history creates the (false) 'certainty that time will dispense nothing without restoring it in a reconstituted unity'.[107] It is this unity that the spectre of the Blanketmen has gone some way to disturbing and, as such, they find themselves not only outside the realms of history but also somewhere beyond the limits of language. In their raw, unassimilated state, they struggle to signify to a society accustomed to lending speech to those historical traces 'which, in themselves, are often not verbal or which say in silence something other than what they actually say'.[108]

Hunger registers this difficulty by becoming a victim of its inhibited historical arrangement. As this pivotal scene reaches its climax, the film's intrinsic description of the H-Blocks is transformed into a more familiar, but historically devalued, discourse. The camera unlocks its static gaze and pans on to Sands, who now recounts his childhood memories of a cross-country race in Donegal: it was the 'most beautiful place in Ireland', a landscape of 'woods and streams' and 'little silver fish', he explains. These stand-out images, redolent of Yeats's 'The Song of Wandering Aengus', transport us to an abstracted world – a realm of Celtic purity far removed from the piss and shit of the H-Block crisis.[109] Yet, despite its Romanticised contours, this dreamscape is somehow more knowable – more recognisable and coherent in its imagery than the visceral prison life the film has carefully reconstructed. *Hunger* pushes deeper into this more legible terrain, searching it for correlatives. On discovering a wounded foal within the stream, Sands recalls how he took the decision to drown the animal, rather than let it suffer a presumed and protracted death from exhaustion. Sands had a keen interest in nature, documented in his own prison writings, but here the rural landscape is loaded with allegorical implications. His decision to kill the foal, witnessed by a Priest who has misconstrued the event and will punish Sands as a consequence, becomes an allegory for the necessity of self-sacrifice. Sands looks directly at the camera, now positioned from Dom's point-of-view, and declares:

> SANDS: I could take the punishment for all our boys. I had the respect of them other boys now and I knew that. I'm clear of the reasons Dom. And I'm clear of all the repercussions. But I will act, and I will not stand by and do nothing.

Taking this lead, the final section of the film presents Sands's fast in startlingly individualistic terms – a path to death shorn of the collectivist attitude *Some Mother's Son* and *H3* have hinted at, albeit in problematic ways. Seen only in the prison hospital, and isolated from all those 'boys' he supposedly represents, Sands dies a beautiful, if terrible, death. 'A shoulder, an arm, a haunch sometimes shine with Caravaggesque sensuality', notes the artist Brian O'Doherty.[110] There is undoubtedly a frisson of subversion in McQueen's visual vocabularies during this final section. In a perceptive reading of the film, Alison Garden notes how Sands's naked and emaciated body comes to mimic Hans Holbein the Younger's sixteenth-century painting *The Body of the Dead Christ in the Tomb*. Crucially, writes Garden, this visual parallel is also 'highly feminised' because Sands's penis also remains out of shot. Leaving viewers 'only with a mound of pubic hair', McQueen manages to feminise Sands's body in such a way that he now becomes the subject of the camera's desire.[111] Yet because of this eerie attraction to Sands's demise, *Hunger* also falls back into that same monotonous trap: translating the H-Block crisis from a moment of rupture into an exhausted imagery of myth and martyrology. As Lloyd has written in relation to this final sequence, 'the hunger strike is at once aestheticized, in however cold and clinical a light, and by the same token mythologized again as an act of "passion"'.[112]

Hunger is certainly loaded with a radical gender politics but, as Garden goes on to conclude, McQueen's broader depiction of the H-Block crisis serves to silence the disruption even its transgressive masculinity could otherwise represent. 'The feminisation of Sands' body works to cancel the excessive, troubled reaches of his masculinity, as a violent member of the Provisional IRA', writes Garden.[113] While, in the film's concomitant elevation of Thatcher's hard-line response to the hunger strike – carried by her disembodied voice, often overlaying prisoners in pain – McQueen's use of the feminine also only seems 'to absolve his male subjects of their violent pasts'.[114]

McQueen has always maintained that his film disavows the political in favour of a focus on humanity: 'for me it's essentially about what we, as humans, are capable of, morally, physically, psychologically'.[115] Yet, the critical charge against his film is that he jeopardises his putative neutrality by depicting the hunger strike in Christological terms; that in presenting death as an act of passion he produces a storyline 'that has already been written by the hunger strik-ers'.[116] For Chris Tookey, *Hunger* is nothing more than 'a love letter to Sands'.[117] My contention is that, on the contrary, McQueen steers a more impartial course by reiterating this mythological version of the strike. Were he to have pursued Sands's heartfelt desire to expand the H-Block struggle, McQueen would have created a far more disruptive film – one that might have even come close to acknowledging how Sands's death actually sought 'to blast a specific era out of the homogeneous course of history'.[118] As the former IRA prisoner Richard O'Rawe reminds us: 'Bobby was a left-winger. He did not think a united Ireland was worth it unless it was a socialist Ireland.'[119] Placed within this context, *Hunger*'s ultimate emphasis upon what McNamee terms 'the transformation of dehumanised figures … into figures of humanity who are worth remembering' is a relatively conservative statement.[120] By focusing on Sands's 'humanity', McQueen downplays the radicalism of his politics, creating an evolutionary narrative which could, much to O'Rawe's discomfort, 'take us from Bobby's struggle to the political situation we are in today'.[121] In his individualised death, what was a collective – socialist – gesture becomes, instead, a story of bodily transformation, and one that allows the image of Sands to be absorbed (for better or for worse) within the structures of a post-conflict, neoliberal Northern Ireland. 'The film opened and ran in Belfast without any protests or demonstra-tions of any kind', remarks McNamee. 'An illustration, perhaps, that the form of memory was, if not something that could be shared equally by all, at least one that was tolerable.'[122]

Ultimately, *Hunger*, *H3* and *Some Mother's Son* make a similar intervention. While each film acknowledges the alternative sociality the Blanketmen embodied, they also all assert (although to varying degrees) that the 1981 hunger strike was a means of resolving, rather than intensifying, the struggle they were in. Death becomes a mode of purification in these films, cleansing the prisoners of their alterity so that they can be reincorporated within those social structures they once fought against. In this way, the unsettling potentiality of the H-Blocks is circumscribed by the continuum of a totalising history, or rather, to use Foucault's terminology, each of these films eventually proves unable 'to con-ceive of the *Other* in the time of our own thought'.[123] Indeed, in their final insistence on historical evolution, they also tentatively reinforce the image by which the Maze/Long Kesh Commission has promoted the site's distinction: namely, that the H-Blocks can become 'a symbol of the ongoing transformation from conflict to peace'. As ever, what is lost in this progression is the historical disorder the H-Blocks used to demarcate. In fact, it is partly for this reason that Peter Robinson's claim that the H-Blocks are 'a symbol of "a societal failure"' has a certain pertinence.[124] The being-in-common espoused within the H-Blocks did indeed fail to integrate with the capitalist ideologies that were aggressively imposed upon Northern Irish society throughout the years of conflict. Faced with a Maze/Long Kesh development energised by a passive and monotonous narrative, it is worth remembering the historical rupture the H-Blocks came to represent. After all, in its fragmented, layered and unstable form, this historical raw material gives us a glimpse into a very different future, an alternative if you like, to the banality that shrouds post-conflict 'reimaginings' of the Troubles.

Notes and references

1   Seamus Heaney, 'Christmas 1971', in *Preoccupations: Selected Prose 1968–1978* (London: Faber, 1985), p. 32.

2   Maze Long Kesh Development Corporation, *From Peace to Prosperity Vision* (YouTube, 2013) www.youtube.com/watch?v=sxsnfQvMS6Q [accessed 24 July 2017].

3   Maze Long Kesh Development Corporation, 'Press Release: Maze Long Kesh Is Northern Ireland's Largest Development Site' (24 April 2013) http://mazelongkesh. com/assets/pdf/Press-Release-Vision-Plan.pdf [accessed 24 July 2017].

4   Liam Clarke, 'Hunger strike hospital key to Maze project success: report', *Belfast Telegraph*, 14 May 2014. www.belfasttelegraph.co.uk/news/local-national/north ern-ireland/hunger-strike-hospital-key-to-maze-project-success-report-30272119. html [accessed 24 July 2017].

5   Quoted in Allen Feldman, *Formations of Violence: The Narrative of the Body and Political Terror in Northern Ireland* (Chicago: University of Chicago Press, 1991), p. 231.

6   'Declaration of Support', *The Agreement: Agreement Reached in the Multi-Party Negotiations* (Good Friday Agreement, 1998), Paragraphs 2, www.gov.uk/government/uploads/ system/uploads/attachment_data/file/13665 2/agreement.pdf.

7   'Thomas "Dixie" Elliott interviewed about Peace and Reconciliation Centre', *Breakfast*, BBC Radio Foyle, 19 August 2013.

8   Colin Graham, 'Luxury, Peace and Photography in Northern Ireland', *Visual Culture in Britain*, 10.2 (2009), 143.

9   MLKDC, 'Northern Ireland's Largest Development Site'.

10   Slavoj Žižek, *The Sublime Object of Ideology* (London: Verso, 1989), p. 138.

11   David Harvey, *Rebel Cities: From the Right to the City to the Urban Revolution* (London: Verso, 2013), p. 96.

12   *Ibid.*, p. 103.

13   See Coiste na n-Iarchimí's, *A Museum at Long Kesh or the Maze? Report of Conference Proceedings* (Belfast: Coiste na n-Iarchimí, 2003).

14   Coiste na n-Iarchimí, *A Museum at Long Kesh or the Maze*, p. 31.

15   Masterplanning Consortium, *Maze/Long Kesh: Masterplan and Implementation Strategy. Final Report* (Belfast: HMSO, 2006), pp. 5, 23.

16 MLKDC, 'Northern Ireland's Largest Development Site'.
17 Quoted in Laura McAtackney, *An Archaeology of the Troubles: The Dark Heritage of Long Kesh/Maze Prison* (Oxford: Oxford University Press, 2013), p. 243.
18 Harvey, *Rebel Cities*, pp. 108–110.
19 Thomas Dumm, *A Politics of the Ordinary* (London: New York University Press, 1999), p. 14.
20 Michel Foucault, *The Archaeology of Knowledge*, trans. by A.M. Sheridan Smith (London: Routledge, 2002), p. 6.
21 Foucault, *Archaeology of Knowledge*, pp. 10–11.
22 Walter Benjamin, 'Theses on the Philosophy of History', in *Illuminations* ed. by Hannah Arendt, trans. by Harry Zohn (London: Fontana Press, 1992), p. 248.
23 *Ibid.*, p. 254.
24 Elizabeth Goodstein, *Experience without Qualities: Boredom and Modernity* (Stanford: Stanford University Press, 2005), p. 382. While Benjamin foregrounds the 'sad' element of acedia, it is important to realise that this quality creates a sense of inertia. Acedia is a condition 'leading to listlessness and lack of interest in life; apathy, lethargy, torpor' (*Oxford English Dictionary*) www.oed.com/view/Entry/1068#eid39596420 [accessed 24 July 2017].
25 Heaney, 'Christmas 1971', p. 32.
26 Brian Graham and Sara McDowell, 'Meaning in the Maze: The Heritage of Long Kesh', *Cultural Geographies*, 14.3 (2007), 361.
27 Louise Purbrick, 'The Architecture of Containment', in *Donovan Wylie: The Maze* (London: Granta Books, 2004), p. 11.
28 Feldman, *Formations of Violence*, p. 152.
29 David Lloyd, *Irish Culture and Colonial Modernity: The Transformation of Oral Space* (Cambridge: Cambridge University Press, 2011), p. 132.
30 Quoted in Feldman, *Formations of Violence*, p. 161.
31 *Ibid.*, p. 157.
32 Lloyd, *Colonial Modernity*, p. 145.
33 Ned Flynn describes this process in *Nor Meekly Serve My Time* ed. by Brian Campbell, Laurence McKeown and Felim O'Hagan (Belfast: Beyond the Pale, 1994), p. 22.
34 Feldman, *Formations of Violence*, p. 185.
35 *Ibid.*, p. 212.
36 Melanie McMahon, 'Irish as Symptom: Language, Ideology and Praxis in the Post/Colony' (unpublished doctoral thesis, King's College London, 2012), p. 82.
37 David Beresford, *Ten Men Dead: The Story of the 1981 Hunger Strike* (London: Grafton Books, 1987), pp. 27–28.
38 Quoted in Feldman, *Formations of Violence*, p. 183.
39 *Ibid.*, pp. 193–195.
40 Foucault, *The Archaeology of Knowledge*, p. 6.
41 Quoted in Feldman, *Formations of Violence*, pp. 164–165.
42 Giorgio Agamben, *Homo Sacer: Sovereign Power and Bare Life*, trans. by Daniel Heller-Roazen (Stanford: Stanford University Press, 1998), pp. 159, 142.

43   George Legg, 'Biopolitical Ireland: Text, Culture, Theory', *Irish Review*, 53 (2016), 5.

44   See Graham and McDowell, 'Meaning in the Maze', 357–358.

45   Denis O'Hearn, *Nothing but an Unfinished Song: Bobby Sands, the Irish Hunger Striker wwho Ignited a Generation* (New York: Nation Books, 2006), p. 227.

46   Feldman, *Formations of Violence*, p. 220.

47   Quoted in Feldman, *Formations of Violence*, p. 240.

48   *Ibid.*, p. 224.

49   Ed Moloney, *A Secret History of the IRA*, 2nd edn (London: Penguin, 2007), p. 75.

50   Quoted in Kevin Bean and Mark Hayes, *Republican Voices* (Monaghan: Seesyu Press, 2001), p. 75.

51   Quoted in Feldman, *Formations of Violence*, p. 222.

52   *Ibid.*, p. 224.

53   Bobby Sands, *The Diary of Bobby Sands: The First Seventeen Days of Bobby's H-Block Hunger-Strike to Death* (Dublin: Republican Publications, 1990), p. 46.

54   Foucault, *Archaeology of Knowledge*, p. 14.

55   Seamus Deane, 'Civilians and Barbarians', in *Ireland's Field Day: Field Day Theatre Company* ed. by Seamus Deane (London: Hutchinson, 1985), p. 42.

56   Padraig O'Malley, *Biting at the Grave: The Irish Hunger Strikes and the Politics of Despair* (Boston, MA: Beacon Press, 1990), p. 6.

57   Lloyd, *Colonial Modernity*, p. 121.

58   *Ibid.*, p. 154.

59   McAtackney, *Archaeology of the Troubles*, p. 177.

60   Foucault, *Archaeology of Knowledge*, p. 9.

61   Masterplanning Consortium, *Maze/Long Kesh Masterplan*, p. 64.

62   *Ibid.*, p. 27.

63   Historic Buildings Council for Northern Ireland, *16th Annual Report: 2004–2006* (Belfast: HMSO, 2007), p. 26.

64   *Ibid.*, p. 27.

65   Foucault, *Archaeology of Knowledge*, p. 24.

66   David Webb, *Foucault's Archaeology* (Edinburgh: Edinburgh University Press, 2013), p. 51.

67   MLKDC, 'Northern Ireland's Largest Development Site'.

68   Harvey, *Rebel Cities*, p. 109. As Tunbridge and Ashworth have argued, sites of atrocity have increasingly become 'one of the most marketable of heritages' (J.E. Tunbridge and Gregory John Ashworth, *Dissonant Heritage: The Management of the Past as a Resource in Conflict* (New York: John Wiley and Sons, 1996), p. 94).

69   Graham and McDowell, 'Meaning in the Maze', 363.

70   Tunbridge and Ashworth, *Dissonant Heritage*, p. 22.

71   Deane, *Strange Country*, p. 164.

72   A clear example of this desire for destruction is the 'Raze the Maze Petition', organised by the TUV, UUP and UKIP. The petition gathered around ten thousand signatures and led to a suspension of the redevelopment plans ('Thousands oppose Maze Prison

peace centre', *Belfast Daily*, 21 June 2013) www.belfastdaily.co.uk/2013/06/21/thousands-oppose-maze-prison-peace-centre/ [accessed 24 July 2017].

73 Deane, *Strange Country*, p. 168.

74 *Ibid.*, p. 168.

75 R.J. Raack, 'Historiography as Cinematography: A Prolegomenon to Film Work for Historians', *Journal of Contemporary History*, 18 (1983), 416, 418.

76 Conor McCarthy, *Modernisation, Crisis and Culture in Ireland, 1969–1992* (Dublin: Four Courts Press, 2000), p. 165.

77 Harvey, *Rebel Cities*, p. 103. *Some Mother's Son* received funding from the Irish Film Board and *H3* secured EU funds through the Northern Ireland Film Commission (John Hill, *Cinema and Northern Ireland: Film, Culture and Politics* (London: BFI, 2006), p. 177). *Hunger* also received public moneys through Northern Ireland Screen (formerly Northern Ireland Film Commission).

78 John Myerscough, *The Economic Importance of the Arts* (London: Policy Studies Institute, 1988), pp. 148–150.

79 Harvey, *Rebel Cities*, p. 110.

80 Quoted in Feldman, *Formations of Violence*, p. 257.

81 Gary Crowdus and O'Mara Leary, 'The "Troubles" He's Seen in Northern Ireland: An Interview with Terry George', *Cineaste*, 23.1 (Winter 1997), 24.

82 Brian Neve, 'Cinema, the Ceasefire and "the troubles"', *Irish Studies Review*, 5.20 (1997), 6.

83 Fredric Jameson, 'The End of Temporality', *Critical Inquiry*, 29.4 (Summer 2003), 710, 714.

84 *Ibid.*, 715.

85 Crowdus and O'Leary, 'The "Troubles" He's Seen', 25.

86 Peter Mahon, *Violence, Politics and Textual Interventions in Northern Ireland* (Basingstoke: Palgrave Macmillan, 2010), p. 117.

87 'The producers of *H3* reconstructed the prison interior in Ardmore Studios, relying on Maze Prison exteriors for authenticity. Blair made "every effort to be as authentic as possible"' (Cahal McLaughlin, 'Cold, Hungry, and Scared: Prison Films about the "Troubles"', in *Ireland in Focus: Film, Photography, and Popular Culture* ed. by Eóin Flannery and Michael Griffin (New York: Syracuse University Press, 2009), p. 51). McQueen recounts how he built the set 'exactly to the specifications of the actual H-block, so there were no breakaway walls. We had to manoeuvre ourselves within the space with the cameras … What was fascinating to me was the contrast between the chaos inside the prisoners' cells, and outside the cells where there was this sort of formal construction, this regimentation and order' (quoted in Steven Rea, '*Hunger* director explores Maze prison hunger strike of '81', *Philadelphia Inquirer* (28 April 2009) www.popmatters.com/article/73519-hunger-director-explores-maze-prison-hunger-strike-of-81/) [accessed 24 July 2017].

88 Interview with Les Blair, in 'Special Features: The Making Of', *H3*, Element Pictures Distribution, 2001. DVD.

89 Interview with Juanita Wilson, in 'Special Features: The Making Of', *H3*. DVD.

90   Jason Solomons interviews Steve McQueen, in 'Special Features', *Hunger*, Pathé Distribution Ltd, 2009. DVD.
91   Feldman, Formations of Violence, p. 165.
92   Eugene McNamee, 'Eye Witness: Memorialising Humanity in Steve McQueen's *Hunger*', *International Journal of Law in Context*, 5.3 (2009), 290.
93   Interview with Wilson, *H3*. DVD.
94   Solomons interviews McQueen, *Hunger*. DVD.
95   Feldman, *Formations of Violence*, p. 205.
96   Quoted in Feldman, *Formations of Violence*, p. 205.
97   Lloyd, *Colonial Modernity*, p. 155.
98   Solomons interviews McQueen, *Hunger*. DVD.
99   *Ibid.*
100 Jeff Reichert, 'Hunger Pains: An Interview with Steve McQueen', *Reverse Shot*, 27 March 2009, www.reverseshot.com/interviews/entry/416/steve-mcqueen [accessed 24 July 2017].
101 Deane, 'Civilians and Barbarians', p. 41.
102 Feldman, *Formations of Violence*, p. 164.
103 Michel Foucault, *The Order of Things: An Archaeology of the Human Sciences*, trans. anon (London: Routledge, 2001), p. xix.
104 Foucault, *The Order of Things*, p. xix.
105 Lloyd, *Ireland after History*, p. 59.
106 Foucault, *Archaeology of Knowledge*, p. 13.
107 *Ibid.*, p. 13.
108 *Ibid.*, pp. 6–7.
109 The language here surely reminds us of the opening stanza to Yeats's extraordinary poem: 'I went out to the hazel wood', 'I dropped the berry in a stream / And caught a little silver trout' (W.B. Yeats, 'The Song of Wandering Aengus', in *The Major Works* ed. by Edward Larrissy (Oxford: Oxford University Press, 1997), p. 29).
110 Brian O'Doherty, 'Terrible Beauty', *Artforum*, 47.5 (January 2008), 61.
111 Alison Garden, 'Proving Their "Virility"? Steve McQueen's *Hunger* and Transgressive Masculinity', in *Transgression in Anglo-American Cinema: Gender, Sex and the Deviant Body* ed. by Joel Gwynne (London: Wallflower Press, 2016), p. 68.
112 Lloyd, *Colonial Modernity*, p. 156.
113 Garden, 'Transgressive Masculinity', p. 68.
114 *Ibid.*, p. 69.
115 Quoted in Sean O'Hagan, 'McQueen and country', *Observer*, 12 October 2008. www.theguardian.com/film/2008/oct/12/2 [accessed 24 July 2017].
116 Fintan O'Toole, '*Hunger* fails to wrest the narrative from the hunger strikers', *Irish Times*, 22 November 2008 http://cain.ulst.ac.uk/victims/docs/newspapers/irish_times/otoole_it_221108.pdf [accessed 24 July 2017].
117 Chris Tookey, '*Hunger*: More pro-terrorist propaganda', *Daily Mail*, 30 October 2008. www.dailymail.co.uk/tvshowbiz/reviews/article-1081911/Hunger-More-pro-terrorist-propaganda.html#ixzz3Hd0XEEMJ [accessed 24 July 2017].

118   Benjamin, 'Theses on the Philosophy of History', p. 254.

119   Quoted in Vanessa Thorpe and Henry McDonald, 'Anger as new film of IRA hero
      Bobby Sands screens at Cannes', *Observer* (11 May 2008) www.theguardian.com/
      film/2008/may/11/cannesfilmfestival.northernireland [accessed 24 July 2017].

120   McNamee, 'Memorialising Humanity', p. 292.

121   Quoted in Thorpe and McDonald, 'Bobby Sands screens at Cannes'.

122   McNamee, 'Memorialising Humanity', p. 293.

123   Foucault, *Archaeology of Knowledge*, p. 13.

124   Quoted in Liam Clarke, 'Sort it, or we will be left with a sorry site', *Belfast Telegraph*
      (21 August 2013) www.belfasttelegraph.co.uk/debateni/blogs/liam-clarke/sort-it-
      or-we-will-be-left-with-a-sorry-site-29514934.html [accessed 24 July 2017].

Conclusion: *Alternative Ulster?*

This book has examined key moments of capitalism within Northern Ireland's cultural history. In chapters on bourgeois apathy and geographical inertia, on state surveillance and sectarian psychogeography, I have highlighted how a fraught interface exists between sites of conflict and ideologies of capital. Conceptions of place and individuality are radically reconfigured at this intersection, giving way to experiences of exhaustion, depletion and ennui. The condition of boredom congeals the diversity of these moments, foregrounding the unwritten rapacity of capital. Through this, I have uncovered the inverse of what is often termed a 'capitalist peace'.[1] Capitalism, I argue, is neither peaceful nor conciliatory. Northern Ireland's animosities and divisions still persist under the auspices of accumulation, albeit in more nebulous and amorphous forms. Examining the cultural history of capitalism in Northern Ireland, I have consciously rubbed against the official mantra of its peace – what the Good Friday Agreement has termed the 'fresh start' by which we can 'best honour' the 'tragedies of the past'.[2] This book has returned to those traumatic moments, apprehending within their ruins both the monotony capitalism can create and the radical politics such boredom contains.

This is more than nostalgia – a forlorn longing for a forgotten history.[3] Instead, as McKenzie Wark has argued in *#Celerity: A Critique of the Manifesto for an Accelerationist Politics* (2013), a backward glance can be understood as a means of 'drawing on the past to imagine a future'.[4] The method may be retrospective, but its target is always tilted forward. 'There are', Wark writes, 'many resources in aesthetic alter-modern spaces of the past via which to experiment with steps forward'.[5] Wark's comments were made in response to Alex Williams and Nick Srnicek's *#Accelerate: Manifesto for an Accelerationist Politics* (2013), but through its critique *#Celerity* forms something of a manifesto in itself. In the following concluding remarks, I draw upon this document, but I do so in the context of another manifesto or movement of sorts, namely Northern Irish punk. My focus is on the punk fanzine *Alternative Ulster* and, more particularly, a polemic piece – '(I don't wanna go to …) Bangor' – written by one of its founding members, Gavin Martin, in 1978. I look to these texts in order to summarise and reiterate the themes of this book and to highlight, thereby, the politicised sense of boredom I have managed to establish.

Punk culture is particularly valuable in this respect. As an expression of disenchantment with, amongst other things, 'the consumer boom of the 1960s', punk can speak of the dispossession and disgust that underpin ideologies of capitalist accumulation.[6] It can do so by emphasising the personal and political exhaustion this entails. 'Boredom', writes Andy Medhurst, is 'perhaps the truest punk trope of all'.[7] In the localised phenomenon that was the Northern Irish punk scene – the Troubles having made the North 'a problem destination for international rock acts'[8] – punk also helps to crystallise Northern Ireland's unique location within the rhizomes and tendrils of a non-capitalist discourse. Looked at with hindsight Martin's article pre-empts, in startling ways, the insufficiencies of Northern Ireland's peace dividend. Yet when read alongside Wark's *#Celerity*, Martin's piece can also be seen to initiate a popular poetics that speaks to a wider geographical spectrum. The depletion and despair uncovered in this study merge with Martin's discontent. These shared semantics do not enact change in and of themselves, nor do they pine for a past that is now foreclosed. Rather they mark a possible path out of the present and provide a conscious opening on to the future. They make the call for an alternative focused, direct and loud.

Northern Irish punk is often remembered for its ecumenical ethos; its groups, its gigs and its venues all transcended the North's broader sectarian commitments.[9] 'For the first time in my life I had the pleasure to be part of an audience which are made up of people of all religious creeds and denominations', writes Ziggy in a 1978 edition of *Alternative Ulster*. 'This is something for which all the bands should be congratulated. They have done something politicians have not been able to or not wanted to do in endless years of Trouble.'[10] As one reads through the remnants of *Alternative Ulster*, however, it is striking how often this non-sectarian imperative is positioned more as a coincidence than a conscious ambition. Instead, if anything can be said to have motivated *Alternative Ulster*'s production, then it was perhaps the desire to redress and reignite a music scene widely held to be 'meaningless, futile, predictable … boring'.[11]

The causes for this drudgery were multiple, but *Alternative Ulster*'s critique was perhaps at its most vehement when inflected by an anti-capitalist agenda. 'You use words to make money for yourself, not to communicate meaningfully', states one editorial, written in response to Colin 'Mucky Press-Cat' McClelland's journalistic snipe at the fanzine's punk credentials. 'Now you're trying to do the same with music – do us a favour, you worthless smug and evil piece of dog's vomit, stick to satisfying Mr. and Mrs. Average of Cave Hill with your printed diarrhoea.'[12] Returning us to the geography and psychology of

Derek Mahon's Glengormley, it is not difficult to hear the same anger and frustration that Mahon's poetry came to espouse. Here, as elsewhere in this book, capital is seen to destroy meaning, producing an apathetic shell of contentment and complacency so as to deny other forms of agency.

Alternative Ulster's critique was pointed and precise, focusing upon the regional networks that largely defined Northern Irish punk. '*Alternative Ulster* … represents our answer to the "everything-of-importance-based-in-London" myth', states an early declaration of the fanzine's intent. 'Our long-term objective is to gradually turn A.U. into a *sort-of* Ulster N.M.E'.[13] In many ways, *Alternative Ulster* was a fanzine that embodied what later feminist 'grrrl zine' collectives would call an 'autobiographical approach': 'personal opinions and aspirations that were by their very nature a critique of the punk zines that had come before'.[14] Yet, in its disenchantment with consumerism – the Cave Hills of Northern Ireland – *Alternative Ulster* still embodied something of punk's 'culture of dissent'.[15] Championing local issues but still channelling punk's broader discontent, *Alternative Ulster* produced a liminal lexicon: a capitalist critique, inflected by the peculiarities of the North.

Nowhere is this clearer than in Martin's 1978 article, '(I don't wanna go to …) Bangor'. Taking, as its starting point, a détoured lyric from The Clash ('Bangor's Burning With Boredom Now'), Martin's piece is notable for its distillation of 'wealth and accompanying stagnation' within a pointedly Northern Irish sphere.[16] What makes Martin's assessment of this capitalist monotony particularly valuable, however, is its grounding within a cessation of the Troubles. Bangor, Martin tells us, is 'Ulster's most peaceful town', and it is the abeyance of conflict that makes the 'cancerous complacency' of Bangor's bourgeoisie all the more pronounced. As Martin writes:

> Some people say kids nowdays [*sic*] have no future, in Bangor they have no present. It's a disgrace coz this is a peaceful spot in Ulster's confusion and turmoil, there should be provisions for people from all over the province in Bangor, there's certainly the money to provide people with something worthwhile.[17]

Juxtaposing the inequalities of Bangor's peace with the 'confusion and turmoil' of the Northern Troubles, Martin unravels a crucial argument of this study. The logic of capital is – as Karl Marx, Gilles Deleuze and Guy Debord have demonstrated – an inherently violent phenomenon, but the pervasive presence of Northern Ireland's conflictual ethnic–national divide manages to mask these aggressive incursions under a discourse of progress and improvement. As Seamus Deane has observed, in order that economic development might 'proceed', 'the two communities in the north' are told that they must 'surrender' their 'archaic language of difference'.[18] Like the chapters in this book, Martin seeks to put the onus back on capital. He shifts his gaze from the North's embedded divisions so as to highlight the pain and disruption capitalist ideologies generate independently. Capital may promote a rhetoric of reconciliation, but it cannot efface old divides. Indeed, as the chapters in this book have served to demonstrate, to do so would be to lose sight of those potential blockage points that give capitalism's monotonous logic such unrestrained momentum. Capitalism merely repackages sectarianism, while simultaneously creating its own forms of exclusion and separation: people and places where money still simply refuses to flow.

Viewed from our current vantage, Martin's article paints an ominously precise portrait of what Northern Ireland has become. Bangor, like a post-Troubles North, claims to be at peace. In both cases, moreover, there can be 'no future' because the present remains so vacuous that it is essentially invisible. To live 'in that godforsaken place', writes Martin, is to live 'a life of terminal sedation'.[19] As the previous chapters have argued, under the rubric of capital the only way to neutralise the North's 'confusion and turmoil' is to create a society replete with boredom and ennui – a fakeland scene like those with which this study started. 'Seen in these terms', write Greg McLaughlin and Stephen Baker in *The Propaganda of Peace* (2010), 'Northern Ireland is not only undergoing a peace process aimed at settling the conflict over its constitutional position, it is potentially undergoing a process of pacification, a denial of politics upon which the free market depends'.[20] 'Forget all the crap about democracy', writes Martin about Bangor in 1978, 'council strategy panders to the town's bountiful complacency … and no-one asks any questions'.[21]

Martin's article seeks to challenge these conditions, however. Adopting the apparent localism of Northern Irish punk, Martin is entirely committed to an understanding of economic oppression through a consciously personal perspective. 'Some people have said this is too parochial an article' jots Martin, almost as an afterthought at the end of his piece. 'But I think it was necessary to write from personal experience to give a clearer and more direct insight into authoritarianism than to do an article based on vague generalising and suppositions'.[22] I have been equally specific in my outlook. Across the preceding chapters, I am highly critical of the monocular nature of the Peace Process and its refusal to countenance anything but a capitalist solution to the Troubles. All the moments of capitalism that I have considered delineate the terms of this singular narrative. But they also harbour the germs for its undoing. By charting the depleted politics and personhoods that capital creates, I have sought to supply 'a clearer and more direct insight' into the processes by which capitalism can be disrupted and potentially displaced.

At the centre of Wark's #Celerity, he suggests that an effective critique of capitalism will always depend upon 'insight and information from the popular struggles in and against [the] commodity economy'.[23] Williams and Srnicek's *#Accelerate* had disavowed 'a *folk politics* of localism' in favour of 'an *accelerationist politics* at ease with a modernity of abstraction',[24] but in his response Wark outlines how '"folk politics" and technical politics need to talk to each other'. Through this, Wark continues, it might finally be possible 'to open cracks towards new futures' – alternative, non-capitalist tomorrows. Like Martin's article, this book has considered what Wark would term 'local and specific grievances'. Yet in so doing I have aimed, if only briefly, to 'talk' to that 'larger picture of a metabolic rift' that Wark's *#Celerity* describes. 'What we need is neither abstraction nor occupying', asserts Wark, 'but *the occupying of abstraction*'.[25] Northern Ireland's strange status as an underdeveloped region within the United Kingdom's over-developed economy means that it is, I would argue, uniquely placed to initiate this local/global conversation, this '*occupying of abstraction*'.[26]

In hindsight, punk appears almost as an aberration – what Simon Reynolds has called 'a brief blip in an otherwise unbroken continuum of art-rock spanning the seventies from start to finish'.[27] Punk always dreamed of 'unit[ing] a motley array of malcontents as a force *against*', Reynolds continues, 'but when the question shifted to "What are we *for?*", the moment/movement disintegrated and dispersed'.[28] Indeed, if anything can be said to epitomise punk's semantic repertoires, then perhaps it was this desire to disaggregate. Punk's rich and complex history is layered with discord and division, arguments and disagreements which have wedded its 'belief in the power of music' to a recurrent sense of failure.[29] 'Built into Punk from the beginning was not only a tendency to self-destruction, but a short shelf-life', writes Jon Savage in his analysis of punk-rock. 'Despite what many of the groups professed, the movement enshrined failure: to succeed in conventional terms meant that you had failed on your own terms; to fail meant that you had succeeded.'[30]

Understood in these terms, punk's fanzines are possibly the closest we can come to accessing the movement's self-destructive core. Made with punk's DIY ethic, the fanzines' Xeroxed pages have deteriorated and decayed; the staples that once bound their spines have rusted over time. 'For the most part fanzines, or "zines", remain hidden', writes Teal Triggs, 'flying beneath the radar of mainstream publishing and its conventions'.[31] Certainly *Alternative Ulster* defied the chronology of the archive. It deployed a numbering system that was 'hacky' and 'providential', making its various issues almost impossible to trace. The first edition is labelled as volume number 7, its second as number 72. 'I have not got one copy of any edition of *Alternative Ulster* now', states Martin. 'I'm not even sure I could tell you how many copies there were (fucked by my own surreal numerological scheme)'.[32]

The momentary, fractious nature of punk has important repercussions on how we are to understand the species of boredom politicised by this study. Like punk, boredom tends towards diffusion and dispersal: its manifestations are painful and disruptive, while also being fleeting and obscure. Emanating in different ways and under diverse historical conditions, the strands of boredom uncovered in this book have the potential to disintegrate. Yet they are all united by their recurrent apparition at that charged interface between the ideologies of capitalism and the persistence of ethnic–national division. By exposing these continuities, I have orientated boredom away from its common diagnosis as 'the mark of a singular consciousness' and propagated, instead, an understanding of boredom as being, in Saikat Majumdar's phrase, 'an affective consequence of exclusion and disempowerment'.[33] Collating these disaggregated experiences under a shared syntax of powerlessness and pacification, I have politicised boredom – casting it not as a singular affliction internally digested, but as a communal condition externally imposed.

This book has rendered boredom in a different, broken rhythm – as a soundscape through which a collectivised deletion can be heard. In this I have, to return to Wark's manifesto, isolated the ways in which capital 'renders more and more molecular the points of conflict and struggle', while also deploying boredom as a 'semantic glue to stitch such actions together'.[34] The emancipatory potential of this shared, politicised poetics must be carefully understood, however. Jonathan Crary's discussion of *Late Capitalism and the Ends of Sleep* (2013), for example, bestows considerable agency upon a similar sense of collective inertia – embodied, in his case, by the monotonous cadence of sleep. Crary writes of how, 'the restorative inertness of sleep counters the deathliness of all the accumulation, financialization, and waste that have devastated anything once held in common'.[35] Attractive as this sounds, the extent to which 'inertness' can 'counter' capitalism's insatiable desires must be tempered and reconceived. While monotony's restorative alterity can provide respite from a world of relentless accumulation, its torpor does not possess the energy to enact change of its own accord. As with punk's nihilistic nature, boredom represents only a means by which we can comprehend and rail against capitalism's predatory incursions. Boredom does not pose a political alternative in and of itself, but rather creates a space in which we can, to borrow Wark's terminology, 'imagine and experiment with emerging gaps and cracks in the gamespace that the commodity economy has become'.[36]

Throughout this study, I have suggested that boredom is a symptom of repression that can also give way to moments of startling revelation. The Dolly Mixtures embodied, perhaps more than anyone, the radical potential that this could inspire. Inhabiting a landscape replete with the rhythms of ennui, they responded by creating a lexicon of their own. The poetry and prose of this creative writing group established an architecture of collectivity, or 'through-otherness',[37] in a planned environment that had otherwise become, in Henri Lefebvre's phrase, 'closed, sterilized, emptied out'.[38] Boredom did not enact this change, but it did produce the conditions through which this alterity could emerge. In my chapter on internment, I have illustrated how the female dependants of those detained reacted to the homogeneous timescape of state surveillance. Their innovative system of bin-lid bashing established a network of resistance – one that was built in direct response to the monotony of social control. Similarly, in my chapter on Derek Mahon's poetry, the phenomenon of political apathy is seen to motivate a far more threatening form of political 'dissensus'.[39] Here apathy becomes a plastic concept, one able to evolve, as Tony Cliff writes, 'into its opposite, swift mass action'.[40] Boredom does not perform this dissidence, but it can certainly inspire such celerity.

Yet for all their emancipatory potential, these countercultures – these alternative Ulsters – are temporary and transient. The power of the capitalist spectacle is such that these moments of rupture are soon reincorporated within that universal system. It was not long after women started banging bin-lids, for example, that they, too, were interned. The opportunity for a radical politics today is, therefore, a difficult undertaking. As Wark conjectures in #Celerity, what is at stake in a critique of the capitalist economy

> is a question of whether boredom with the commodity economy will work fast enough, as it spreads from the overdeveloped world to the underdeveloped, to open up a new path before metabolic rifts like climate crisis forces the planet towards more violent, disorganizing, and frankly fascist 'solutions' to its problems.[41]

At the level of Northern Ireland's political economy, the question is whether boredom with the Peace Process can ever be co-ordinated – or made known – before the brutal sectarian violence that dominated the Troubles returns to the surface. My chapters on the Maze/Long Kesh development and the psycho-geography of sectarianism have both demonstrated how these divisive patterns of relating can still be seen to dominate the North. Their persistence can be disregarded no longer, nor can their histories be sterilised or displaced. To do so amounts to nothing more than an act of repression: an overkilling of that which 'glistens with the not-so-gold of the Troubles' to the extent that the history of that conflict actually becomes a spectre or a ghost.[42] And, as Jacques Derrida reminds us, 'a ghost never dies, it remains always to come and to come-back'.[43]

'The task', concludes Wark in #Celerity, 'is one of co-ordinating the latent energies of a people bored with what the commodity has to offer'.[44] As I have demonstrated, once boredom is politicised it can inspire counter-discourses and different ways of being. Through this, boredom, while not creating social activism, can undoubtedly produce the conditions for its becoming. Boredom can, in other words, open an avenue through which something else might be able to 'counter', to return to Crary's statement, 'the deathliness of all the accumulation, financialization, and waste that have devastated anything once held in common'. An understanding of boredom is, as Roland Barthes has suggested, 'not simple'.[45] But for all the complexity involved in its formation there is, as I have shown throughout this book, one circumstance which adds particular weight to its occurrence: to be faced with boredom is to germinate the conditions for resistance. In this sense, to experience boredom is not simply to be subjected to a structure of mass constriction. Rather, through its collective experience and politicised figuration, boredom can also reveal new spaces and alternative modes of being.

Notes and references

1   See Erik Gartzke, 'The Capitalist Peace', *American Journal of Political Science*, 51.1 (January 2007), 166–191.

2   'Declaration of Support', *The Agreement: Agreement Reached in the Multi-Party Negotiations* (Good Friday Agreement, 1998), Para 2, www.gov.uk/government/uploads/ system/uploads/attachment_data/file/13665 2/agreement.pdf.

3   As Mark Fisher writes, 'it seems strange to have to *argue* that comparing the present unfavourably with the past is not automatically nostalgic in any culpable way, but such is the power of the dehistoricising pressures of populism and PR that the claim has to be explicitly made' (Mark Fisher, *Ghosts of My Life: Writings on Depression, Hauntology and Lost Futures* (Winchester: Zero Books, 2014), p. 25).

4   McKenzie Wark, *#Celerity: A Critique of the Manifesto for an Accelerationist Politics*, 0.0 https://speculativeheresy.files.wordpress.com/2013/05/wark-mckenzie-celerity. pdf [accessed 24 July 2017].

5   *Ibid.*, 2.3.

6   Martin McLoone, 'Punk Music in Northern Ireland: The Political Power of "what might have been"', *Irish Studies Review*, 12.1 (2004), 32.

7   Andy Medhurst, 'What Did I Get? Punk, Memory and Autobiography', in *Punk Rock: So What? The Cultural Legacy of Punk* ed. by Roger Sabin (London: Routledge, 1999), pp. 227–228.

8   Gerry Smyth, *Noisy Island: A Short History of Irish Popular Music* (Cork: Cork University Press, 2005), p. 49.

9   See, for example, Sean Campbell, '"Pack Up Your Troubles": Politics and Popular Music in Pre- and Post-ceasefire Ulster', *Popular Musicology Online*, 4 (2007) www. popular-musicology-online.com/issues/04/campbell-01.html [accessed 24 July 2017].

10   Ziggy, 'The Story So Far', *Alternative Ulster*, 34 (1978), 24.

11   'L.A.M.F', *Alternative Ulster*, 34 (1978), 2.

12   *Ibid.*, 2. McClelland was responsible for helping the English Journalist Gordon Ogilvie politicise the lyrics of Northern Irish punk band Stiff Little Fingers – a band often accused of exploiting the Troubles with 'a generically British – rather than a specifically local – audience in mind' (Campbell, '"Pack Up Your Troubles"'). Stiff Little Fingers' track 'Alternative Ulster' (1978) took its title from the fanzine.

13   'L.A.M.F', 2.

14   Teal Triggs, *Fanzines* (London: Thames and Hudson, 2010), p. 130. See also Marion Leonard, 'The riot grrrl network: grrrl power in indie rock', *Gender in the Music Industry: Rock, Discourse and Girl Power* (Aldershot: Ashgate, 2007), pp. 115–136.

15   McLoone, 'Punk music in Northern Ireland', 35.

16   Gavin Martin, '(I don't wanna go to ....) Bangor', *Alternative Ulster*, 72 (1978), 21. The title is taken from the Clash song, 'London's Burning (with boredom now)'.

17   *Ibid.*, 22.

18   Seamus Deane, *Strange Country: Modernity and Nationhood in Irish Writing since 1790* (Oxford: Oxford University Press, 1997), p. 163.

19   Martin, 'Bangor', 21.

20   Greg McLaughlin and Stephen Baker, *The Propaganda of Peace: The Role of the Media and Culture in the Northern Ireland Peace Process* (Bristol: Intellect, 2010), p. 94.

21   Martin, 'Bangor', 21–22.

22   *Ibid.*, 22.

23   Wark, *#Celerity*, 3.1.

24   Alex Williams and Nick Srnicek, '03: MANIFEST: On the Future', in *#Accelerate: Manifesto for an Accelerationist Politics*, para. 1. https://syntheticedifice.files.wordpress.com/2013/06/accelerate.pdf [accessed 24 July 2017].

25   Wark, *#Celerity*, 3.1.

26   Remembering their 1982 gig in Belfast, Crass's lead singer Penny Rimbaud writes that 'nowhere else could the hard truth of colonialism and capitalist statism be so readily observed, for this surely was its nerve-end' (Penny Rimbaud, 'Crass in Belfast, 1982', in *It Makes You Want to Spit! The Definitive Guide to Punk in Northern Ireland 1977–1982* ed. by Sean O'Neill and Guy Trelford (Dublin: Reekus Music, 2003), p. 12).

27   Simon Reynolds, *Rip It pp and Start Again: Post-Punk 1978–1984* (London: Faber, 2005), p. xxi.

28   *Ibid.*, pp. xxix–xxx.

29   *Ibid.*, p. xxx.

30   Jon Savage, *England's Dreaming: Sex Pistols and Punk Rock* (London: Faber, 1991), p. 141.

31   Triggs, *Fanzines*, p. 7.

32   Spit Records, 'Fanzines' www.spitrecords.co.uk/fanzines.htm [accessed 24 July 2017].

33   Saikat Majumdar, *Prose of the World: Modernism and the Banality of Empire* (New York: Columbia University Press, 2013), p. 15.

34   Wark, *#Celerity*, 1.6.

35 Johnathan Crary, *24/7: Late Capitalism and the Ends of Sleep* (London: Verso, 2013), p. 128.

36 Wark, *#Celerity*, 2.4.

37 Estyn Evans, *The Personality of Ireland: Habitat, Heritage and History* (Cambridge: Cambridge University Press, 1973), p. 60.

38 Henri Lefebvre, *The Production of Space*, trans. by Donald Nicholson-Smith (Oxford: Blackwell, 1991), p. 165.

39 Jacques Rancière, 'Comment and Responses', *Theory and Event*, 6.4 (2003), para. 4.

40 Quoted in Chris Harman, 'Thinking it Through: Out of Apathy', *Socialist Review*, 219 (May 1998), http://pubs.socialistreviewindex.org.uk/sr219/harman.htm [accessed 24 July 2017].

41 Wark, *#Celerity*, 3.2.

42 Colin Graham, '"Every Passer-by a Culprit?" Archive Fever, Photography and the Peace in Belfast', *Third Text*, 19.5 (September 2005), 568.

43 Jacques Derrida, *Spectres of Marx: The State of the Debt, the Work of Mourning and the New International*, trans. by Peggy Kamuf (London: Routledge, 1994), p. 123.

44 Wark, *#Celerity*, 3.1.

45 Roland Barthes, *The Pleasure of the Text*, trans. by Richard Miller (London: Jonathan Cape, 1976), p. 25.

Bibliography

For sources where there is no named author, items are listed with the title first.

'£2 million recreation forum planned', *Portadown Times*, 5 January 1973, p. 25.

'£70 million spent in the past five years but the next few months are crucial for Craigavon', *Craigavon Times*, 28 January 1976, p. 6.

'A new roof over your head – and hard cash in your hand', *Craigavon Progress* (= *Craigavon Times*), 21 January 1976, p. 7.

Ackroyd, Carol, Karen Margolis, Jonathan Rosenhead and Tim Shallice, *The Technology of Political Control*, 2nd edn (London: Pluto Press, 1980).

Adams, Gerry, *Cage Eleven* (Kerry: Brandon, 2002).

Adorno, Theodor W., *The Culture Industry: Selected Essays on Mass Culture* ed. by J.M. Bernstein (London: Routledge, 1991).

Agamben, Giorgio, *Homo Sacer: Sovereign Power and Bare Life*, trans. by Daniel Heller-Roazen (Stanford: Stanford University Press, 1998).

Alberro, Alexander, 'Picturing Relations: Images, Text, and Social Engagement', in *Barbara Kruger* ed. by Alexander Alberro, Martha Gever, Miwon Kwon and Carol Squires (New York: Rizzoli, 2010), pp. 193–200.

Alexander, Anthony, *Britain's New Towns: Garden Cities to Sustainable Communities* (London: Routledge, 2009).

Alexander, Neal, 'Deviations from the Known Route: Walking and Writing in Ciaran Carson's Belfast', *Irish Studies Review*, 16.1 (2008), 41–51.

——*Ciaran Carson: Space, Place, Writing* (Liverpool: Liverpool University Press, 2010).

Allen, Luther A., 'New Towns and The Troubles: Some Political Observations on Northern Ireland', *Town and Country Planning*, 50 (November–December 1981), 283–289.

Althusser, Louis, *Lenin and Philosophy and Other Essays*, trans. by Ben Brewster (London: NLB, 1971).

Angell, Norman, *The Great Illusion* (New York: Putnam, 1933).

Aretxaga, Begoña, *Shattering Silence: Women, Nationalism and Political Subjectivity in Northern Ireland* (Princeton: Princeton University Press, 1997).

Auden, W.H., *The English Auden* (London: Faber, 1986).

Auden, W.H., and John Garrett, *The Poet's Tongue* (London: G. Bell & Sons, 1935).

Augé, Marc, *Non-Places: Introduction to an Anthropology of Supermodernity*, trans. by John Howe (London: Verso, 1995).

Azoulay, Ariella, *The Civil Contract of Photography* (New York: Zone Books, 2008).

Bannerman, A.H., 'Craigavon – the "rural city"' *Town and Country Planning*, 36.1–2 (January–February 1968), 119–120.

Barber, Fionna, 'Ghost Stories: An Interview with Willie Doherty', *Visual Culture in Britain*, 10.2 (2004), 189–199.

——*Art in Ireland since 1910* (London: Reaktion Books, 2013).

Bardon, Jonathan, *A History of Ulster* (Belfast: Blackstaff Press, 2001).

Barthes, Roland, *The Pleasure of the Text*, trans. by Richard Miller (London: Jonathan Cape, 1976).

——*Image Music Text*, trans. by Stephen Heath (New York: The Noonday Press, 1977).

Bassett, Keith, 'Walking as an Aesthetic Practice and a Critical Tool: Some Psychogeographic Experiments', *Journal of Geography in Higher Education*, 28.3 (2004), 397–410.

Bean, Kevin, and Mark Hayes, *Republican Voices* (Monaghan: Seesyu Press, 2001).

Beckett, J.C., and R.E. Glasscock, eds, *Belfast: The Origin and Growth of an Industrial City* (London: BBC, 1967).

Beckett, Mary, *Give Them Stones* (London: Bloomsbury, 1988).

Bell, J.B., *The Secret Army: The IRA*, 3rd edn (New Brunswick, NJ: Transaction, 2003).

Benjamin, Walter, *Illuminations* ed. by Hannah Arendt, trans. by Harry Zohn (London: Fontana Press, 1992).

Bennet, Huw, and Rory Cormac, 'Low Intensity Operations in Theory and Practice: General Sir Frank Kitson as Warrior-Scholar', in *The Theory and Practice of Irregular Warfare: Warrior-Scholarship in Counter-Insurgency* ed. by Andrew Mumford and Bruno C. Reis (Abingdon: Routledge, 2014), pp. 105–125.

Beresford, David, *Ten Men Dead: The Story of the 1981 Irish Hunger Strike* (London: Grafton Books, 1987).

Bew, Paul, and Gordon Gillespie, *Northern Ireland: A Chronology of the Troubles 1968–1993* (Dublin: Gill and Macmillan, 1993).

Bew, Paul, Peter Gibbon and Henry Patterson, *Northern Ireland 1921/2001: Political Forces and Social Classes* (London: Serif, 2002).

Bexton, W.H., W. Heron, and T.H. Scott, 'Effects of Decreased Variation in the Sensory Environment', *Canadian Journal of Psychology*, 8.2 (1954), 70–76.

Bird, Eric Leslie, *The Work of the Northern Ireland Housing Trust* (London: Hudson and Kearns, 1950).

Bishop, Patrick, and Eamonn Mallie, *The Provisional IRA* (London: Heinemann, 1987).

Blackman, Tim, 'Craigavon: The Development and Dismantling of Northern Ireland's New Town', *Capital and Class*, 11.2 (Summer 1987), 117–141.

——'Housing Policy and Community Action in County Durham and County Armagh: A Comparative Study' (unpublished doctoral thesis, University of Durham, 1987).

Blair, John G., *The Poetic Art of W.H. Auden* (Princeton: Princeton University Press, 1965).

Blair, Tony, 'Speech by Tony Blair to the Royal Agricultural Society Belfast', 14 May (1998) http://cain.ulst.ac.uk/events/peace/docs/tb14598.htm [accessed 24 July 2017].

Bloom, Robert, 'The Humanization of Auden's Early Style', *PMLA*, 83.2 (May 1968), 443–454.

Boland, Eavan, 'The Northern writers' crisis of conscience: part 2', *Irish Times*, 13 August 1970, p. 12.

——'The Northern writers' crisis of conscience: part 3', *Irish Times*, 14 August 1970, p. 12.

Bourdieu, Pierre, *Distinction: A Social Critique of the Judgement of Taste*, trans. by Richard Nice (London: Routledge, 1984).

Boyle, Kevin, Tom Hadden and Paddy Hillyard, *Law and State: The Case of Northern Ireland* (London: Martin Robertson & Company, 1975).

Brady, Brian J., Denis Faul and Raymond Murray, *Internment 1971–1975* (Dungannon: St Patrick's Academy, 1975).

Brady, Evelyn, Eva Patterson, Kate McKinney, Rosie Hamill and Pauline Jackson, *In the Footsteps of Anne: Stories of Republican Women Ex-Prisoners* (Belfast: Shanway Press, 2011).Brennock, Mark, 'Guess who's coming to Belfast 9?', *Irish Times*, 23 March 1991, p. 1.

Brett, C.E.B., *Buildings of Belfast 1700–1914* (London: Weidenfeld and Nicolson, 1967).

——*Housing a Divided Community* (Belfast: Institute of Irish Studies, 1986).

Brewer, John. D, 'Sectarianism and Racism, and Their Parallels and Differences', *Ethnic and Racial Studies*, 15.3 (3 July 1992), 352–364.

Buckler, Chris, 'Craigavon: City of Hope and Fear', 11 March 2009 http://news.bbc.co.uk/1/hi/uk/7938663.stm [accessed 24 July 2017].

Burbank, Jane and Frederick Cooper, *Empires in World History: Power and the Politics of Difference* (Princeton: Princeton University Press, 2010).

Burgin, Victor, ed., *Thinking Photography* (London: Macmillan, 1982).

Burton, Anthony, and Joyce Harley, eds, *The New Towns Record, 1946–2002* (London: IDOX Information Services in association with Logical Innovations, 2002).

Cameron, David, 'David Cameron's speech at the Northern Ireland Investment Conference', 11 October 2013 www.gov.uk/government/speeches/david-camerons-speech-at-the-northern-ireland-investment-conference.

Campany, David, 'Saftey in Numbness: Some Remarks on the Problems of "Late Photography"' (2003) http://davidcampany.com/safety-in-numbness/ [accessed 24 July 2017].

Campbell, Brian, Laurence McKeown and Felim O'Hagan, eds, *Nor Meekly Serve My Time* (Belfast: Beyond the Pale, 1994).

Campbell, Sean, '"Pack Up Your Troubles": Politics and Popular Music in Pre- and Post-Ceasefire Ulster', *Popular Musicology Online*, 4 (2007).

Carson, Ciaran, *Collected Poems* (Oldcastle: The Gallery Press, 2013).

Carville, Justin, and Ken Grant, *Victor Sloan: Drift* (Banbridge: F.E. McWilliam Gallery, 2015).

Cattermole, Paul, *Building Titanic Belfast: The Making of a Twenty-First-Century Landmark* (Belfast: Titanic Belfast Publications, 2013).

Chandler, David, 'The Uncritical Critique of "liberal peace"', *Review of International Studies*, 36 (2010), 137–155.

Cheng, Wendy, '"New Topographics": Locating Epistemological Concerns in the American Landscape', *American Quarterly*, 63.1 (March 2011), 151–162.

'City poised for success', *Craigavon Progress* (= *Craigavon Times*), 21. January 1976, p. 1.

Clapson, Mark, *Invincible Green Suburbs, Brave New Towns: Social Change and Urban Dispersal in Postwar England* (Manchester: Manchester University Press, 1998).

Clarke, Liam, *Broadening the Battlefield: The H-Blocks and the Rise of Sinn Féin* (Dublin: Gill and Macmillan, 1987).

——'Sort it, or we will be left with a sorry site', *Belfast Telegraph*, 21 August 2013 www.belfasttelegraph.co.uk/debateni/blogs/liam-clarke/sort-it-or-we-will-be-left-with-a-sorry-site-29514934.html.

——'Hunger strike hospital key to Maze project success: report', *Belfast Telegraph*, 14 May 2014 www.belfasttelegraph.co.uk/news/northern-ireland/hunger-strike-hospital-key-to-maze-project-success-report-30272119.html [accessed 24 July 2017].

Cleary, Joe, 'Introduction: Ireland and Modernity', in *The Cambridge Companion to Modern Irish Culture* ed. by Joe Cleary and Claire Connolly (Cambridge: Cambridge University Press, 2005), pp. 1–21.

——*Outrageous Fortune: Capital and Culture in Modern Ireland* (Dublin: Field Day Publications, 2007).

Coiste na n-Iarchimí, *A Museum at Long Kesh or the Maze?: Report of Conference Proceedings* (Belfast: Coiste na n-Iarchimí, 2003).

Community Relations Commission Research Unit, *Flight: A Report on Population Movement in Belfast during August 1971* (Belfast: Northern Ireland Community Relations Commission, 1971).

Compton, Sir Edmund, *Report of the Enquiry into Allegations against the Security Forces of Physical Brutality in Northern Ireland Arising out of Events on the 9th August, 1971* (London: HMSO, 1971).

Connolly, James, 'Labour and the Proposed Partition of Ireland', *Irish Worker*, Saturday 14 March 1914, p. 2.

Connolly, Maeve, 'Looking Backwards into the Future: Steadicam Cinematography, Urban Regeneration and Artists Cinema', *Irish Review*, 39 (Winter 2008), 78–92.

Corcoran, Mary, *Out of Order: The Political Imprisonment of Women in Northern Ireland, 1972–1998* (Cullompton: Willan Publishing, 2006).

Corcoran, Neil, *The Poetry of Seamus Heaney: A Critical Guide* (London: Faber, 1998).

Coulter, Colin, 'Direct Rule and the Unionist Middle Classes', in *Unionism in Modern Ireland: New Perspectives on Politics and Culture* ed. by Richard English and Graham Walker (Basingstoke: Macmillan, 1996), pp. 169–192.

——'The Culture of Contentment: The Political Beliefs and Practice of the Unionist Middle Classes', in *Who Are 'the people'?: Unionism, Protestantism and Loyalism in Northern Ireland* ed. by Peter Shirlow and Mark McGovern (London: Pluto Press, 1997), pp. 114–139.

——'Peering in from the Window Ledge of the Union: The Anglo-Irish Agreement and the Attempt to Bring British Conservatism to Northern Ireland', *Irish Studies Review*, 21.4 (2013), 406–424.

——'Under Which Constitutional Arrangement Would You Still Prefer to Be Unemployed? Neoliberalism, the Peace Process, and the Politics of Class in Northern Ireland', *Studies in Conflict and Terrorism*, 37.9 (2014), 736–776.

Coulter, Colin and Michael Murray, 'Introduction', in *Northern Ireland After the Troubles: A Society in Transition* ed. by Colin Coulter and Michael Murray (Manchester: Manchester University Press, 2008), pp. 1–26.

Coverley, Merlin, *Psychogeography* (Harpenden: Pocket Essentials, 2007).

'Craigavon – 4,500 houses by 1971', *Portadown News*, 24 February 1967, p. 1.

'Craigavon's House-Building Target Is Eight Hundred Per Annum', *Ulster Commentary*, 279 (May 1969), 14.

'Craigavon strides out towards 2000 AD', *Portadown News*, 9 June 1967, p. 3.

Crary, Jonathan, *24/7: Late Capitalism and the Ends of Sleep* (London: Verso, 2013).

Crawford, Mairtín, 'Ambiguous Images', *Fortnight*, 393 (March 2001), 28.

Cresswell, Tim, *Place: A Short Introduction* (Malden, MA: Blackwell, 2004).

Crowdus, Gary, and O'Mara Leary, 'The "Troubles" He's Seen in Northern Ireland: An Interview with Terry George', *Cineaste*, 23.1 (Winter 1997), 24–29.

'Crowe hits out at thugs', *Craigavon Echo*, 22 October 2003, p. 1.

Cusack, Jim, '450 homes face demolition in "new city" of Craigavon', *Irish Times*, 7 July 1982, p. 9.

Daly, Mary, *Sixties Ireland: Reshaping the Economy, State and Society, 1957–1973* (Cambridge: Cambridge University Press, 2016).

Darby, John, ed., *Northern Ireland: The Background to the Conflict* (Belfast: Appletree Press, 1983).

Deane, Seamus, *Gradual Wars* (Shannon: Irish Academic Press, 1972).

——'An Irish Intelligentsia: Reflections on Its Desirability', *Honest Ulsterman*, 46–47 (November 1974–February 1975), 27–34.

——'Civilians and Barbarians', in *Ireland's Field Day: Field Day Theatre Company* ed. by Seamus Deane (London: Hutchinson, 1985), pp. 33–42.

——*Strange Country: Modernity and Nationhood in Irish Writing since 1790* (Oxford: Oxford University Press, 1997).

——'The Famous Seamus', *The New Yorker*, 20 March 2000, 54–80.

Debord, Guy, 'Introduction to a Critique of Urban Geography', in *Situationist International Anthology* ed. by Ken Knabb (Berkeley: Bureau of Public Secrets, 1981), pp. 5–8.

——*Comments on the Society of the Spectacle*, 1988 www.notbored.org/commentaires.html [accessed 24 July 2017].

——'Theory of the dérive', *Internationale Situationniste*, 2 www.bopsecrets.org/SI/2.derive.htm [accessed 24 July 2017].

——*The Society of the Spectacle*, foreword by Martin Jenkins, trans. by Ken Knabb, 2nd edn (Eastbourne: Soul Bay Press, 2012).

Deleuze, Gilles, 'Postscript on the Societies of Control', *October*, 59 (Winter 1992), 3–7.

Deleuze, Gilles, and Félix Guattari, *Anti-Oedipus: Capitalism and Schizophrenia*, trans. by Robert Hurley et al. (Minneapolis: University of Minnesota Press, 2000).

Derrida, Jacques, *Spectres of Marx: The State of the Debt, the Work of Mourning and the New International*, trans. by Peggy Kamuf (London: Routledge, 1994).

'Details of the city plan', *Portadown Times*, 11 December 1964, p. 17.

Deutsch, Richard, and Vivien Magowan, *Northern Ireland 1968–73: A Chronology of Events – Volume 1, 1968–71* (Belfast: Blackstaff, 1973).

Devlin, Bobby, *An Interlude with Seagulls: Memories of a Long Kesh Internees*, 2nd edn (London: Information on Ireland, 1985).

Dewar, Colonel Michael, *The British Army in Northern Ireland* (London: Arms and Armour, 1996).

de Wolfe, Ivor, 'Sociable Housing', *The Architectural Review*, 154.920 (October 1973), 203–204.

Dickens, Peter, Simon Duncan and Mark Goodwin, *Housing, States and Localities* (London: Methuen, 1985).

Dillon-Malone, Aubrey, 'Middle Third', *Books Ireland*, 116 (September 1987), 171–172.

'Dissidents blamed for recent bomb hoaxes', *Craigavon Echo*, 23 February 2005, p. 1.

'District commander questioned over police role in Brownlow estates', *Craigavon Echo*, 17 December 2003, p. 12.

Dixon, Hugh, *An Introduction to Ulster Architecture* (Belfast: Ulster Architectural Heritage Society, 1975).

Doherty, Willie, *Dark Stains* (San Sebastián: Kulturunea, 1999).

——*Ghost Story* (Belfast: British Arts Council, 2007).

——*Disturbance* (Dublin: The Hugh Lane Gallery, 2011).

——*Photo/Text/85/92* (London: Matt's Gallery, 2012).

Donnelly, Ann, and Victor Sloan, eds, *My Country Is Where I Am* (Craigavon: Arts Development, Craigavon Borough Council, 2009).

Donovan, Katie, *Irish Women Writers: Marginalised by Whom?* (Dublin: Raven Arts, 1988).

Dorian, Hugh, *The Outer Edge of Ulster: A Memoir of Social Life in Nineteenth-Century Donegal* ed. by Breandán Mac Suibhne and David Dickson (Dublin: Lilliput Press, 2000).

Douds, Stephen, 'All Croppies Together', *Fortnight*, 353 (September 1996), 18–19.

Downey, Karen, ed., *Where Are the People? Contemporary Photographs of Belfast 2002–2010* (Belfast: Belfast Exposed Photography, 2010).

Duffield, Mark, *Global Governance and the New Wars: The Merging of Development and Security*, 2nd rev. edn (London: Zed Books, 2014).

Dumm, Thomas, *A Politics of the Ordinary* (London: New York University Press, 1999).

Duncan, John, *Bonfires*, with essays by Colin Graham and Mary Warner Marien (Belfast: Belfast Exposed Photography, 2008).

Dunne, Aidan, *Victor Sloan Selected Works* (Belfast: Ormeau Baths Gallery, 2001).

Durcan, Paul, 'The World of Derek Mahon', *Magill*, 8.5 (Christmas 1984), 38–46.

Edgerton, Lynda, 'Public Protest, Domestic Acquiescence: Women in Northern Ireland', in *Caught up in Conflict: Women's Responses to Political Strife* ed. by Rosemary Ridd and Helen Callaway (Basingstoke: Macmillan Education, 1986), pp. 61–83.

Emerson, Newton, *The Lost City of Craigavon* (Double-Band Films, BBC NI, 2007).

'Engulfed', *Lurgan Mail*, 12 June 1965, p. 1.

Enloe, Cynthia, *Does Khaki Become You? The Militarization of Women's Lives* (London: Pandora Press, 1988).

Enniss, Stephen, *After the Titanic: A Life of Derek Mahon* (Dublin: Gill and Macmillan, 2014).

Evans, Estyn, *The Personality of Ireland: Habitat, Heritage and History* (Cambridge: Cambridge University Press, 1973).

——*Irish Folk Ways* (Mineola: Dover, 2000).

Evans, Jessica, ed., *The Camerawork Essays: Context and Meaning in Photography* (London: Rivers Oram, 1997).

Evelegh, Robin, *Peace Keeping in a Democratic Society: The Lessons of Northern Ireland* (London: C. Hurst & Company, 1978).

'Fears for Goodyear jobs in Ulster', *Guardian*, 4 March 1983, p. 17.

Feldman, Allen, *Formations of Violence: The Narrative of the Body and Political Terror in Northern Ireland* (Chicago: Chicago University Press, 1991).

Fiacc, Padraic, ed., *The Wearing of the Black: An Anthology of Contemporary Ulster Poetry* (Belfast: Blackstaff Press, 1974).

Fisher, Mark, *Capitalist Realism: Is There No Alternative* (Winchester: Zero Books, 2009).

——*Ghosts of My Life: Writings on Depression, Hauntology and Lost Futures* (Winchester: Zero Books, 2014).

Fisher, Mark, and Jeremy Gilbert, 'Capitalist Realism and Neoliberal Hegemony: A Dialogue', *New Formations*, 80–81 (Winter 2013), 89–101.

'Focus on Craigavon', *Portadown Times*, 12 January 1973, p. 1.

Foster, John Wilson, *The Titanic Complex* (Vancouver: Belcouver Press, 1997).

Foster-Rice, Greg, and John Rohrbach, eds, *Reframing the New Topographics* (Chicago: University of Chicago Press, 2010).

Foucault, Michel, *The Order of Things: An Archaeology of the Human Sciences*, trans. anon. (London: Routledge, 2001).

——*The Archaeology of Knowledge*, trans. by A.M. Sheridan Smith (London: Routledge, 2002).

Franklin, Seb, 'Humans and/as Machines: Beckett and Cultural Cybernetics', *Textual Practice*, 27.2 (2013), 249–268.

——'The Context of Forms', *World Picture*, 11 (Summer 2016) www. worldpicturejournal.com/WP_11/pdfs/Franklin_WP_11.pdf.

Friedman, Thomas, *The World Is Flat: The Globalized World in the Twenty-First Century* (London: Allen Lane, 2005).

Frisk, Robert, 'Army's computer has data on half the population in Ulster', *The Times*, 5 December 1974, p. 1.

'Funny Things at the Forum', *Craigavon Times*, 4 February 1976, p. 1.

Gallagher, Philomena, ed., *Troubles and Joys – An Anthology of Craigavon Women Writers* (Lurgan: Ronan Press Limited, 1992).

Galloway, Alexander R., *Gaming: Essays on Algorithmic Culture* (Minneapolis: University of Minnesota Press, 2006).

Garden, Alison, 'Proving Their "Virility"? Steve McQueen's *Hunger* and Transgressive Masculinity', in *Transgression in Anglo-American Cinema: Gender, Sex and the Deviant Body* ed. by Joel Gwynne (London: Wallflower Press, 2016), pp. 57–72.

Gartman, David, *Culture, Class and Critical Theory* (London: Routledge, 2013).

Gartzke, Erik, 'The Capitalist Peace', *American Journal of Political Science*, 51.1 (January 2007), 166–191.

Geoghegan, Peter, *A Difficult Difference: Race, Religion and the New Northern Ireland* (Dublin: Irish Academic Press, 2010).

Gilligan, Chris, 'Peace or Pacification Process? A Brief Critique of the Peace Process', in *Peace or War? Understanding the Peace Process in Northern Ireland* ed. by Chris Gilligan and Jon Tonge (Aldershot: Ashgate, 1997), pp. 19–34.

Gilroy, Paul, '"We Got To Get Over Before We Go Under": Fragments for a History of Black Vernacular Neoliberalism', *New Formations*, 80–81 (Winter 2013), 23–38.

Goldstein, Richard, 'Just Say Noh: The Esthetics of Banality', *Artforum*, 26.6 (January 1988), 77–82.

'Gone with the Wind!', *Portadown Times*, 19 January 1973, p. 1.

Goodstein, Elizabeth S., *Experience without Qualities: Boredom and Modernity* (Stanford: Stanford University Press, 2005).

Gorst, Thom, 'Maritime Myths and Meanings', *Architecture Today*, 228 (May 2012), 58–61.

Government of Northern Ireland, *Census of Population of Northern Ireland 1951: General Report* (Belfast: HMSO, 1955).

Graham, Brian, and Sara McDowell, 'Meaning in the Maze: The Heritage of Long Kesh', *Cultural Geographies*, 14.3 (2007), 343–361.

Graham, Colin, '"Every Passer-by a Culprit?": Archive Fever, Photography and the Peace in Belfast', *Third Text*, 19.5 (September 2005), 567–580.

———'A Persisting Anachronism: Luxus, a Collaboration by Victor Sloan and Glenn Patterson', *Source: Photographic Review*, 50 (Spring 2007), 139–154.

———'"Let's Get Killed": Culture and Peace in Northern Ireland', in *Irish Postmodernisms and Popular Culture* ed. by Wanda Balzano, Anne Mulhall and Moynagh Sullivan (Basingstoke: Palgrave Macmillan, 2007), pp. 171–184.

———'Luxury, Peace and Photography in Northern Ireland', *Visual Culture in Britain*, 10.2 (2009), 139–154.

———'Motionless Monotony: New Nowheres in Irish Photography', *In/Print*, 1 (2012), 1–21.

———*Northern Ireland: 30 Years of Photography* (Belfast: Belfast Exposed, 2013).

Grennan, Eamonn, 'Derek Mahon, the Art of Poetry', *The Paris Review*, 154 (Spring 2000) www.theparisreview.org/interviews/732/the-art-of-poetry-no-82-derek-mahon [accessed 24 July 2017].

Haladyn, Julian Jason, *Boredom and Art: Passions of the Will to Boredom* (Alresford: Zero Books, 2015).

Hall, Michael, *A Question of 'Community Relations': Protestants Discuss Community Relations Issues*, Island Pamphlets No. 32 (Newtownabbey: Island Publications, 2000).

Hall, Stuart, 'Cultural Identity and Diaspora', in *Identity: Community, Culture, Difference* ed. by Jonathan Rutherford (London: Lawrence and Wishart, 1990), pp. 222–237.

———'Conclusion: The Multi-cultural Question', in *Un/Settled Multiculturalism: Diasporas, Entanglements, 'Transruptions'* ed. by Barnor Hesse (New York: Zed Books, 2000), pp. 209–241.

Harcourt Developments, *TQ: Titanic Quarter – Regenerating Belfast* (London: Fox International, 2007).

Hardt, Michael, and Antonio Negri, *Empire* (Cambridge, MA: Harvard University Press, 2001).

Harman, Chris, 'Thinking It Through: Out of Apathy', *Socialist Review*, 219 (May 1998) http://pubs.socialistreviewindex.org.uk/sr219/harman.htm [accessed 24 July 2017].

Harris, Helen, and Eileen Healy, eds, *'Strong about it all …': Rural and Urban Women's Experiences of the Security Forces in Northern Ireland* (Derry: North West Women's / Human Rights Project Publications, 2001).

Harvey, David, *The New Imperialism* (Oxford: Oxford University Press, 2003).

———*The Limits to Capital*, 2nd edn (London: Verso, 2006).

———*The Enigma of Capital: And the Crises of Capitalism* (London: Profile, 2011).

———*Rebel Cities: From the Right to the City to the Urban Revolution* (London: Verso, 2012).

Haughton, Hugh, '"The bright garbage on the incoming wave": Rubbish in the Poetry of Derek Mahon', *Textual Practice*, 16.2 (2002), 323–343.

——*The Poetry of Derek Mahon* (Oxford: Oxford University Press, 2010).

Hayes, Maurice, *Whither Cultural Diversity?* (Belfast: Community Relations Council, 1993).

Heaney, Seamus, *Wintering Out* (London: Faber, 1972).

——*Preoccupations: Selected Prose 1968–1978* (London: Faber, 1985).

Heidegger, Martin, *The Fundamental Concepts of Metaphysics: World, Finitude, Solitude*, trans. by William McNeill and Nicholas Walker (Bloomington: Indiana University Press, 1995).

Heidemann, Birte, *Post-Agreement Northern Irish Literature: Lost in a Liminal Space?* (Basingstoke: Palgrave Macmillan, 2016).

Hill, Lord George, *Facts from Gweedore*, with an introduction by E. Estyn Evans (Belfast: Queen's University of Belfast, Institute of Irish Studies, 1971).

Hill, John, *Cinema and Northern Ireland: Film, Culture and Politics* (London: BFI, 2006).

Historic Buildings Council for Northern Ireland, *16th Annual Report: 2004–2006* (Belfast: HMSO, 2007).

House of Commons Debate, Vol. 642, col. WA7 (9 December 2002) www.publications.parliament.uk/pa/ld200203/ldhansrd/vo021209/text/21209 w02.htm#21209w02_spnew5 [accessed 24 July 2017].

——Vol. 855, cols 279–280, 17 April (1973) http://hansard.millbanksystems.com/commons/1973/apr/17/northern-ireland-emergency-provisions [accessed 24 July 2017].

Iggulden, Annette, 'Women's Silence: In the Space of Words and Images' (unpublished doctoral thesis, Deakin University, 2002).

'Image of city plan', *Portadown Times*, 11 December 1964, p. 18.

Jameson, Fredric, 'Cognitive Mapping', in *Marxism and the Interpretation of Culture* ed. by Cary Nelson and Lawrence Grossberg (Chicago: University of Illinois Press, 1988), pp. 347–360.

——*The Seeds of Time* (New York: Columbia University Press, 1994).

——'The End of Temporality', *Critical Inquiry*, 29.4 (Summer 2003), 695–718.

——*A Singular Modernity: Essay on the Ontology of the Present* (London: Verso, 2011).

Jarman, Neil, 'Troubling Remnants: Dealing with the Remains of Conflict in Northern Ireland', in *Matériel Culture: The Archaeology of Twentieth Century Conflict* ed. by John Schofield, William Gray Johnson and Colleen M. Beck (London: Routledge, 2002), pp. 281–296.

Jennings, Anthony, ed., *Justice under Fire: The Abuse of Civil Liberties in Northern Ireland* (London: Pluto Press, 1990).

Johns, Stephen, *Socialist Labour League Pocket Library No. 2, Torture Casebook: The Ulster Dossier* (London: Plough Press, 1971).

Johnson, James H., 'The Geography of a Belfast Suburb', *Irish Geography*, 3.3 (1956), 150–161.

Kant, Immanuel, *Anthropology from a Pragmatic Point of View*, trans. by Robert B. Louden (Cambridge: Cambridge University Press, 2006).

Kelly, Aaron, 'Geopolitical Eclipse: Culture and the Peace Process in Northern Ireland', *Third Text*, 19.5 (September 2005), 545–553.

——*Twentieth-Century Irish Literature: A Reader's Guide to Essential Criticism* (Basingstoke: Palgrave Macmillan, 2008).

——'Introduction: Troubles with the Peace Process: Contemporary Northern Irish Culture', *Irish Review*, 40–41 (2009), 1–17.

Kelly, Brian, 'Neoliberal Belfast: Disaster Ahead?', *Irish Marxist Review*, 1.2 (2012), 44–59.

Kelly, Liam, *Thinking Long: Contemporary Art in the North of Ireland* (Kinsale: Gandon Editions, 1996).

Kelly, Richard, *Alan Clarke* (London: Faber, 1998).

Kennard, Peter, *Images for the End of the Century: Photomontage Equations* (London: Journeyman Press, 1990).

Kennedy-Pipe, Caroline, *The Origins of the Present Troubles in Northern Ireland* (London: Longman, 1997).

Kierkegaard, Søren, *Repetition and Philosophical Crumbs*, trans. by M.G. Piety (Oxford: Oxford World Classics, 2009).

Kilmurray, Avila, 'Peace II – A Shadow of its former self?', *Scope* (December–January 2002–2003), 10–11.

Kirkland, Richard, *Identity Parades: Northern Irish Culture and Dissident Subjects* (Liverpool: Liverpool University Press, 2002).

——'The Spectacle of Terrorism in Northern Irish Culture', *Critical Survey*, 15.1 (2003), 77–90.

——'Visualising Peace: Northern Irish Post-Conflict Cinema and the Politics of Reconciliation', *Review of Irish Studies in Europe*, 1.2 (2017), 12–25.

Kirkpatrick, Kathryn, ed., *Border Crossings: Irish Women Writers and National Identities* (Tuscaloosa: University of Alabama Press, 2000).

Kitson, Frank, *Low Intensity Operations: Subversion, Insurgency, Peace-Keeping* (London: Faber and Faber, 1971).

Kuhn, Reinhard, *The Demon of Noontide: Ennui in Western Literature* (Princeton: Princeton University Press, 1976).

'L.A.M.F.', *Alternative Ulster*, 31 (1978), 2.

'L.A.M.F.', *Alternative Ulster*, 34 (1978), 2.

Lefebvre, Henri, *The Production of Space*, trans. by Donald Nicholson-Smith (Oxford: Blackwell, 1991).

Legg, George, 'Biopolitical Ireland: Text, Culture, Theory', *Irish Review*, 53 (2016), 1–8.

Leonard, Marion, *Gender in the Music Industry: Rock, Discourse and Girl Power* (Aldershot: Ashgate, 2007).

Lesjack, Carolyn, 'Reading Dialectically', *Criticism*, 55.2 (2013), 233–277.

Levine, Caroline, *Forms: Whole, Rhythm, Hierarchy, Network* (Princeton: Princeton University Press, 2015).

Liechty, Joseph, and Cecelia Clegg, *Moving Beyond Sectarianism: Religion, Conflict, and Reconciliation in Northern Ireland* (Dublin: The Columba Press, 2001).

Lijphart, Arend, *The Politics of Accommodation: Pluralism and Democracy in the Netherlands* (Berkeley: University of California Press, 1968).

——*Democracy in Plural Societies: A Comparative Exploration* (New Haven: Yale University Press, 1977).

——*Patterns of Democracy: Government Forms and Performance in Thirty-Six Countries* (New Haven: Yale University Press, 2012).

Linfield, Susie, *Cruel Radiance: Photography and Political Violence* (Chicago: University of Chicago Press, 2010).

Lippard, Lucy R., 'Ireland's Long Division', *The Village Voice*, 29.50 (15 May 1984), 89.

Little, Adrian, *Democracy and Northern Ireland: Beyond the Liberal Paradigm?* (Basingstoke: Palgrave Macmillan, 2004).

Lloyd, David, *Irish Times: Temporalities of Modernity* (Dublin: Field Day, 2008).

——*Irish Culture and Colonial Modernity 1800–2000: The Transformation of Oral Space* (Cambridge: Cambridge University Press, 2011).

Lodge, Tom, 'Northern Ireland: Between Peace and Reconciliation', *OpenSecurity: Conflict and Peacebuilding*, 3 June 2009.

Long, Declan, *Visual Art and the Conflict in Northern Ireland: Troubles Archive Essays* (Belfast: Arts Council of Northern Ireland, 2009).

——*Ghost-Haunted Land: Contemporary Art and Post-Troubles Northern Ireland* (Manchester: Manchester University Press, 2017).

Longley, Edna, *Poetry in the Wars* (Newcastle: Bloodaxe, 1986).

——*The Living Stream: Literature and Revisionism in Ireland* (Newcastle: Bloodaxe, 1994).

——'Looking Back from *The Yellow Book*', in *The Poetry of Derek Mahon* ed. by Elmer Kennedy-Andrews (Gerrards Cross: Colin Smythe, 2002), pp. 29–48.

Lowe, David, '14 years after Good Friday Agreement, Belfast is still divided', *Sun*, 6 April 2012, p. 23.

Lundy, Patricia, and Mark McGovern, 'The Politics of Memory in Post-Conflict Northern Ireland', *Peace Review: A Journal of Social Justice*, 13.1 (2001), 27–33.

Mac Ginty, Roger, *International Peacebuilding and Local Resistance: Hybrid Forms of Peace* (Basingstoke: Palgrave Macmillan, 2011).

Mac Ginty, Roger, and John Darby, *Guns and Government: The Management of the Northern Ireland Peace Process* (Basingstoke: Palgrave, 2006).

Mahon, Derek, 'Subsidy Bungalows', *Icarus*, 32 (December 1960), 22.

——*The Sea in Winter* (Dublin: The Gallery Press, 1986).

——'The Coleraine Triangle', in *Journalism*, ed. by Terence Brown (Oldcastle: Gallery Press, 1996), pp. 216–220.

——*New Collected Poems* (Oldcastle: The Gallery Press, 2012).

Mahon, Peter, *Violence, Politics and Textual Interventions in Northern Ireland* (Basingstoke: Palgrave Macmillan, 2010).

Major, John, 'Mr Major's Speech to the Institute of Directors in Belfast', 21 October (1994) www.johnmajor.co.uk/page1961.html [accessed 24 July 2017].

——'Mr. Major's Speech at the International Investment Forum', 14 December (1994) www.johnmajor.co.uk/page2268.html [accessed 24 July 2017].

Majumdar, Saikat, *Prose of the World: Modernism and the Banality of Empire* (New York: Columbia University Press, 2013).

Martin, Gavin, '(I don't wanna go to ....) Bangor', *Alternative Ulster*, 72 (1978), 21.

Martinez, Daniel E., 'Beyond Disciplinary Enclosures: Management Control in the Society of Control', *Critical Perspectives on Accounting*, 22.2 (February 2011), 200–211.

Marx, Karl, *The Class Struggles in France 1848–1850*, intro. by Frederick Engels, trans. by Henry Kuhn (New York: New York Labor News Company, 1924).

——*Capital Vol. I*, trans. by Ben Fowkes (London: Penguin, 1990).

——*Grundrisse*, trans. by Martin Nicolaus (London: Penguin, 1993).

Marx, Karl, and Frederick Engels, *Selected Correspondence 1846–1895*, trans. by Dona Torr (London: Lawrence and Wishart, 1943).

——*Manifesto of the Communist Party*, trans. by Samuel Moore (Moscow: Progress Publisher, 1967).

——*The German Ideology*, ed. and intro. by C.J. Arthur (London: Lawrence and Wishart, 1970).

Mason, Roy, *Paying the Price* (London: Robert Hale, 1999).

Masterplanning Consortium, *Maze/Long Kesh: Masterplan and Implementation Strategy. Final Report* (Belfast: HMSO, 2006).

Matthew, Robert H., *The Belfast Regional Survey and Plan* (Belfast: HMSO, 1963).

Maze Long Kesh Development Corporation, *From Peace to Prosperity Vision* (YouTube, 2013) www.youtube.com/watch?v=sxsnfQvMS6Q [accessed 24 July 2017].

——'Press Release: Maze Long Kesh Is Northern Ireland's Largest Development Site', 24 April 2013.

McAtackney, Laura, *An Archaeology of the Troubles: The Dark Heritage of Long Kesh/ Maze Prison* (Oxford: Oxford University Press, 2014).

McAvera, Brian, *Marking the North: The Work of Victor Sloan* (Dublin: Open Air, 1990).

McCabe, Conor, *The Double Transition: The Economic and Political Transition of Peace* (Belfast: Irish Congress of Trade Unions and Labour After Conflict, 2013).

McCarthy, Conor, *Modernisation, Crisis and Culture in Ireland, 1969–1992* (Dublin: Four Courts Press, 2000).

McCleery, Martin J., 'The Creation of the "New City" of Craigavon: A Case Study of Politics, Planning and Modernisation in Northern Ireland in the Early 1960s', *Irish Political Studies*, 27.1 (2012), 89–109.

——'Debunking the Myths of Operation Demetrius: The Introduction of Internment in Northern Ireland in 1971', *Irish Political Studies*, 27.3 (2012), 411–430.

McConnell, Gail, *Northern Irish Poetry and Theology* (Basingstoke: Palgrave, 2014).

McCoy, Alfred W., *A Question of Torture: CIA Interrogation, from the Cold War to the War on Terror* (New York: Metropolitan Books, 2006).

McCreary, Alf, 'The Creation of a City', *Belfast Telegraph*, 3 May 1965, p. 6.

McDiarmid, Lucy, and Michael Durkan, 'Q. and A. with Derek Mahon', *Irish Literary Supplement*, 10.2 (Fall 1999), 27–28.

McDonald, Patrick J., *The Invisible Hand of Peace: Capitalism, the War Machine and International Relations Theory* (Cambridge: Cambridge University Press, 2009).

McDonald, Peter, 'Incurable Ache', *Poetry Ireland: Review*, 56 (Spring 1998), 116–119.

McDonough, Tom, ed., *Boredom* (Cambridge, MA: MIT Press, 2017).

McDowell, Sarah, 'Negotiating Places of Pain in Post-Conflict Northern Ireland: Debating the Future of the Maze Prison/Long Kesh', in *Places of Pain and Shame: Dealing with 'Difficult Heritage'* ed. by William Logan and Keir Reeves (London: Routledge, 2009), pp. 215–230.

McGarry, John, and Brendan O'Leary, eds, *The Future of Northern Ireland* (Oxford: Clarendon Press, 1990).

——*Explaining Northern Ireland: Broken Images* (Oxford: Blackwell, 1995).

——*The Northern Ireland Conflict: Consociational Engagements* (Oxford: Oxford University Press, 2004).

McGuffin, John, *Internment* (Tralee: Anvil Books, 1973).

——*The Guineapigs* (Hamondsworth: Penguin, 1974).

McIlroy, Brian, *Shooting to Kill: Filmmaking and the 'Troubles' in Northern Ireland* (Richmond: Steveston Press, 2001).

McLaughlin, Cahal, 'Cold, Hungry, and Scared: Prison Films about the "Troubles"', in *Ireland in Focus: Film, Photography, and Popular Culture* ed. by Eóin Flannery and Michael Griffin (New York: Syracuse University Press, 2009), pp. 35–53.

McLaughlin, Greg, and Stephen Baker, *The Propaganda of Peace: The Role of the Media and Culture in the Northern Ireland Peace Process* (Bristol: Intellect, 2010).

McLoone, Martin, 'Punk Music in Northern Ireland: The Political Power of "what might have been"', *Irish Studies Review*, 12.1 (2004), 29–38.

McMahon, Melanie, 'Irish as Symptom: Language, Ideology and Praxis in the Post/Colony' (unpublished doctoral thesis, King's College London, 2012).

McNamee, Eugene, 'Eye Witness: Memorialising Humanity in Steve McQueen's *Hunger*', *International Journal of Law in Context*, 5.3 (2009), 281–294.

'Meadowbrook – "a jungle"', *Portadown News*, 16 January 1970, p. 3.

Medhurst, Andy, 'What Did I Get? Punk, Memory and Autobiography', in *Punk Rock: So What? The Cultural Legacy of Punk* ed. by Roger Sabin (London: Routledge, 1999), pp. 219–231.

Mill, John Stuart, *Principles of Political Economy: with Some of Their Applications to Social Philosophy*, intro. by V.W. Bladen; ed. by J.M. Robson (Toronto: University of Toronto Press, Routledge & Kegan Paul, 1965).

'Moira goes to town', *Lurgan Times*, 18 June 1965, p. 1.

Moloney, Ed, *A Secret History of the IRA*, 2nd edn (London: Penguin, 2007).

'More than planning is required', *Portadown Times*, 9 June 1967, p. 23.

Morrison, Danny, *Then the Walls Came Down: A Prison Journal* (Dublin: Mercier Press, 1999).

Murray, R., and F.W. Boal, 'The Social Ecology of Urban Violence', in *Social problems and the [RUN ON]City: Geographical Perspectives on the Northern Problem* ed. by D.T. Herbert and D.M. Smith (Oxford: Oxford University Press, 1979), pp. 139–157.

Myerscough, John, *The Economic Importance of the Arts* (London: Policy Studies Institute, 1988).

——*The Arts and the Northern Ireland Economy* (Belfast: Northern Ireland Economic Council, 1995).

Nagle, John, 'Potemkin Village: Neo-Liberalism and Peace-Building in Northern Ireland?', *Ethnopolitics*, 8.2 (June 2009), 173–190.

Nairn, Ian, *Britain's Changing Towns* (London: BBC, 1967).

Nairn, Tom, *The Break-Up of Britain* (London: New Left Books, 1977).

Neill, William J.V., Michael Murray and Berna Grist, eds, *Relaunching Titanic: Memory and Marketing in the New Belfast* (London: Routledge, 2014).

Netz, Reviel, *Barbed Wire: An Ecology of Modernity* (Middletown, CT: Wesleyan University Press, 2004).

Neve, Brian, 'Cinema, The Ceasefire and "the troubles"', *Irish Studies Review*, 5.20 (1997), 2–8.

'New hope for the home hunters', *Craigavon Times*, 12 January 1976, p. 1.

'Newtownabbey means little to its citizens-to-be', *Larne Times*, 27 March 1958, p. 8.

'New towns bill gets a flaying', *Lurgan Mail*, 19 February 1965, p. 1.

'"No future for bitter plays," says Lord Major', *Belfast Newsletter*, 19 May 1959, p. 1.

Northern Ireland Economic Council, *Through Peace to Prosperity: Proceedings of the Peace Seminar Hosted by the Economic Council* (Belfast: Northern Ireland Economic Development Office, 1995).

Northern Irish Civil Rights Association, *Information Sheet on Women Internees* (Belfast, 23 May 1973).

Obama, Barack, 'Remarks by President Obama and Mrs. Obama in Town Hall with Youth of Northern Ireland', 17 June (2013) http://iipdigital.usembassy.gov/st/english/texttrans/2013/06/20130617276442.html#axzz3Pdgnslqn [accessed 24 July 2017].

O'Doherty, Brian, 'Terrible Beauty', *Artforum*, 47.5 (January 2008), 61.

O'Doherty, Malachi, 'Peace process piffle makes me want yo hit out', *Belfast Telegraph*, 1 August 2012 www.belfasttelegraph.co.uk/opinion/news-analysis/peace-process-piffle-makes-me-want-to-hit-out-16191837.html [accessed 24 July 2017].

O'Dowd, Liam, 'Social Class', in *Social Attitudes in Northern Ireland* ed. by Peter Stringer and Gillian Robinson (Belfast: Blackstaff Press, 1991), pp. 39–50.

——'Craigavon: Locality, Economy and the State in a Failed "New City"', in *Irish Urban Cultures* ed. by Chris Curtain, Hastings Donnan and Thomas Wilson (Belfast: Institute of Irish Studies, 1993), pp. 39–62.

O'Gorman, Eddie, 'Peace ranks high as North and US get down to business', *Irish Times*, 13 December 1994, p. 17.

O'Hagan, Sean, 'McQueen and Country', *Observer*, 12 October 2008 www.theguardian.com/film/2008/oct/12/2 [accessed 24 July 2017].

O'Hearn, Denis, 'Peace Dividend, Foreign Investment, and Economic

Regeneration: The Northern Irish Case', *Social Problems*, 47.2 (May 2000), 180–200.

——*Nothing but an Unfinished Song: Bobby Sands, the Irish Hunger Striker Who Ignited a Generation* (New York: Nation Books, 2006).

O'Leary, Brendan, 'The Shackles of the State and Hereditary Animosities: Colonialism in the Interpretation of Irish History', *Field Day Review*, 10 (2014), 149–187.

O'Malley, Padraig, *Biting at the Grave: The Irish Hunger Strikes and the Politics of Despair* (Boston, MA: Beacon Press, 1990).

——*Northern Ireland: Questions of Nuance* (Belfast: Blackstaff Press, 1990).

'Opposition MPs plan to "carpet" O'Neill', *Belfast Telegraph*, 10 May 1969, p. 1.

Ormsby, Frank, ed., *A Rage for Order: Poetry of the Northern Ireland Troubles* (Belfast: Blackstaff Press, 1992).

Osborn, Fredric, and Arnold Whittick, *The New Towns: The Answer to Megalopolis* (London: Leonard Hill, 1963).

Osborne, Peter, *Anywhere or Not at All: Philosophy of Contemporary Art* (London: Verso, 2013).

O'Toole, Fintan, '*Hunger* fails to wrest the narrative from the hunger strikers', *Irish Times*, 22 November 2008.

Ó Tuathail, Séamas, *They Came in the Morning* (Dublin: Sinn Féin (Official), 1972).

Paine, Thomas, *Rights of Man, Common Sense, and Other Writings* ed. by Mark Philip (Oxford: Oxford University Press, 1995).

Palmer, Patricia, *The Severed Head and Grafted Tongue: Literature, Translation and Violence in Early Modern Ireland* (Cambridge: Cambridge University Press, 2014).

Paris, Roland, 'Saving Liberal Peacebuilding', *Review of International Studies*, 36.2 (April 2010), 337–365.

Parker, Lord, J.A. Gardiner and Lord Gardiner, *Report of the Committee of Privy Counsellors Appointed to Consider Authorised Procedures for the Interrogation of Persons Suspected of Terrorism* (London: HMSO, 1972).

Pascal, Blaise, *Pensées*, trans. A.J. Krailsheimer (London: Penguin, 1966).

Patterson, Henry, *Ireland since 1939: The Persistence of Conflict* (London: Penguin, 2006).

——'Unionism after the Good Friday and St Andrews', *The Political Quarterly*, 83.2 (April–June 2012), 247–255.

Patterson, Henry, and Eric Kaufmann, *Unionism and Orangeism in Northern Ireland since 1945: The Decline of the Loyal Family* (Manchester: Manchester University Press, 2007).

Pease, Allison, *Modernism, Feminism and the Culture of Boredom* (Cambridge: Cambridge University Press, 2012).

Peatling, G.K., *The Failure of the Northern Ireland Peace Process* (Dublin: Irish Academic Press, 2004).

Pezze, Barbara Dalle, and Carol Salzani, eds, *Essays on Boredom and Modernity* (New York: Rodopi, 2009).

Pickering, Sharon, *Women, Policing and Resistance in Northern Ireland* (Belfast: Beyond the Pale, 2002).

Pinder, David, 'Old Paris Is No More: Geographies of Spectacle and Anti-Spectacle', *Antipode*, 32.4 (2000), 357–386.

'Piped Radio, Television and Telephone!', *Ulster Commentary*, 310 (March 1972), 2.

Pitzl, Gerald R., *Encyclopaedia of Human Geography* (Westport, CT: Greenwood Press, 2004).

'Plan is "rotten"', *Lurgan Mail*, 12 March 1965, p. 1.

'Planners face the farmers', *Lurgan Mail*, 23 December 1964, p. 9.

Pollak, Andy, ed., *A Citizen's Inquiry: The Opsahl Report On Northern Ireland* (Dublin: Lilliput Press, 1993).

'Pro-city folk "told off"', *Lurgan Mail*, 18 December 1964, p. 6.

Purbrick, Louise, 'The Architecture of Containment', in *Donovan Wylie: The Maze* (London: Granta Books, 2004), pp. 3–22.

Raack, R.J., 'Historiography as Cinematography: A Prolegomenon to Film Work for Historians', *Journal of Contemporary History*, 18 (1983), 411–438.

Ragg, Nicholas M., Tracy Doherty, Joe O'Hara and Brian Buckley, *Survey of Internees' Families* (Belfast: NICRA, 1972).

Ramsey, Phil, '"A Pleasingly Blank Canvas": Urban Regeneration in Northern Ireland and the Case of Titanic Quarter', *Space and Polity*, 17.2 (2013), 164–179.

Rancière, Jacques, 'Comment and Responses', *Theory and Event*, 6.4 (2003), 28 pars.

Reichert, Jeff, 'Hunger Pains: An Interview with Steve McQueen', *Reverse Shot*, 27 March 2009.

Relph, Edward, *Place and Placelessness* (London: Pion, 1976).

Reynolds, Simon, *Rip It Up and Start Again: Post-Punk 1978–1984* (London: Faber, 2005).

Rimbaud, Penny, 'Crass in Belfast, 1982', in *It Makes You Want to Spit!: The Definitive Guide to Punk in Northern Ireland 1977–1982* ed. by Sean O'Neill and Guy Trelford (Dublin: Reekus Music, 2003), pp. 12–15.

Robinson, Peter, ed., *The Oxford Handbook of Contemporary British and Irish Poetry* (Oxford: Oxford University Press, 2013).

Rodwell, Bob, 'Goodyear closure costs 700 jobs in Ulster', *Guardian*, 26 July 1983, p. 1.

Rolston, Bill, 'The Contented Classes', *Irish Reporter*, 9 (1993), 7.

Ruane, Joseph, and Jennifer Todd, *The Dynamics of Conflict in Northern Ireland: Power, Conflict and Emancipation* (Cambridge: Cambridge University Press, 2000).

Salvesen, Britt and Alison Nordström, eds, *New Topographics* (Eastman House: New York, 2010).

Samuel, Raphael, *Theatres of Memory: Past and Present in Contemporary Culture* (London: Verso, 2012).

Sands, Bobby, *The Diary of Bobby Sands: The First Seventeen Days of Bobby's H-Block Hunger-Strike to Death* (Dublin: Republican Publications, 1990).

Savage, Jon, *England's Dreaming: Sex Pistols and Punk Rock* (London: Faber, 1991).

Seawright, Paul, *Inside Information: Paul Seawright Photographs 1988–1995* (London: The Photographers' Gallery, 1995).

Shallice, Tim, 'The Ulster Depth Interrogation Techniques and Their Relation to Sensory Deprivation Research', *Cognition*, 1.4 (1972), 385–405.

Sharrock, David, 'From bad to verse', *Guardian*, 22 August 1994, p. A11.

Shinkle, Eugénie, 'Boredom, Repetition, Inertia: Contemporary Photography and the Aesthetics of the Banal', *Mosaic*, 37.4 (December 2004), 165–183.

Shirlow, Peter, 'Belfast: the "post-conflict" City', *Space and Polity*, 10.2 (2006), 99–107.

'Ski Slope at Craigavon', *Ulster Commentary*, 331 (February 1974), 11.

Sloan, Victor, and Gerry Burns, 'Craigavon: The Heart Is Missing', *Circa*, 5 (July–August 1982), 13–15.

Smith, Stan, ed., *The Cambridge Companion to W.H. Auden* (Cambridge: Cambridge University Press, 2005).

Smith, William Beattie, *The British State and the Northern Crisis 1969–73: From Violence to Power-Sharing* (Washington: US Institute of Peace Press, 2011).

Smyth, Gerry, *The Novel and the Nation: Studies in the New Irish Fiction* (London: Pluto, 1997).

——*Noisy Island: A Short History of Irish Popular Music* (Cork: Cork University Press, 2005).

Sontag, Susan, *On Photography* (Harmondsworth: Allen Lane, 1978).

Spacks, Patricia Meyer, *Boredom: The Literary History of a State of Mind* (Chicago: University of Chicago Press, 1996).

Spit Records, 'Fanzines' www.spitrecords.co.uk/fanzines.htm [accessed 24 July 2017].

Spjut, R.J., 'Internment and Detention without Trial in Northern Ireland

1971–1975: Ministerial Policy and Practice', *The Modern Law Review*, 49.6 (November 1986), 712–739.

Stallabrass, Julian, 'Sebastiao Salgado and Fine Art Photojournalism', *New Left Review*, 223 (May–June 1997), 131–160.

Steele, Nigel, and Jonny Kerr, *Craigavon Safari* (YouTube, 2006) www.youtube.com/watch?v=mW8W1WA47tM [accessed 24 July, 2017].

Stewart, Heather, 'Eurozone boost of €1.1tn in "shock and awe" plan by Central Bank', *Guardian*, 22 January 2015 www.theguardian.com/business/2015/jan/22/ecb-boosts-eurozone-mario-draghi-kickstart-growth.

'Stormont attacked over "New City"', *Irish Times*, 15 August 1964, p. 11.

Sullivan, Megan, 'Mary Becket: An Interview by Megan Sullivan', *Irish Literary Supplement* (Fall 1995), 10–12.

——*Women in Northern Ireland: Cultural Studies and Material Conditions* (Gainesville: University Press of Florida, 1999).

Sunday Times Insight Team, *Ulster* (Harmondsworth: Penguin, 1972).

Svendsen, Lars, *A Philosophy of Boredom*, trans. by John Irons (London: Reaktion Books, 2008).

Tadiar, Neferti X.M., 'Life-Times in Fate Playing', *South Atlantic Quarterly*, 111.4 (2012), 783–802.

Taylor, Charles, 'The Politics of Recognition', in *Multiculturalism: Examining the Politics of Recognition* ed. by Amy Gutmann (Princeton: Princeton University Press, 1994), pp. 25–73.

The Agreement: Agreement Reached in the Multi-Party Negotiations (Good Friday Agreement) www.gov.uk/government/uploads/system/uploads/attachment_data/file/13665 2/agreement.pdf.

'The task facing the housing chiefs in attracting people to move to Brownlow', *Craigavon Times*, 28 January 1976, pp. 6–7.

Thorpe, Vanessa, and Henry McDonald, 'Anger as new film of IRA hero Bobby Sands screens at Cannes', *Observer*, 11 May 2008 www.theguardian.com/film/2008/may/11/cannesfilmfestival.northernireland [accessed 24 July 2017].

'Thousands oppose Maze Prison peace centre', *Belfast Daily*, 21 June 2013 www.belfastdaily.co.uk/2013/06/21/thousands-oppose-maze-prison-peace-centre/ [accessed 24 July 2017].

Thrift, Nigel, 'The Material Practices of Glamour', *Journal of Cultural Economy*, 1.1 (2008), 9–23.

Tiqqun, 'The Cybernetic Hypothesis', *Tiqqun 2* (Paris: Belles-Letters, 2001).

Toohey, Peter, *Boredom: A Lively History* (New Haven: Yale University Press, 2011).

Tookey, Chris, '*Hunger*: more pro-terrorist propaganda', *Daily Mail*, 30

October 2008 www.dailymail.co.uk/tvshowbiz/reviews/article-1081911/Hunger-More-pro-terrorist-propaganda.html#ixzz3Hd0XEEMJ.

Townshend, Charles, *Political Violence in Ireland* (Oxford: Oxford University Press, 1984).

Tracy, Robert, 'An Ireland / The Poets have Imagined', *The Crane Bag*, 3.2 (1979), 82–88.

Triggs, Teal, *Fanzines* (London: Thames and Hudson, 2010).

Trinity College Dublin, '1641 Depositions Project', online transcript (January 1970) http://1641.tcd.ie/depositions.php?depID=836101r054 [accessed 24 July 2017].

Tuck, Sarah, *After the Agreement: Contemporary Photography in Northern Ireland* (London: Black Dog Publishing, 2015).

Tunbridge, J.E., and G.J. Ashworth, *Dissonant Heritage: The Management of the Past as a Resource in Conflict* (Chichester: John Wiley and Sons, 1996).

'Ulster: The Battle that Is Coming', *The Economist*, 244 (16 September 1972), 24.

Vischer, A.L., *Barbed Wire Disease: A Psychological Study of the Prisoner of War* (London: John Bale, Sons & Danielsson, 1919).

'Vital year ahead', *Craigavon Progress* (= *Craigavon Times*), 21 January 1976, p. 3.

Walsh, Michael, 'Thinking the Unthinkable: Coming to Terms with Northern Ireland in the 1980s and 1990s', in *British Cinema, Past and Present* ed. by Justine Ashby and Andrew Higson (London: Routledge, 2000), pp. 288–300.

'Wanted – any type of house, barn or outhouse', *Craigavon Times*, 8 September 1976, p. 6.

Wark, McKenzie, *#Celerity: A Critique of the Manifesto for an Accelerationist Politics* https://speculativeheresy.files.wordpress.com/2013/05/wark-mckenzie-celerity.pdf [accessed 24 July 2017].

Webb, David, *Foucault's Archaeology* (Edinburgh: Edinburgh University Press, 2013).

Weininger, Elliot B., 'Foundations of Pierre Bourdieu's Class Analysis', in *Approaches to Class Analysis* ed. by Erik Olin Wright (Cambridge: Cambridge University Press, 2005), pp. 82–119.

Whalen, Lachlan, '"Our Barbed Wire Ivory Tower": The Prison Writings of Gerry Adams', *New Hibernia Review*, 10.2 (Summer 2006), 123–139.

'Will anything worthwhile come from this trip to Holland?', *Craigavon Times*, 19 May 1976, p. 4.

Williams, Alex, and Nick Srnicek, *#Accelerate: Manifesto for an Accelerationist Politics* https://syntheticedifice.files.wordpress.com/2013/06/accelerate.pdf [accessed 24 July 2017].

Williams, Val, *Martin Parr* (London: Phaidon Press, 2002).

Williams, Raymond, *Keywords: A Vocabulary of Culture and Society* (London: Fontana Press, 1988).

Wilkinson, Paul, *Terrorism and the Liberal State*, 2nd edn (Basingstoke: Macmillan, 1986).

Wilson, William, 'A Theoptic Eye: Derek Mahon's *The Hunt by Night*', *Éire-Ireland*, 25.4 (Winter 1990), 120–131.

Yeats, W.B., *The Major Works*, ed. by Edward Larrissy (Oxford: Oxford University Press, 1997).

Ziggy, 'The Story So Far', *Alternative Ulster*, 34 (1978), 24.

Žižek, Slavoj, 'Multiculturalism, Or, the Cultural Logic of Multinational Capitalism', *New Left Review*, 225 (September–October 1997), 28–51.

——*The Sublime Object of Ideology* (London: Verso, 1989).

Index